MW00446072

From Bulldog *to* Bengal

From Bulldog *to* Bengal

THE **JOE BURROW STORY**
THROUGH THE EYES OF HIS HOMETOWN

SCOTT BURSON *with* **SAM SMATHERS**

ORANGE *frazer* PRESS
Wilmington, Ohio

ISBN 978-1949248-678

Published by:
Orange Frazer Press
37½ West Main St.
P.O. Box 214
Wilmington, OH 45177

For price and shipping information, call: 937.382.3196
Or visit: www.orangefrazer.com

Book and cover design by: Orange Frazer Press with Catie South

Front cover, back cover top photo, back cover screened photo
and back flap photo by: Trisha Doudna (www.tsphoto1.com)

Library of Congress Cataloging-in-Publication Data

Names: Burson, Scott, author. | Smathers, Sam, author.
Title: From Bulldog to Bengal : the Joe Burrow story through the eyes of his hometown / Scott Burson with Sam Smathers.
Description: Wilmington, Ohio : Orange Frazer Press, [2023] | Includes bibliographical references and index. | Summary: "This is the story of Cincinnati Bengals quarterback, Joe Burrow and how he became such an amazing football player. The story is told through interviews with Joe's parents, childhood friends, teammates and coaches"-- Provided by publisher.
Identifiers: LCCN 2022057382 | ISBN 9781949248678 (paperback)
Subjects: LCSH: Burrow, Joe, 1996- | Burrow, Joe, 1996---Friends and associates. | Quarterbacks (Football)--United States--Biography. | Quarterbacks (Football)--Ohio--Athens--Biography. | Athens (Ohio)--Biography.
Classification: LCC GV939.B873 B87 2023 | DDC 796.33092 [B]--dc23/eng/20221219
LC record available at https://lccn.loc.gov/2022057382

First Printing

"Thank you to all the people who have supported Joe and our family throughout this amazing journey. From The Plains and Athens to Baton Rouge to Cincinnati, special people have helped along the way. Many have been mentioned by Scott in this book and we appreciate that. The journey continues."

—The Burrow Family

"To my father, Robert Burson, who coached The Plains Indians and Athens Bulldogs for many years. He was the first Athens City Recreation Director and the biggest Athens County sports fan I have ever known. I wish he had lived long enough to see this magical story unfold. Writing this book has brought me closer to him and my Southeastern Ohio roots. This project has been a sacred labor of love."

—Scott Burson
1980 Athens High School graduate

"We want to thank all the people who gave their time to Athens Youth Football and allowed the kids in our community to have a chance to participate. Without these people volunteering their time, whether it be coaching, cheerleading, working concessions, cleaning up, or helping work every fundraiser we could find, our program would not be where it is today. They say it takes a community to raise a child; well, we have had many community members over the years help this Bulldog Family. So, I guess it takes an entire Bulldog Community to help raise a Heisman Trophy winner!"

—The Smathers Family

Acknowledgments

This book could not have been written without the contributions of many people.

First and foremost, thank you to Robin and Jimmy Burrow for supporting this project and reading through the manuscript. Your feedback was invaluable.

I want to thank the following people who were interviewed for this book. Many also provided photographs: Ryan Adams; Kaitlin Baker; Troy Bolin; Travis Brand; Karin Bright; Les Champlin; Don, Beth and Evan Cooley; Mike and Pam Dailey; Kevin and Karli Davis; Dominique Doseck; Trisha Doudna; Will Drabold; Bill Finnearty; Matt Frazee; Fred Gibson; Kevin and Kristi Goldsberry; Bryce Graves; Liz, Bill, Adam and Ryan Luehrman; Keith and Brody McGrath; Ryan Mack; John Pugh; Ron Ricketts; David, Micah and Zacciah Saltzman; Jeff and Heather Skinner; Alan Smathers; Stanley Smathers; Chad Springer; Machelle Stewart;

Rusty Thomas; Tom, Marikay and Sam Vander Ven; Ann Welsh; Mary Ann Welsh; Nathan White; Randy and Susan Wolfe; and Dustin Zofchak.

A special thank you to Tom Vander Ven and Fred Gibson for reading the manuscript and offering helpful notes.

It has been great to work with the folks at Orange Frazer Press. A special Who Dey goes out to Sarah Hawley for her advocacy and patience. Orange Frazer was the perfect publisher for this book.

A big thank you to Sam and Terri Smathers for working with me on this project. And to their daughter, Trisha, for serving as the chief photographer. The whole Smathers clan is the best.

The biggest thank you goes out to my family. To my children—Ashley, Bryan and grandson Jensen; Ryan and Nicole; and Lindsey and Ethan—for encouragement and understanding. To my brother and sister-in-law, Mark and Marie, and their boys, Bruno and Keenan, for filming Sam Smathers in the Dawg Pound. Most important to my wife, Deb, for patiently enduring many long days, nights, weeks, and months of research and writing. You get to pick what we do next summer.

—Scott Burson

I would like to say thank you to my wife, Terri, for always supporting and helping me with Athens Youth Football. She is the greatest woman in my life: To my daughter, Trisha, for all the photos that she has contributed over the years; my sons, Alan and Stanley for always helping with youth football, getting equipment down and putting away and whatever else was needed; the Burrow Family for giving me the blessing to be a part of this book and letting me and my family share this amazing ride; Scott Burson for including me on this project and letting me relive this experience, reconnect with past players and coaches. It has brought back many fond memories.

—Sam Smathers

Table of Contents

Introduction

JUST A KID FROM SOUTHEAST OHIO

"I think it's easily the worst feeling in the world.
The worst day of my life."[1]

—Joe Burrow
December 4, 2014

Ever since he was a small boy, Joe Burrow dreamed of playing in The Horseshoe. On December 4, 2014, his dream came true.

The trip to Ohio Stadium, home of the storied Ohio State Buckeyes, was an early birthday present. Just six days before Burrow turned eighteen, he and his teammates took the seventy-five-mile bus ride up Route 33 from The Plains to Columbus, where the 14–0 Athens High School Bulldogs would compete for the Ohio State Division III Football title.

Despite their unblemished record, the small-town Bulldogs entered the game as underdogs. Toledo Central Catholic was bigger, stronger and faster. But Athens had one thing Central Catholic did not—the two-time Ohio High School Gatorade Player of the Year, 6-foot-4, 210-pound quarterback Joe Burrow.

To those who watched Joe grow up in Athens, his exploits in The Shoe that night came as no surprise. They'd seen it many times before. The crisp,

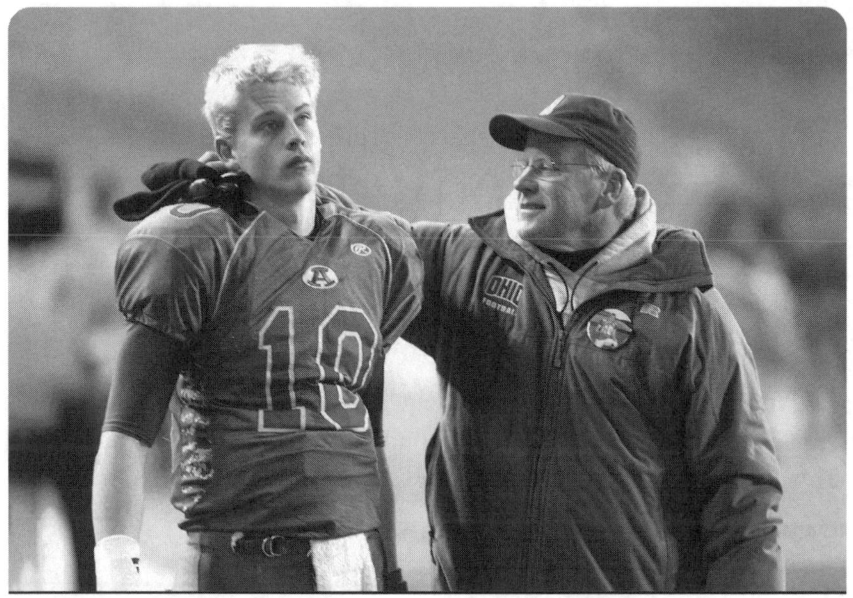

Father, Jimmy, consoles a heartbroken Joe after losing to Toledo Central Catholic in the Ohio high school state title game. *Photo credit: Tony Coles*

pinpoint passes. The elusive escapes from a collapsing pocket. The quick decision-making. The poise under pressure. The leadership. The physical toughness. Joe even played defensive back in the second half, delivering a devastating blow that sent Central Catholic running back Michael Warren II limping off to the sidelines. Warren, who went on to star at the University of Cincinnati, would later tell Burrow it was one of the hardest hits he's ever taken.[2] As Burrow's father, Jimmy, says: "Joe's a football player first, a quarterback second."[3]

By the end of the night, Burrow had thrown for an eye-popping 446 yards and six touchdowns, while adding an additional 69 yards on the ground. The six touchdowns tied an Ohio high school championship game record.

But Burrow's dazzling performance wasn't enough. Central Catholic mounted a dramatic final drive to score with fifteen seconds remaining to

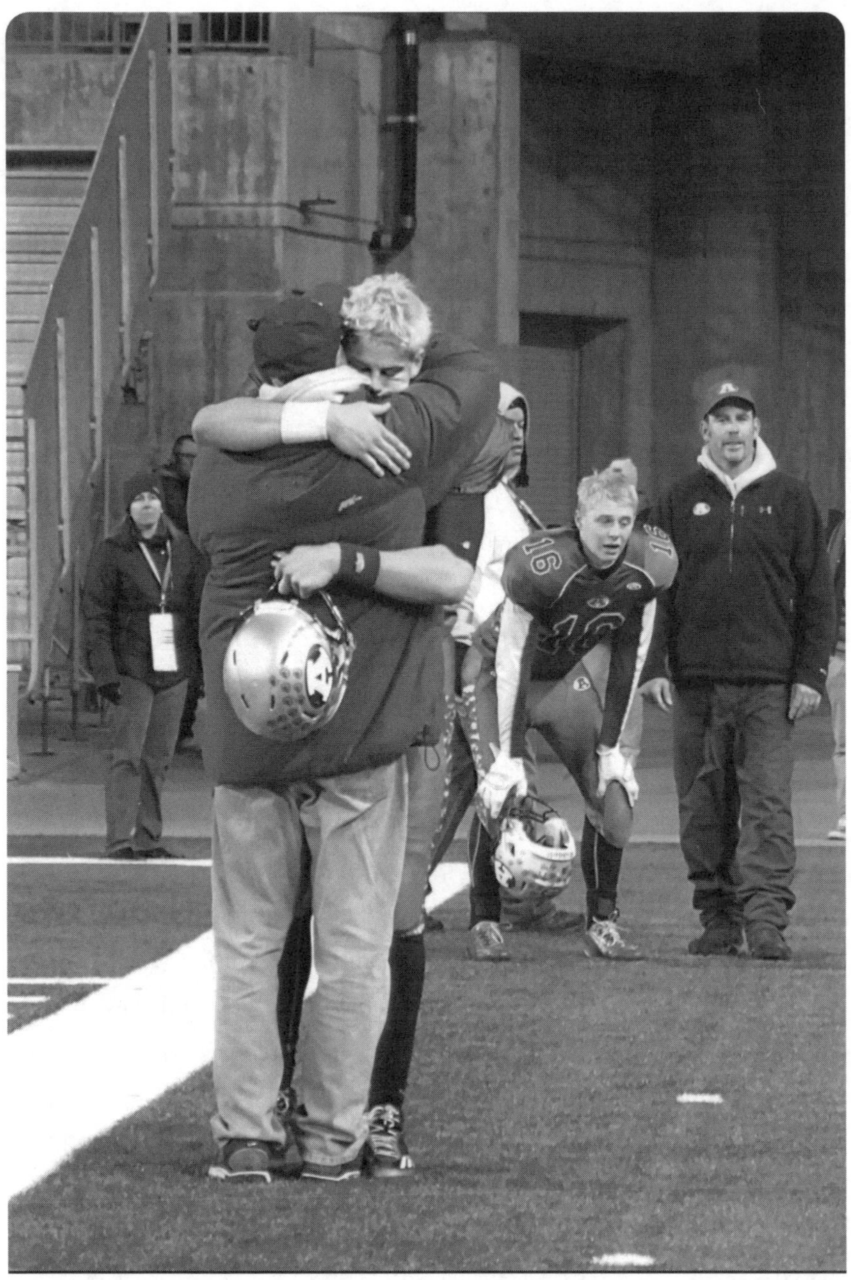

Joe embraces his father after the state championship defeat. An exhausted Ryan Luehrman and Bulldog head coach, Ryan Adams, look on. *Photo credit: Trisha Doudna*

pull out a 56–52 victory. One of the TV announcers called it the greatest high school game he'd ever seen.[4] Neither team deserved to lose, but it was the Bulldogs who took the silver trophy and somber ride back down Route 33—just a few elusive seconds away from claiming the first state title in school history.

In the postgame press conference, a downtrodden, bleach-blonde Burrow couldn't celebrate the fourteen wins. Or the six touchdown passes. It was too soon. It stung too much. All he could think about was the silver trophy and one uncharacteristic miscue—a third-quarter interception. It was only the second pick he'd thrown all year. "I think it's easily the worst feeling in the world," said a teary-eyed Burrow. "The worst day of my life."[5]

For Joe, the dream of playing in The Horseshoe had actually turned into a nightmare.

Eight Years Later

As an Ohio State recruit, Burrow's impressive debut in The Shoe appeared to be a mere foretaste of scarlet-and-gray greatness to come. But following the loss to Central Catholic, sportswriter Bill Landis couldn't help but wonder: "Will the future Buckeye ever be able to think back fondly on his first game on that field?"[6]

Eight years later, that question was answered. While talking to the media about the upcoming game against Justin Herbert and the Los Angeles Chargers, the Cincinnati Bengals star quarterback was asked if he ever thinks about that high school championship loss. With a heavy sigh and hint of melancholy, Burrow said, "Oh man, I think about that all the time." The surprised reporter responded, "Do you really?" Burrow continued, "Yeah, that's a championship you didn't win. I think about that one a lot. We missed some PATs and turned the ball over. I think about that one all the time." Another member of the media asked Burrow if it was still the worst day of his life. Through a slight smile, instead of tears this time, Joe answered, "I've been kind of lucky with that. I haven't had a ton of bad days, but that one definitely sticks out."[7]

Now, why would an NFL star with a Heisman Trophy and college national championship ring obsess about a high school loss? It's one thing to ponder high school highs and lows when the glory days are over, but three days after you've led your team to a 31-point trouncing of Ben Roethlisberger and the Pittsburgh Steelers? Who cares about a high school championship game?

I'll tell you who. Joe Burrow.

"I've always said that our family, we're not good losers," says Jimmy Burrow, who spent fourteen years as the Ohio University Bobcats Defensive Coordinator. "We don't just jump back into 'everything is great' after a tough loss."[8]

It would be easy to misconstrue Jimmy's comment. It's not that the Burrows are sore losers or bad sports; far from it. They respect their opponents, win or lose. It just speaks to their ultra-competitive nature—which Joe has in spades. Just ask his mother, Robin, who says family vacations with Joe and his older brothers always turn into non-stop competitions—be it paddleball, putt-putt or ping pong.[9]

But there's more to Joe's obsession with the high school title that got away. It not only shows his competitive fire; it reveals his heart—a deep emotional connection to his hometown and the people of Athens County. That's what this book is about.

Just a Kid from Athens

From Bulldog to Bengal is a book about astounding achievements and inspirational relationships. It's an unlikely story about a small-town boy, whose hard work and mental tenacity have taken him to the top of the football mountain—accomplishing more in twenty-five years than most do in a lifetime.

National championship. Check.

Heisman Trophy. Check.

NFL number-one pick. Check.

Super Bowl appearance. Check.

NFL Comeback Player of the Year. Check.

Burrow has ascended to the peak, but not without challenges. His story includes doubters, naysayers, and recruiting snubs. It includes waiting for a turn that would never come at Ohio State. It includes placing a bet on himself and transferring to another school. It includes a devastating injury and facing the toughest test of his life.

Ultimately, this is a story about staying grounded. Joe has made it to the top of the mountain by keeping his head out of the clouds and feet firmly planted in southeastern Ohio soil. Joe has never forgotten his roots and those who helped him along the way—family, friends, coaches, teammates, and classmates. From shining a light on food insecurity during his Heisman speech to wearing clothing and cleats designed by hometown kids, Joe consistently reps Southeast Ohio and gives back to the Athens community.

In the following pages, the Joe Burrow story will be told from a hometown perspective. Both authors of this book have deep roots in Athens County. I (Scott) was born and raised in Athens and was the point guard on a state-ranked Athens High School basketball team thirty years before Joe played the same position for the Bulldogs.

My father, Robert Burson, was known as "Mr. City Recreation" throughout the Athens community, serving as the Recreation Director for sixteen years.[10] He also coached football, basketball and baseball at The Plains High School and was an assistant basketball coach when the Athens

Bob Burson (Mr. City Recreation) was the first Athens City Recreation Director.
Photo credit: Scott Burson

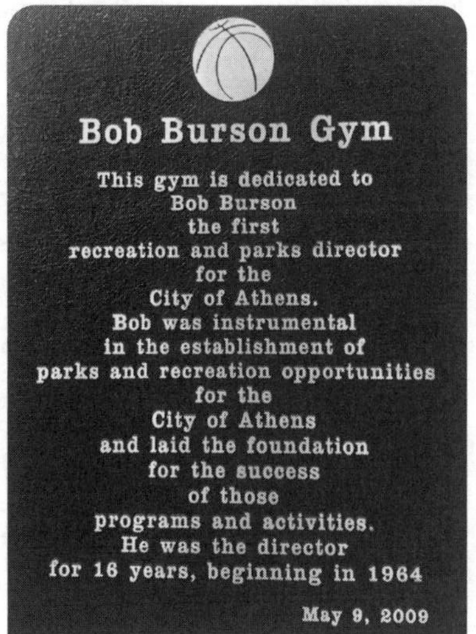

Joe Burrow and his buddies spent thousands of hours playing pick-up basketball in the Bob Burson Gym.
Photo credit: Scott Burson

county schools consolidated into one high school in 1968. The basketball courts at the Athens Community Center are named after my dad.

The youth of Athens especially benefitted from the facilities and programs that were established during my father's tenure. One program, in particular, was a Saturday morning youth tackle football league. The football program ran for many years, but came to an end when some parents raised concerns over the danger of head injuries.

Not all parents agreed with the decision to terminate the program. One such parent was Sam Smathers, who would become Joe's first youth football coach. Sam can't help but think about Athens football. After all, when he walks out his front door at 18 N. McDonald Street in The Plains, he sees the high school football stadium staring him directly in the face.

When Sam's son entered second grade in the mid-'90s, Smathers started asking why Athens didn't have a youth tackle football program. Nearby

Nelsonville, Trimble, and other Southeastern Ohio towns were all part of a travel league. But not Athens. Sam wondered what the AHS gridiron teams might be like if they had a legitimate feeder program. Basketball and baseball fielded youth travel teams. Why not football?

So, he and another parent hosted a town hall meeting at Athens Middle School. "We passed out leaflets and had some people talk," recalls Sam. The concern over contact was addressed. "I remember one guy saying you pad a kid up that weighs sixty pounds and another kid that weighs sixty pounds and fully padded they can't get no head of steam. They just bounce off each other. It's really just kinda cute, you know?"[11]

Nothing happened for about a year. Then Sam received a call one day. Athens was joining the youth travel league. Sam coached his son as he progressed from third through sixth grade. Eventually Sam became the commissioner of the entire league and held coaches' meetings in his garage, af-

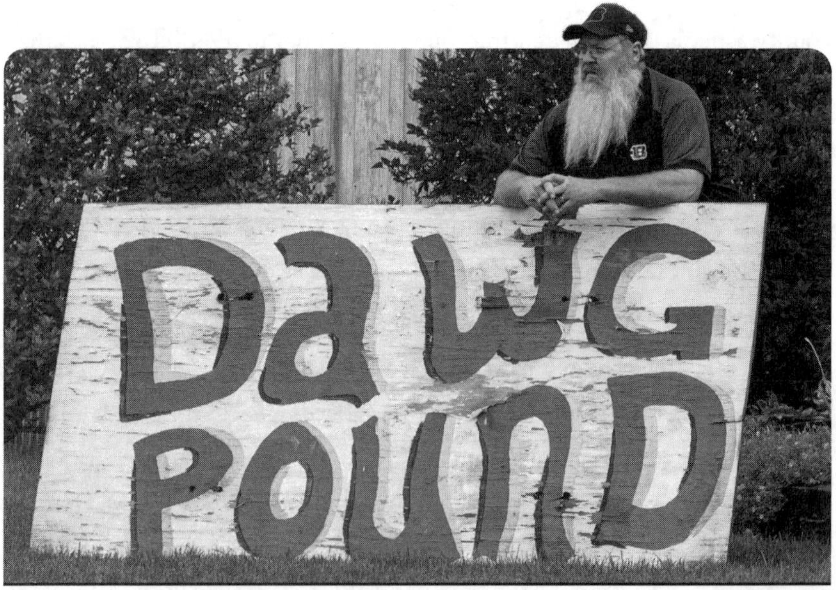

Sam Smathers, Joe Burrow's first youth football coach, was instrumental in jump-starting the Athens youth tackle football program. *Photo credit: Trisha Doudna*

fectionately known as The Dawg Pound. The Dawg Pound was also where Athens players would come pick up their equipment. Sam's garage took on a life of its own. The Dawg Pound is a central character in this story.

So, my father started organized youth tackle football in Athens, it waned for a while, then Sam helped bring it back. Just in time to coach a third-grade boy, whose family had moved to The Plains from Fargo, North Dakota. As Jimmy and Sam both like to say, "That's when the stars started to align."[12]

Warner Wisdom

As the 2021 AFC Champion Cincinnati Bengals emerged from the SoFi Stadium tunnel at the start of Super Bowl LVI, NBC rolled the player introductions. While most players called out their colleges, the Bengals quarterback proudly said, "Joe Burrow. Athens High School." Typical Joe. Always "reppin" the 740.

Perhaps Joe was thinking about his final game as a Bulldog when he recorded those comments. Remarkably, that difficult night in the Horseshoe was the last playoff defeat Burrow had experienced as a starting quarterback. Eight years without a playoff loss. The streak included LSU victories over Oklahoma and Clemson on the way to a national title, as well as dramatic wins over the Raiders, Titans and Chiefs en route to Cincinnati's first Super Bowl appearance in thirty-three years. One more victory and Joe would become the first player to ever win the coveted triple crown: a college national championship, the Heisman Trophy, and a Super Bowl ring.

Yeah, not a ton of bad days.

The triple crown might belong to Burrow one day, but it eluded him on this night. While the Bengals led for much of the second half, the Rams ground out a sustained, five-minute final drive that culminated with a Matthew Stafford to Cooper Kupp game-winning touchdown. The drive was remarkably similar to the one mounted by Toledo Central Catholic eight years prior. It was another heartbreaking defeat for Burrow. Only this time in front of 100 million viewers.

When the crestfallen Bengals captain joined the postgame press conference, one reporter asked Joe to compare this loss with the Central Catholic defeat. With a flicker of a smile, Burrow ran his fingers over his hair and said, "You lose a state championship and a Super Bowl, obviously, different media coverage, but it feels the same to me."

Another reporter asked what he was going to remember most about the Bengals' season. Joe's response was deliberate and telling: "I watched 'A Football Life of Kurt Warner' last week.... [The Rams] lost a [Super Bowl] and later in the documentary Kurt said they let it sting too much. That they didn't celebrate what they had accomplished. Obviously, it stings, but we had a great year, didn't come out this last game the way we wanted it to, but I think we still have something to celebrate.... I'm going to celebrate with the guys and reminisce on the season we had."[13]

Burrow's comments reveal remarkable growth, perspective, and maturity. When Joe lost the state championship in high school, he couldn't see past the runner-up trophy and missed opportunities. He couldn't celebrate the fourteen wins. He let it sting too much. While the Super Bowl loss stings and will undoubtedly fuel the young Bengals into the future, Burrow and his teammates made the wise choice to intentionally celebrate the accomplishments of a magical season.

And who knows? If Joe can celebrate a magical season after a Super Bowl loss, maybe one day he can look back on that first night in The Horseshoe with at least a tinge of fondness, turning that nagging nightmare back into a dream come true.

Celebration seems to be the perfect word for this book. It's a celebration of Joe Burrow's first twenty-five years. Let's get this party started.

From Bulldog *to* Bengal

1

My Bloodline Runs Deep

"Joe Burrow is the most effortlessly cool person on the planet."[14]

—Dan Hoard

The voice of the Cincinnati Bengals

Quarterbacks Joe Burrow and Kurt Warner have a few things in common. Not only have both gone to the Super Bowl, but each knows what it's like to be an underdog.[15] In less than two years, Burrow went from little-known backup to number-one overall selection in the NFL draft. Warner's meteoric rise was even more unlikely, going from second-string signal-caller to league and Super Bowl MVP in a matter of five months.

But Burrow and Warner have something (or someone) else in common—Joe's dad, Jimmy. Kurt and Jimmy met in 1995 when the newly formed Arena League Iowa Barnstormers were assembling a team. Both men were looking to bounce back from professional disappointments. Kurt had been recently cut by the Green Bay Packers and was staying afloat by stocking grocery-store shelves. Jimmy had just finished an eight-year stint as the Iowa State defensive backs coach and was paying the bills as a salesman.

"Once we got let go at Iowa State, I was working for a screen-printing and embroidery shop," recalls Jimmy. "I stayed involved in coaching by volunteering at Ames High School during the fall and working with the Barnstormers during the summer. That was back when the Arena League was crazy. We played at all of the big venues around the country."[16]

Jimmy transferred from Ole Miss to the University of Nebraska, where he excelled as a Cornhusker defensive back. *Photo credit: The Burrow Family*

The Barnstormers went 7–5 the first year, but with Kurt guiding the high-flying offense and Jimmy directing the defense, the new franchise caught fire the next two seasons posting a 23–5 record en route to back-to-back well-earned ArenaBowl appearances. Despite losing both championship games, Jimmy and Kurt ended up forging a lifelong friendship.

Jimmy and Robin's fondest memory from those years, however, was the birth of their son Joseph Lee Burrow on December 10, 1996. Always the accommodating child, Joe came into the world in the offseason—three weeks after Ames High School and Joe's oldest brother, Jamie, fell short to Iowa City in the 4A state title game.

Eight months later, Joe found himself on his mother's lap just a couple seats away from Warner on the charter flight back from Phoenix following an ArenaBowl loss to the Arizona Rattlers. "Kurt quietly read his Bible the whole way," recalls Robin.[17] On the somber return flight to Iowa that night, just a few feet from each other, who could have possibly predicted the inspirational paths that lay ahead for these two underdogs—devout Kurt Warner and little Joe Burrow.

Mo-Joe So Dope

Despite tough high school championship and ArenaBowl losses, the Burrows have been surrounded by winners through the years. In fact, several Super Bowl champion quarterbacks would become family friends. "It's kind of a thing," says Jimmy. Kurt Warner, Mark Rypien, Peyton and Eli Manning, and Drew Brees are all family friends. They all have Super Bowl rings. With a smile, Jimmy adds, "Hopefully we can add Joe to that list one day."[18]

Joe came within eighty-five seconds of joining that elite list on February 13, 2022. Despite the stinging defeat, he took Warner's advice and celebrated a magical season that no one saw coming. Part of that celebration included the Bengals Super Bowl after-party, headlined by Joe's favorite musician Kid Cudi.

Burrow and many of his teammates joined the singer on stage to vibe to a setlist hand-selected by the Bengals QB. Some would say the title to the opening song, "Mojo So Dope," fits Burrow to a "T." Just ask Bengals play-by-play announcer Dan Hoard, who thinks "Joe Burrow is the most effortlessly cool person on the planet."[19]

Hoard is not alone. Before Super Bowl LVI, Rams all-pro receiver Odell Beckham Jr. offered glowing comments about Burrow's swag and demeanor: "If you look up 'cool' in the dictionary, there's a picture of [Joe Burrow] with some Cartier shades. This guy is smooth."[20]

It's not entirely clear where Joe gets his mojo and why it's so dope. No one can put their finger on it. Aura. "It" factor. Call it what you want. Those who know him best don't try to explain it. To them, Joe is just Joe.

Or maybe the answer lies in another lyric from the same Kid Cudi song: "My bloodline runs deep." Joe certainly has some cool customers in his lineage, which can be traced to the Deep South on his father's side of the family.

Only 37 More to Go!

Born in 1953 on Langley Air Force Base in Hampton, Virginia, Jimmy Burrow moved to his parents' hometown of Smithville, Mississippi, when he was just two years old. At age eleven, he and his family relocated to nearby Amory, which was the Magnolia state's first planned city when founded in 1887 by the Kansas City, Memphis & Birmingham Railroad. About two hours southeast of Memphis and an hour northwest of Tuscaloosa, Amory is home to around 7,000 residents.

Jimmy had a pretty dope childhood. Or maybe *swell* would be a more apt adjective, given the Mayberry or *Leave-It-to-Beaver* ambiance of Amory. There were plenty of opportunities for sports—baseball, basketball and football. But nothing could top after-parties at Bill's Hamburgers. Rumor has it, they have some of the best sliders in the state if not the entire country.[21] If you're in the area, it's a must see—and taste. Just cruise down Main Street and look for a weathered red brick building with candy-striped awnings and a large nondescript sign across the facade that reads: "Bill's Hamburgers, Founded 1929." To the side of the door, you'll be welcomed by a charming hand-drawn picture of a smiling fry cook holding a coke and slider. Inside you'll find plenty of memorabilia, including an autographed picture of Ole Miss legend Eli Manning and snapshot of another favorite son—Joe Burrow, wearing a Bill's Hamburger shirt.

Jimmy was a standout athlete at Amory High School during the late '60s. As a hoops star, Burrow was on fire one night only to have his enthusiasm doused by his own mother. "I remember being pretty excited about scoring 45 points in a game and she told me, 'Only 37 more to go!'"[22] (Did I mention the Burrows are competitive?) The good-natured maternal ribbing was a reference to the night Dot scored a state-record 82 points.

Here's the story: The year was 1950. Fifteen-year-old Elvis Presley had just moved from nearby Tupelo to Memphis. Jimmy's father, James Burrow, was a sophomore point guard at Mississippi State. James would tell tales about his 5-foot-10 girlfriend and future wife, Dot Ford, who was tickling the twine for nearby Smithville High School. His teammates rolled their eyes. James finally convinced six of his buddies to come along and see for themselves. Dot flashed moves young Elvis could only dream of, overcoming non-stop double-teaming to light up Hamilton High for 72 points. Next time the whole Bulldog team made the trek from Starkville. That's the night she scorched Caledonia for 82.[23]

During Joe's senior season at LSU, ESPN's Tom Rinaldi reminded Joe that Kobe Bryant dropped 81 in a game, one point shy of Dot. With a twinkle in his eye, the proud grandson quipped, "Never thought about that. Is my grandmother better than Kobe Bryant? I don't know."[24]

While Jimmy inherited his hardwood skills from both parents, he was even better on the diamond and gridiron. He excelled at quarterback and defensive back in high school and seemed destined to play for his childhood team—the Mississippi State Bulldogs. Then, during his senior season, Jimmy broke his arm. "That's when most of the schools pulled away from recruiting me."[25]

Burrow took summer classes at Mississippi State, but chose to walk on at Ole Miss because they gave him the opportunity to play both football and baseball. After starting every game for the freshman team, he approached Ole Miss Football Coach Billy Kinard about a scholarship. The answer was no.

It was time to consider other options.

Vindication Is Sugary Sweet

Amory High School Coach Jim Walden joined Bob Devaney's Nebraska coaching staff in 1969—after Burrow's sophomore season. Walden had previously played quarterback for Devaney at Wyoming. Nebraska showed interest in Burrow, but didn't offer a scholarship out of high school. Walden fondly remembers Jimmy as a talented kid, but a "skinny-assed 125 pounds" when he coached him at Amory.[26]

Now, things were different. The Huskers needed a scout-team quarterback who could run the wishbone and eventually contribute in other ways. Jimmy was a perfect fit. The 5-foot-11, 170-pound Burrow had grown into a hard-nosed, quick-twitch, lean-muscled two-way player. Walden convinced Devaney that Burrow was their guy.

Jimmy packed his bags and headed north.

"While Nebraska recruited me to play scout-team quarterback, the plan was always to move over to defensive back once I became eligible," recalls Jimmy. "It was fun. They had just won two national championships in a row and had one of the best defensive units in all of football."[27]

Devaney handed over the reins of the Husker football program to Tom Osborne after the 1972 season. Burrow proved to be a sure-handed punt-returner and hard-hitting safety, earning second-team All-Big Eight recognition his senior season and Academic All-Big Eight honors, as well. The Huskers went 28–7–1 from 1973–75 with Cotton Bowl and Sugar Bowl victories.

Jimmy's biggest moment came in the 1974 Sugar Bowl when the eighth-ranked Huskers faced the 18th-ranked Florida Gators. In the final Sugar Bowl game played at Tulane Stadium, with ABC's Keith Jackson and Oklahoma's Barry Switzer on the call, the Gators were on the verge of extending their 10–0 lead as time was winding down in the third quarter. Another touchdown would likely put the game out of reach. On fourth and goal from the one-yard line, the Gator quarterback ran the option, but Burrow wasn't fooled. The Nebraska DB shed a blocker, anticipated the pitch, and wrapped up the Florida tailback just shy of the goal line. "Jim Burrow, Number 2, got his man!" exclaimed Jackson.

The Husker sideline erupted.

With newfound energy and resolve, the offense mounted a relentless 18-play, 99-yard touchdown drive. The Husker defense shut down Florida the rest of the way and Nebraska added two field goals for a hard-fought 13–10 win. Burrow's gritty goal-line tackle proved to be the pivotal moment in the game.

The Nebraska faithful still recall that play with great fondness. All-American Rik Bonness, now a lawyer in Omaha, was the Husker center that night. Through the years, Bonness has inspired countless fans with the following life lesson: "When it looks like you might lose, make a stand and start your own 99-yard drive."[28]

In a postgame TV interview, Burrow had his own message to convey. With a well-earned sense of vindication, Jimmy wished Billy Kinard, the coach who didn't offer him a scholarship, a "Happy New Year from the Sugar Bowl."[29] Jimmy bet on himself and the decision to transfer paid off. He was headed to Bourbon Street to celebrate a Sugar Bowl victory and ring in 1975 in style. Kinard, on the other hand, had been fired the previous season, lasting less than three years as the Ole Miss head coach.

Go North Young Man

As if Nebraska wasn't cold enough for this Mississippi boy, Jimmy found himself even farther north when selected by the Green Bay Packers in the eighth round of the 1976 NFL Draft. Lambeau Field, nicknamed the "Frozen Tundra," had been the site for the coldest game in NFL history (thirteen degrees below zero) on New Year's Eve 1967. Dubbed the "Ice Bowl," legendary signal-caller Bart Starr led the Packers to a finger-numbing and heart-pounding 21–17 NFC Championship victory over the Dallas Cowboys.

Nine years later, Starr had moved from quarterback to Green Bay head coach. Burrow joined a defensive backfield room that included two-time Pro-Bowler and Packer Hall-of-Fame inductee Willie Buchanon.

While he learned invaluable lessons from coaches and teammates, Burrow only played in the first three games for the struggling Packers, who finished the season 5–9 and last in the NFC Central standings. In the third game of the season, Jimmy faced future Cincinnati Ring of Honor quarterback Ken Anderson at Riverfront Stadium. In a 28–7 Bengals victory, Anderson threw for a touchdown and Ohio State great Archie Griffin added another one on the ground. The real story of the game, however, was the Bengals secondary, as Ken Riley and Tommy Casanova each took interceptions to the house.

Jimmy Burrow's brief NFL career quietly came to an end that afternoon on the banks of the Ohio River. Ironically, it would turn out to be the very spot where his youngest son would one day rule the Jungle as the undisputed King of the Queen City.

While Jimmy never played another down in the NFL, his professional career continued even farther north in the Canadian Football League. He would play five years in the CFL for the Montreal Alouettes, the Calgary Stampeders and the Ottawa Rough Riders. With the Alouettes, he competed in three Grey Cups (the CFL equivalent of the Super Bowl)—winning the title in 1977. Burrow was twice named CFL Eastern Conference All-Star.

While playing for the Alouettes, Jimmy injured his shoulder. He reached out to his former high school and college coach, Jim Walden, who had just taken over as the Washington State quarterbacks coach. Burrow asked if he could help out with the Cougar football program while rehabbing. It led to a multi-year arrangement. During the CFL offseason, Burrow trained in Pullman and served as a graduate assistant with the football team.

When his playing career ended in 1981, Burrow graduated with a master's degree in Education Administration, building on the bachelor's in education he'd already obtained from Nebraska. He was well-prepared to become a school administrator—a job his father had held back in Amory.

By now, however, Walden had become the Washington State head coach and asked Jimmy to join his full-time staff. Burrow coached tight ends for one season before shifting over to defensive backs for the remainder of his time in Pullman.

The Cougars put together a memorable season in 1981. They finished 8–3–1 and narrowly lost to Brigham Young, 38–36, in a wildly entertaining Holiday Bowl. Two future Super Bowl winning quarterbacks suited up for the game. Jim McMahon, who five years later would lead the Chicago Bears to a victory in Super Bowl XX, slung it around the field for BYU that night, while Mark Rypien, the Redskins Super Bowl XXVI MVP, was a freshman backup for Washington State.

During his years in Pullman, Jimmy was often responsible for recruiting. While he landed some quality players, including Rypien, the biggest fish to get away was Ryne Sandberg. Sandberg was a *Parade* All-American quarterback at North Central High School in Spokane when Jimmy signed him to a letter of intent. Unfortunately for Jimmy and the Washington State coaching staff, Sandberg never played a down for the Cougars. Instead, the Philadelphia Phillies drafted him in the 20th round and agreed to pay him a comparable amount of money to the scholarship he had been offered by Jimmy.[30]

It worked out okay for Sandberg. Not so much for Philadelphia, where he only played one season. The ten-time All-Star was inducted into the Major League Baseball Hall of Fame in 2005. Wearing a Cubs hat.

The Return to Lincoln

In 1987, Walden accepted the head coaching job at Iowa State and Jimmy came along as his defensive backs coach. Burrow was elevated to co-defensive coordinator his final season. Walden, Burrow and the rest of the new Cyclone coaching staff were behind the eight ball from the beginning, inheriting a program facing NCAA sanctions. In each of their first four seasons, Walden's Cyclones played with a reduction of scholarship players.[31]

Young Joe with Jimmy and brother Dan.
Photo credit: The Burrow Family

When Walden and his staff were let go in 1994, it was a major disappointment for Burrow. That said, there were two positive changes looming on the horizon.

First, Jimmy had two sons, Jamie and Dan, from a previous marriage. While he was always deeply involved in their lives, his professional commitments had limited his opportunities to coach them directly. Now he'd be able to coach both of them at Ames High School.

The second positive change? Jimmy met his perfect complement—a farm girl from Nebraska.

Robin Parde was born in Lincoln, but grew up near the town of Cook (population: 300) in the southeastern part of the state. The daughter of Wayne and Marianne, Robin was surrounded by testosterone from the earliest days—sandwiched in between one older brother and two younger ones.

On the farm, Robin learned discipline, hard work, and the difficult reality that "life is short."[32] She baled plenty of hay and put a few miles on the tractor.

Robin excelled in the classroom, graduating with twenty tight-knit classmates from Nemaha Valley High School. In addition to her chores on the farm, she played a sport each season—volleyball, basketball and track. Two of her brothers played college football and her father had been a high school athlete, as well, so sports were always encouraged. So was rooting for the Cornhuskers every Saturday afternoon during Harvest season.

Robin was well-rounded and verbally gifted, but Wayne remembers his daughter as an especially empathetic child with a big heart—even inviting a troubled friend to live with the Pardes during a rough patch.[33]

After high school, Robin studied fashion merchandising at Northwest Missouri State in Maryville, about ninety minutes east of Cook. Her career in women's clothing eventually led to a job in Ames, where she met Jimmy, whom Wayne remembers playing for the Huskers: "He was really small (listed at 165 pounds), but quick. And he enjoyed hitting people."[34]

Robin and Jimmy married and settled into a house on McKinley Drive, less than a mile from Ames High. Young Joe came along early in their marriage. The youngest Burrow had a high motor from the get-go. Whether running around at his brothers' football games, dunking on a Little Tikes hoop, diving for Nerf balls over the couch, or refining his baseball swing in the backyard, Joe was destined to be an athlete.

"He could hit the wiffle ball over the house when he was three and four years old," remembers Robin with a smile. "He always had to have a certain number. He'd choose how many he was going to hit that day. And that's what he did."[35]

While Joe was whacking wiffle balls, his older brothers were bruising ball carriers. Jamie was a linebacker, Dan a safety. After high school, both Burrows followed in their father's footsteps and enrolled at Nebraska.

In 2001, Frank Solich, the fourth-year Cornhusker head coach, offered Jimmy a graduate assistant position on his staff. It was an exciting opportunity for the whole family. Jimmy would get back into college football and help coach his sons at his alma mater. Robin would return to her home state and the town in which she'd been born. And five-year-old Joe would learn how to ride a bike around the iconic Nebraska "N" on the Memorial Stadium turf.

Dan redshirted in 2001, but Jamie played a major role on a Husker team that made it all the way to the national championship game. While Nebraska fell short to Miami that day in the Rose Bowl, the 2001 Huskers had much to celebrate. The accolades were impressive: 11–2 final record; Big-12 co-regular season champions; Heisman trophy-winning quarterback (Eric Crouch); and decisive 20–10 victory over number-one ranked Oklahoma. The midseason win over the Sooners turned out to be Jamie's best game, as the 6-foot-1, 245-pound middle linebacker recorded 17 tackles. A few days later, Burrow was selected as the Bronko Nagurski Defensive National Player of the Week.

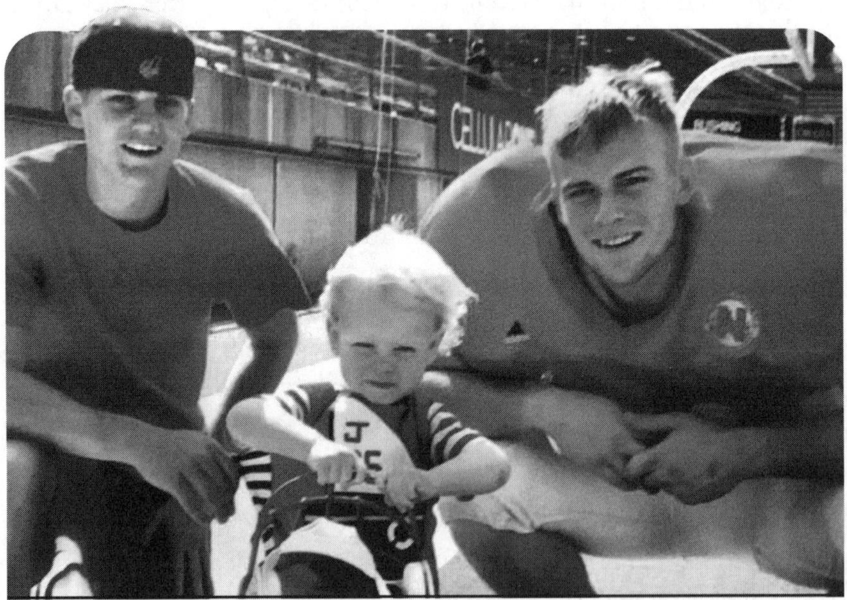

Joe at Memorial Stadium with older brothers Dan and Jamie. *Photo credit: The Burrow Family*

Research shows the first five years of life are the most critical for a child's brain development.[36] By the time Joe Burrow was five, he had already attended two ArenaBowls, an NCAA national championship game, and was hanging around Heisman-trophy and Super Bowl winning quarterbacks. It's hard to imagine an EA SPORTS Madden game developer designing a more perfectly wired five-year-old football brain.

They Have Padded Football, Buddy!

As everyone knows, the life of a football family can be nomadic. After two years in Lincoln, the Burrows were on the move again. When Nebraska assistant coach Craig Bohl was hired as the North Dakota State head coach, he asked Jimmy to join his staff as the Bisons' defensive coordinator and fellow Nebraska graduate assistant Tim Albin came along to oversee the offense.

Burrow's defense was especially stingy in 2004, allowing a league-low 13.6 points and only 285 yards per game. The Bisons finished with an 8–3 record and top-25 ranking in the final NCAA Division I-AA national poll.

While the Burrows and Albins were settling into life in Fargo, Frank Solich was fired by new Nebraska Athletic Director Steve Pederson following the 2003 season. Solich finished his head coaching career at Nebraska with 58 wins in six seasons, which exceeded the number of wins legendary coaches Bob Devaney (53) and Tom Osborne (55) compiled in their first six campaigns.

After taking a year off, Solich accepted the head coaching position at Ohio University in Athens. A native of Cleveland, Frank was no stranger to the Buckeye state. When Solich began assembling his coaching staff, two of the first calls were to Fargo. Burrow and Albin were on the move again.

The decision was made, but Joe was now in second grade and hesitant about moving again. "You're always concerned about uprooting kids when they are young," says Jimmy. "Joe had just started making friends in Fargo. He wasn't sure he wanted to make this transition."[37]

Robin did everything she could to sell Joe on the move. "Not that you had to *sell* it to an eight-year-old, I mean he was moving no matter what, but I was just trying to cushion it a little bit." She read him a book about one of southeastern Ohio's most famous native sons, astronaut John Glenn.[38] Joe was intrigued, but still hesitant.

Not surprisingly, the biggest selling point was sports. Athens had something Fargo did not. "They have padded football, buddy!" said an enthusiastic Robin to young Joe. "Third grade padded football!"[39]

Joe's eyes lit up.

2

Joe Shady

"We saw this eight-year-old kid coming up the hill in a white t-shirt and sunglasses. One of the coaches said to me, 'Look, it's Joe Cool. Your next quarterback.'"[40]

—Sam Smathers
Joe Burrow's first football coach

On January 15, 2022, Joe Burrow tossed a pair of touchdown strikes to lead the Cincinnati Bengals past the Las Vegas Raiders, 26–19. It was the first Cincinnati playoff win in thirty-one years. It was also the first time in three decades that Bengals fans had witnessed their quarterback throw more than one TD pass in a postseason game—going all the way back to Boomer Esiason.

Three decades of postseason heartache. All gone in one glorious night in the Queen City. The drought was over. The curse was broken. The party was on.

With the Jungle still gyrating, Burrow entered the postgame press conference wearing a plain white t-shirt and Cartier glasses.

The media wanted to know how the Bengals' high priest felt about exorcising the demons. Joe Cool was nonchalant. "Yeah, it's exciting. It's exciting for the city, for the state, but we're not going to dwell on that....

Third-grade Joe is picked by Coach Smathers to serve as the Bulldogs' signal-caller. *Photo credit: The Burrow Family*

This was expected. This isn't like the icing on top of the cake or anything. This is the cake, so we're moving on."[41]

After ten minutes of discussing the game, a reporter asked Burrow if his glasses held any significance. For the first time during the presser, Joe broke into a huge smile and said, "Oh no. I just think they're pretty cool. What do you think?"[42]

The room erupted in laughter.

It wasn't long before everyone was rockin' Joe Burrow shades, even a Cincinnati-area third grader, who broke the Internet when he delivered an oral report on the Bengals quarterback—dressed to the nines.[43] JoeyB9's that is.

Joe Cool

Long before JoeyB9 was playing quarterback for the National Champion LSU Tigers and AFC Champion Cincinnati Bengals, he was JoeyB4 on the Athens Bulldogs youth football, baseball and basketball teams. And long before he acquired the nickname "Joe Shiesty," he was known as "Joe Shady."

"Joe's nickname growing up was 'Shady,'" recalls Robin. "He wore sunglasses a lot. Not to be cool, but because his eyes were sensitive to the sun."[44]

Athens' youth football coach Sam Smathers remembers the first time he laid eyes on the third grader. "It was at a summer youth football camp next to the high school. We saw this eight-year-old kid coming up the hill in a white t-shirt and sunglasses. One of the coaches said to me, 'Look it's Joe Cool. Your next quarterback.'"[45]

Joe was quickly anointed the third-grade signal caller—not because of his attire, but because he could memorize and execute the plays to perfection. Sam would end up coaching Joe four seasons. By the time they were in fifth and sixth grade, Joe and his teammates had a playsheet longer than some high school playbooks.

One time Jimmy came to practice and jokingly quipped, "Hey coach, there are an awful lot of plays on that playsheet." Sam responded, "Yeah, but they know them all. And they want more. They're sponges."[46]

It was clear to everyone that Joe was intellectually and physically gifted, but it wasn't just him. He was surrounded by an unusually talented group of kids that eventually became the most accomplished athletic class to ever pass through the halls of Athens High School.

The First Transfer

When new Ohio University football coach Frank Solich hired his staff, many of the coaches' wives made a trip to Athens to explore housing options. Robin's work responsibilities kept her back in Fargo. The town of The Plains, with a population of 3,000 proud residents, proved to be an attractive location. It's home to Athens High School and the city of Athens is just a short drive away via 33 West or scenic 682 South.

Additionally, it was a great place to raise kids. "Tim Albin and his family decided to buy a house in a subdivision there," recalls Jimmy. "We heard a house next to theirs was going up for sale. I asked Tim to go over and take pictures. He sent them to us, and we bought the house sight unseen."[47]

The Burrows moved during the spring of 2005. Joe finished his second-grade year at The Plains Elementary School, which is located on the edge of their neighborhood. Always the diligent parent, Robin did a tour of the other schools in the area and decided Morrison Elementary, about a fifteen-minute drive from their home, would be the best fit for Joe moving forward. Only one problem: The school turned down their request for a transfer.

"We really wanted Joe to go to Morrison, but it was a large class of students, so it was a challenge," said Robin. "We jumped through as many hoops as we could and knocked on windows in the summertime. The whole nine yards."[48] Their persistence paid off. Joe was headed to Morrison for the remainder of his elementary-school years.

The decision to transfer was fortuitous, as many of his future friends and teammates were Morrison students. Robin remembers Joe and his buddies would play football during recess, practicing actual plays they had learned from Coach Sam and his staff.[49]

Little Joey Brrr

But it wasn't just football. Many in Joe's class were three-sport athletes. In fact, it all started with baseball.

Robin must have thought they were still in North Dakota when she took Joe to baseball tryouts at the West State Street Park just a few weeks after moving to Athens. It was one of those Southeastern Ohio spring mornings when winter just wouldn't let go.

As coaches prepared to assess the kids' hitting, throwing and fielding, Keith McGrath remembers "seeing this lady and young boy walking toward us. Big snowflakes were slowly falling. It was colder than hell." McGrath thought to himself, "I bet that's the Burrow kid."[50]

Although he hadn't seen him play, McGrath had heard about a second grader from North Dakota coming to town. He had already spoken with Jimmy on the phone about the prospect of Joe joining the Athens travel team following the regular-league season.

There would be no favoritism. Joe would have to earn it. The Burrows wouldn't have it any other way.

Like the rest of the kids on that frosty morning, little Joey Brrr froze his tookus off. But they didn't care, even at that age they were gamers. This group just loved to compete.

Our Kind of People

After the regular season ended, Joe was chosen to the Athens All-Star team, which would travel around the state and compete in tournaments. In the field, "Shady" patrolled center and pitched; at the plate, he hit cleanup.

"When Joe was young, he was just a stick," remembers McGrath. "He was really thin. His legs probably weren't as big as my arms. But, boy, he had a quick bat whip. It didn't matter if it was an off-speed pitch or fast ball, he'd just turn on it."[51]

The Athens All-Stars: #26 Sam Vander Ven, #41 Alec Sikorski, #17 Wade Lent, #2 Brody McGrath, #8 Liam Tompkins, #55 Chris Reimer, #6 Ryan Luehrman, #44 Adam Luehrman, #4 Joe Burrow, #7 Quinton Hart, #15 Jordan Ward. *Photo credit: Keith McGrath*

Joe was introverted by nature. But it didn't take long for him to bond with his teammates, especially Evan Cooley, Sam Vander Ven, and the imposing Luehrman twins—Ryan and Adam, who were often called the "Twin Towers."[52]

The Luehrmans were so tall for their age, opposing coaches demanded to see their birth certificates before every tournament. Ryan and Adam were overpowering pitchers. When not on the mound, Ryan played first base, and Adam often manned the hot corner.[53] The heart of the batting order—three, four, and five—belonged to Ryan, Joe, and Adam. The Athens youth version of "Murderers' Row."

When Joe hit his growth spurt in middle school, many people thought Ryan, Joe, and Adam were triplets. "They were all tall, thin, and blond," says Jimmy.[54] "Joe was a lot shorter early, but then they all ended up about the same size," adds Robin.[55]

While these kids eventually were more known for gridiron glory, their best youth sport was baseball. At least that's what Don Cooley thinks. He should know. Cooley coached them in multiple sports during their youth years. "Between baseball and basketball, I would have coached Joe, the Luehrmans, Sam, and my son (Evan), probably 400 games."[56]

Cooley got to know each player thoroughly. Strengths, weaknesses, tendencies, tangibles, intangibles. "This is not a knock on Joe, because he was a great athlete, but if you went back in a time machine and asked which one of these kids is going to win the Heisman Trophy, you wouldn't have picked Joe out of the pack," says Cooley. "He wasn't an athletic freak."[57]

Evan Cooley, who is now a videographer for the Cincinnati Bengals, agrees. "In the fourth grade, Joe wasn't the one you would have picked out as a future pro athlete. It probably would have been one of the Luehrman twins."[58]

That said, Joe had plenty of highlights on the diamond. Sam Vander Ven remembers Joe was always at his best when it counted the most. "Joe was just ridiculous at some points," recalls Sam. "One day we were in the loser's bracket, and we won six games to win the championship. I don't remember Joe ever getting out the entire day. It was the most pinnacle performance at the plate, which included a couple home runs."[59]

Sam's dad, Tom Vander Ven, fondly remembers one of those home runs. "For some reason, our mantra for that tournament was 'Far out!'" recalls Vander Ven, who was also one of the coaches. "We even had shirts that said, 'Far out!' Joe, who was generally real quiet and serious on the field, but a kid with a sense of humor, cranks one over the fence. No doubter. He's loping around the bases and a bunch of the parents yell, 'Farrr outtt!' As he's rounding third and heading for home, Joe flashes the double peace sign."[60]

Inside the lines, the kids were all business on the field. "It didn't matter what they played, they were going to win," recalls Liz Luehrman, Ryan and Adam's mother. "But after the game, they didn't talk about it. They moved onto Sponge Bob, Nerf basketball, playing video games, whatever. They loved to cut up and have a good time."[61]

So did the parents.

Liz remembers the Burrows' first travel baseball trip. After the games were over, the group would always eat dinner together before heading next door to the hotel. "Robin and Jimmy stayed in the car for the longest time," recalls Liz. "Robin said they were talking about this being the test. If the parents order Coke, then that's one thing. But if they order beer, then they're our kind of people."[62] Jimmy and Robin walked into the restaurant and saw all the kids at one large table and the parents at another one—with a couple pitchers of beer.

They'd found their tribe.

Piece by Piece by Piece

It didn't matter who they played; the Athens All-Stars rarely lost a game. Even against teams from the highly populated parts of the state.

After beating a team from Cincinnati, the opposing coach came up to Don Cooley and asked, "Where do you draw from? How wide is your talent pool?"

Cooley responded, "All these kids go to the same junior high school. In fact, there is another team from our junior high that is pretty decent. I asked him where they drew from. He said, 'We only draw from three counties: Hamilton, Clermont, and Butler. We're very similar to you guys.'" With a good-hearted chuckle, Cooley quipped, "Yeah, it sounds really similar. I'm taking half the kids from one junior high and you're drawing from three of the largest counties in Ohio."[63]

Although rare, the Athens All-Stars occasionally tasted defeat. It usually didn't go down well. "This group hated to lose," remembers McGrath. "They were just super-competitive."[64] Evan Cooley adds, "We were never sore losers, but we weren't great in defeat."[65]

Especially when the other team didn't win fair and square.

McGrath remembers a time when that's exactly what happened. The umpire and the other team's head coach were tight as brothers. In fact, they *were* brothers. The calls were outrageous. Sam Vander Ven remembers strike calls that were not only inches, but feet off the plate.[66] Ultimately the "home-field advantage" decided the tournament in the other team's favor.

"I remember Ryan Luehrman immediately threw his second-place trophy into the trash," says McGrath. "Adam broke his trophy in half. Joe, on the other hand, was completely stoic. No emotion. Then later that night I got a call from Robin. She said, 'I don't know if I should be proud or disturbed, but Joe has spent the last two hours dismantling that second-place trophy, piece by piece by piece. Then he threw it in the trash can.'"[67]

Shortstop and lead-off hitter Brody McGrath, who would go on to play baseball at Butler University, remembers the ride home. “It was just so crazy that we all wanted to torture this inanimate object, because we knew we deserved the championship trophy.”[68]

When Athens first started playing teams from around the region, McGrath and the other coaches wondered how their players would respond to a higher level of competition. They were never intimidated.

Just the opposite.

Cooley remembers a Sunday afternoon when they were in eighth grade. Even the most intense, competitive kids need an occasional day off. The boys had already played several games that weekend to win a tournament in Parkersburg, West Virginia. Now, it was a beautiful day, and they were missing a pool party to play some random team at their home field in Athens.

“None of our kids even wanted to warm up,” recalls Cooley. “Joe even said, ‘This is stupid. Who scheduled this game? We want to go to the pool.’”

Then the opposing team’s coach came over to the Athens dugout to exchange lineups.

Everything changed.

“The other coach asked me, ‘What’s your team called?’” says Cooley. “I told him we were Athens. He said, ‘Well, Athens what?’ I said, ‘I don’t know, we’re like eleven guys from Athens Middle School.’ And he says, ‘Well, we’re the Ohio Valley Destroyers and we’re rated number two (in some rating I’d never heard of).’ Then he just starts bragging about how good their team is. But he’s doing this at the dugout in front of our whole team. And my players are all sitting there watching. Finally, he leaves, and Joe says something to the effect of, ‘We can’t beat this team bad enough.’ If the coach had kept his mouth shut, our kids probably would have forfeited that day. But once he started running his mouth, it was game on.”[69]

Athens proceeded to dismantle the Destroyers, 11–0.

Piece by piece by piece.

What's the Rocket Play?

On Christmas Day 2019, approximately seventy-two hours before Joe Burrow calmly carved up the Oklahoma defense to send LSU to the national title game, the Sooners and Tigers competed in a friendly basketball shootout.

One at a time, five representatives from each team had sixty seconds to make as many buckets as possible. It appeared Oklahoma had the competition in hand. That is, until LSU's final shooter strolled onto the court. With tension in the air and the clock winding down, Joe Burrow calmly hit 10 of 12 shots, including a three-point dagger at the buzzer to seal the victory.[70]

Clutch. As always.

"A lot of people thought basketball was Joe's best sport when he was growing up," says Jimmy. "I think he could have at least played in the Mid-American Conference."[71]

Joe and Brody McGrath were two of the most intense players on the Athens youth travel teams. They were always trying to outduel each other. It didn't matter how much or how little was on the line. Brody remembers, "If you said to Joe that you could brush your teeth better than him, he'd say, 'Oh yeah?'"[72]

That said, Brody and Joe might not have been the most intense players on their youth basketball team. According to Cooley, that honor went to a player who did go on to play Mid-American Conference basketball, a girl by the name of Dominique Doseck. Dominique was so talented, she played with the boys until sixth grade. Later she would star for the hometown Ohio University Bobcats.

"Dominique was an assassin," remembers Cooley. "Very confident. Very skilled at a young age. We would break the opposing team's press by giving her the ball and sending everyone else to the other end of the court. If the opposing team put five guys on her, it was unfair. Five wasn't enough—they had to go out and get more."[73]

While having a girl excelling on a boy's youth team might create a strange dynamic for some, that wasn't the case for Joe and his buddies. "We all loved having Dominique on our team," recalls Sam Vander Ven. "She was as good a youth basketball player as we had. Great athlete, great player, and got along with all the boys very well."[74]

Mary Ann Welsh's daughter, Kaitlin Baker, played with Dominique as they got older. Mary Ann remembers a girl's middle-school game in which Doseck fell while back peddling. She came out of the game with a severely injured arm. Athens lost. "Dominique refused to go to the hospital until after the game," recalls Mary Ann, "She was tough. There's a picture of her with the team holding up the second-place trophy. She was turning green, but didn't shed a tear."[75]

While it took sixty seconds for Burrow to take over the shootout against Oklahoma, Tom Vander Ven remembers it only took Joe half as long to work his magic in a game against Maysville.

"We were up in Columbus at what they call the state tournament, and we were down by eight points with thirty seconds left," recalls Vander Ven, who shared coaching duties with Cooley. "And Joe, as a nine-year-old, scores nine straight points in thirty seconds, most of them from the free throw line. Just draining free throws and making steals. He just completely took over without any show of emotion. Just this flat affect. There was no coaching involved. We were just standing there watching this happen."[76]

Against clearly inferior opponents, Cooley remembers Joe's cutting wit as much as his slashing moves to the basket. One time, Athens was playing a team called the Rockets.[77] "They would come down the floor and the point guard always raised his hand and yelled, 'Rocket,'" recalls Cooley.

"They'd run this play over and over, but hardly ever got a shot off. We were in the huddle and another kid asked, 'What's the 'Rocket' play?' Completely deadpan, Joe goes, 'That's the one where the kid puts his head down, tries to dribble and then kicks it out of bounds.'"[78]

Sam Vander Ven also recalls Joe's off-beat sense of humor that often surfaced when the score wasn't close.

Case in point: a summer scrimmage at Marietta College.

"Joe was in transition, and he 'broke this kid's ankles' like I've never seen in my life; the kid went flying five feet," says Sam with a grin. "Joe just stood there and stared at the kid on the ground for a good two seconds."

Instead of taking the wide open 15-footer, however, Joe passed the ball to Sam, who made the shot. The opposing coach called a timeout. As they were jogging to the bench, Sam said to Joe, "What are you doing? Shoot the shot." Joe responded, "I didn't want to miss it. Watching that kid fly through the air was cool enough."[79]

This Is All Your Fault

The humorous and quick-witted side of Joe Burrow was on full display on May 17, 2022, when he interacted with the media for the first time since the Super Bowl.

"Did you miss us?" asked one reporter. Flashing that million-dollar smile, Joe responded, "Can't say that I did."

The room erupted in laughter.

"A little?" A clearly refreshed and light-hearted Burrow conceded, "Maybe a little."

About a third of the way through the presser, Bengals announcer Dave Lapham asked what kind of offensive changes we could expect going into next season. As dry as a drought, Joe responded, "We're going to completely overhaul the offense. We're going to run the Wing-T a little bit this year. Maybe our division can start watching some Georgia Tech or something."[80]

The room again erupted in laughter.

Now, if Joe's deadpan joke is lost on you, it's probably because you aren't familiar with offensive football schemes.

Quick lesson: The Wing-T is an under-center, run-centric scheme that relies on timing and deception rather than power—about as far away from the shotgun, empty-backfield, pass-heavy approach that Joe and his top-rated Bengals receiving corps often use to carve up opposing defenses.[81]

Got it?

Well, don't feel bad if it's still a bit unclear. You aren't the only one who missed the full depth of his quip. In fact, few in the room would have realized there was another layer to Joe's joke. An esoteric layer that only Joe and his Athens youth football family would have known—Joe was once a master at running the Wing-T. In fact, it's why he became a quarterback in the first place.

During his youth coaching career Sam Smathers had seven different varsity coaches. Since the youth teams run the same schemes as the varsity, this meant installing seven different offenses and defenses through the years.[82]

When Joe and his class entered third grade, the varsity head coach, Cory Miller, was running the Wing-T. It's an offense that requires a smart quarterback who can execute with timing and precision. Joe was Sam's guy. That said, if Miller had been running a passing offense, Sam would have chosen Ryan Luehrman.[83] "I threw the ball way better than Joe," says Ryan with a playful grin.[84]

That would have been fine with Joe. He wanted to play running back or wide receiver. "I know why he didn't want to play quarterback," remembers Smathers. "Joe wanted to catch the ball and run the ball. I told him, 'Don't worry, you will.'" [85]

Many years later, when he started experiencing success in Baton Rouge, Joe would jokingly say to Coach Sam, "You know, this is all your fault." Smathers remembers the day his phone blew up after Joe dropped his name at a press conference. Joe was "blaming" his youth football coach for making him play quarterback against his will. With a twinkle in his eye, Sam told Jimmy, "Remind me to kick Joe's butt when he gets home." Jimmy's response: "He's making us all famous."[86]

Truth is, Sam almost missed out on the chance to coach Joe. He was scheduled to coach fifth- and sixth-grade football the year Joe moved from Fargo. But third- and fourth-grade coach Kevin Schwartzel wanted to keep coaching his son, Skylar, who was going into fifth. "Kevin said, 'Hey coach, do you mind if I move up and keep coaching my son?'" recalls Smathers. "So, I agreed to drop back down and coach whatever third- and fourth-grade kids showed up. As Jimmy always says, 'The stars aligned right there.'"[87]

The Dawg Pound

For the three-sport athletes, sandwiched in between baseball and basketball was football. Sam Vander Ven fondly recalls heading to Coach Sam's garage each August.

"The start of every football season was going over to the Dawg Pound to get our helmets fitted and collect our uniforms," says a nostalgic Vander Ven, who now coaches the quarterbacks at Notre Dame Cathedral Latin High School in Chardon, Ohio. "I just remember a lot of energy and being really excited to go to Coach Smathers' house because that meant it was time for football."[88]

Sam and Terri Smathers purchased their property on N. McDonald Street in 1988. The Friday night lights from every Athens High School home football game have flooded their front yard for the past thirty-five years.[89] A spirited bunch, that's where as many as fifty family and friends have shown up to tailgate and watch games. The local radio station does their version of ESPN's College Gameday from their house.

At first, Sam's crew watched games from their rooftop. Then, during a renovation one year, Sam elevated the front porch so they could come down from the upper deck. A red maple tree on the right side of the front yard gets a little bigger each season. "On really crowded game nights, the newest person has to sit behind the tree," jokes Sam.

"I would always know Coach Sam was over there every time we scored a touchdown," recalls Vander Ven. "He was barking, and his A-Train horn was blaring. That was always in the back of my mind."[90]

While the Smathers clan has had a ton of fun through the years, they've also endured a lot of rough seasons. "I got tired of seeing our teams go 2–8, 1–9," says Smathers. "That's what motivated me to help bring back youth tackle football in Athens. We needed to get going early and teach them the same techniques and terminology all the way up to varsity. We needed a feeder system."[91]

Inside the Dawg Pound, Sam and his youth coaching staff would gather every night after practice. With either a bourbon or Budweiser in hand, the coaches discussed how they were going to get each and every kid into the game on Sunday. By Joe's sixth-grade season, Sam had forty-eight kids on the roster. "We had a complete green team and a complete gold team," says Smathers. "The whole idea of youth football is playing time. Keep kids interested."[92]

Sam's a planner. Every detail covered. There's even a makeshift urinal in the back corner of the Dawg Pound behind a banner and the pickup truck. The last thing Terri needs is a bunch of coaches using her bathroom when planning sessions go a bit too long.

Happy wife, happy life.

Through the years, the Dawg Pound slowly but surely became the ultimate Athens Bulldog Man Cave—one item at a time. Memorabilia and photos of his kids and former players line the walls. Take one photo off the wall and you'll find ten more hidden behind it—each layer revealing a different era of Athens football. Sam tends to the Dawg Pound with as much care as his bountiful vegetable garden just outside the garage.

Sam doesn't do Facebook. "This is the only wall I post to," says Smathers pointing to the rows of photos. "Only my friends get to see my wall."[93] Today, the Dawg Pound is the ultimate Joe Burrow Museum rivaled only by Jimmy and Robin's collection of memories a few miles away.

It's Just a Game

The Athens youth teams had the privilege of playing their Sunday afternoon home games at Peden Stadium, where the Ohio University Bobcats shine on Saturdays. It was a thrill for the kids. Not many nine- and ten-year-olds get to compete on Division I turf. For the Luehrman twins it turned out to be especially sweet since both went on to play tight end for the hometown Bobcats.

It was a perfect arrangement for Jimmy, whose office overlooked the field. As OU's defensive coordinator, he worked Sundays, but could swivel back and forth between breaking down film and watching Joe break down the opposition.

"I was fortunate to be able to watch most of Joe's games even though I was coaching," remembers Jimmy. "I didn't get to play tackle football until seventh or eighth grade, and neither did Jamie or Dan. So, it was just neat to watch Joe and those boys get better each year."[94]

One of Sam's assistant coaches, John Pugh, remembers Joe's growth throughout his youth football career. "Joe was very athletically there, very talented. You could see he knew a lot. A lot of stuff some of the other kids had no idea about," says Pugh. "It was amazing to watch through those four years how he developed and what he picked up. Little nuances here and there. Knowing when to be a motivator. Putting kids in the right positions. He knew exactly where everything was supposed to go. He was like another coach on the field."[95]

With a father and two older brothers as defensive standouts, it's not surprising Joe favored defense over offense at first. On the defensive side of the ball, he played multiple positions—cornerback, safety, linebacker. "In the beginning Joe was defensively minded," continues Pugh. "He loved to hit. When he was quarterbacking in third and fourth grade, he was doing some stuff where I was wondering, 'How does this kid know how to do this?' But it was because he understood how defenders think."[96]

Joe directing the offense. *Photo credit: The Smathers Family*

As third graders, the young Bulldogs went 7–3, finishing second in the Tri-County Youth League. In fourth grade, they improved to 8–2 and won the league title. Smathers remembers running into former AHS assistant coach Ryan Adams at Applebee's. "I told Ryan he needed to take the head coaching job at the high school because there's a really special class coming up soon."[97]

Sure enough, Adams took over as the head varsity coach in 2007 as Joe and his teammates were moving into fifth grade. The old Wing-T was out, and Adams installed a pro-style offense. Smathers asked his son, Alan, who coached the youth offensive linemen, if he could find a player to handle the shotgun snap. He did. "So, fifth-grade year we played with it," says Smathers. "Worked on it all season—shotgun wide double slot with twins. I told Joe, 'If you're going to throw it, throw it where they're the only ones who can catch it or it's going to go out of bounds."[98]

Sam focused more on the defense, so he asked former AHS coach Les Champlin to come to practice one day to help Joe with his footwork. "I said, teach him how to roll out of the pocket. So, Les came over and drilled Joe, teaching him how to roll out right, left, and attack the line of scrimmage. Keeping the ball up, stuff like that. We then practiced those drills every day."[99]

Joe and the rest of that fifth-grade team impressed Champlin, who would later call all of their high school games on local TV. "The amazing thing to me was how quickly Joe adapted to everything. That whole group of kids was so easy to work with," remembers Champlin. "Very smart and athletic. They'd complete passes 30 to 40 yards down field. To see them execute the spread offense unbelievably well at that age was just phenomenal. Unheard of. It was a lot of fun."[100]

Sam's Bulldogs finished 5–4 their fifth-grade season, but it all came together the following year. As sixth graders, Joe and his teammates ran the regular-season table, outscoring their Tri-County League opponents 185–34.

It was a taste of things to come.

"We had a script of ten plays for each game, but we scored so quickly, we couldn't get through the script," says Sam. "Joe didn't play in the second half in any of those games. None of them. Just like in high school."[101]

There was one exception. A comeback for the ages. The gridiron equivalent of Joe's 9-point, thirty-second basketball barrage against Maysville.

"We were down by two touchdowns with 4:50 to go at Nelsonville York," explains Smathers. "In youth football, that's death. You can't come back from that."

Unless, of course, you have sixth graders by the name of Burrow and Luehrman.

Sam and his offensive coordinator drew up a play right there in the Nelsonville dirt. "We told Ryan, who was playing tailback, to sell the fake pitch and hit the edge," recalls Smathers. "We just had to freeze the safety over the top. Adam then ran a straight out-route. Straight flag. Joe would fake the pitch, roll back and launch it up there where only Adam could catch it. We ran that play three times and scored all three times. We won 20–14 in overtime. They couldn't defend it."[102]

While they won their fair share of games over that four-year stretch, Sam wanted his kids to have fun along the way. At the conclusion of each season, the Tri-County League champion played the nearby Muskingum Valley League champion in the region's own version of the Super Bowl. The Bulldogs were the Tri-County representative in fourth grade.

As Athens prepared to face Sheridan in the game of all games, Sam addressed his team. "You're the only ones in the area practicing this week. Football's over. Even the high school is done." He then asked them what kind of offense they wanted to run. They could stick to the Wing-T they'd used all season or air it out. Joe and his teammates didn't hesitate: "We want to throw the ball!" Sam said, "Okay."[103]

The first half of the Super Bowl didn't go as planned. Athens had some opportunities, but several dropped passes. As Sam puts it, "We couldn't catch a cold." They entered halftime down 21–0. "All their heads were down, they were all dejected," remembers Sam. "I just told them, 'Hey don't worry about it. We tried it your way, now let's go back to running the offense we've used all year.'"

In the second half, Athens almost pulled it out by putting two touchdowns on the board and preventing Sheridan from scoring any points the rest of the game.

Why would Sam give the players such a strong voice in the biggest game of the year? "Hey, if you can't have fun in youth football, and let them be the general, let them be the boss once in a while, then what's the point? After all, it's just a game."[104]

A Family Affair

Robin Burrow has always been there for Joe, every step of the way. It's always been family first. "I will always do everything I can to be at all of Joe's stuff," says Robin. "Just as I've done for like a million years."[105]

With all the games Joe has played since third grade, it probably seems like a million years. "But in some ways, it seems like yesterday," continues Robin. "Bill Luehrman and I sitting in our lawn chairs under those trees at every youth football practice."[106]

While in Fargo, Robin had already made a family-first decision. She transitioned from fashion merchandising to a part-time job at Joe's elementary school. "With Jimmy gone so much with coaching, it just fit better with Joe's schedule," says Robin. When they came to Athens, Robin went back to school and earned a degree in elementary education. She taught for several years at Morrison before accepting her current role as principal of Eastern Elementary in nearby Meigs County.

"Eastern is the perfect fit for Robin," says Liz Luehrman. "She grew up in a small town. She understands the culture. Robin is such a hard worker. She's the first to get there in the morning and the last one to leave."[107]

Her hard work extended to supporting Joe's sports teams in any way she could. Sam remembers when the concession sign-up sheet went around, Robin's name was always on it.[108]

"I loved it so much. I wanted to be that team Mom that had all the snacks, and the drinks," says Robin. "I had the band aids in my bag in case anybody wanted one or needed one. Ice packs. I wanted to be all that. We definitely had a lot of fun with Joe's little football teams, baseball teams, basketball teams. All of it. We gained a lot of great friends through all of his athletic teams."[109]

The youth football team practiced just a stone's throw away from the Dawg Pound on a field next to the old Plains High School. The same field where my father, Bob Burson, helped coach The Plains Indians football teams during the 1950s and '60s.

As a coach, Sam was tough, but fair. It all started at practice. When he spoke, they'd all listen. He'd hold up a football, and everything stopped. All eyes went to Coach Sam.

It required discipline and a commitment to schoolwork, as well. "Before each practice, I'd ask the kids if they had their homework done," says Sam. "If not, they had to go over to their parent's car and finish it before they could come back to the field."[110]

If your name wasn't called out during practice, it probably meant you were doing everything right. That meant Joe hardly heard his name. Except for this one time. Joe was serving as the scout team quarterback going against Coach Sam's starting sixth-grade defense. The scout team was supposed to run the opponent's plays to prepare the defense for the upcoming game—this week it was arch rival Nelsonville.

Coach Pugh remembers giving the play to Joe in the huddle. "Joe says, 'Mind if I modify that?' I say, 'Go ahead.' So, Joe takes over and tells his teammates, 'Here's what we're going to do. I'm going to fake the handoff here and the pass is going to be there.'"

Sure enough, Joe and his teammates execute the play perfectly. The defense is dumbfounded. But instead of celebrating, Smathers just says, "Will you run the cards that I gave you please! Nelsonville can't do that." Joe comes back to the huddle and Pugh says, "That one's on me, buddy."[111]

Practices were never optional. Sam's teams practiced three or four times a week and if you missed a practice, then you didn't play a quarter in the next game. No exceptions. Well, there was this one time. "Joe said he was going to miss practice because he wanted to go to the demolition derby," recalls Sam. "I said, 'You know my rule about missing practice.' Then I looked around and it became clear they all wanted to go to demo night at the fair. I just gave in and said, 'Oh, okay, go to the fair.'"[112]

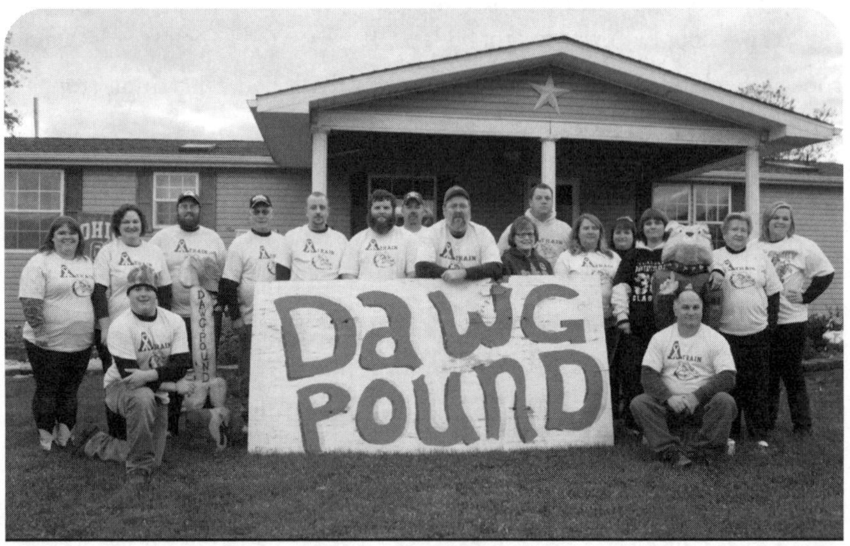

Sam and Terri Smathers with the Friday night Dawg Pound crew. *Photo credit: Trisha Doudna*

Most important, Sam cultivated a sense of belonging. From top to bottom, they were all part of something larger than themselves.

"I always told my players, we're a family," says Sam. "Everyone on this team, we're brothers. If kids would get into arguments or fights in practice, they'd run a lap holding hands. This is what family does. We can fight amongst ourselves, but we will make up."[113]

On November 30, 2008, Joe's final season in youth football, the practice field was named Smathers Field in honor of the entire Smathers family. Youth football in Athens has definitely been a Smathers family affair:

- Sam not only coached, but served as the league commissioner for many years.
- Terri was in charge of concessions and oversaw cheerleading.
- Trisha cheered, then took over cheerleading training as she got older.
- Alan and Stanley played for Sam, then assisted with coaching and filled in pretty much anywhere else they were needed.

Each kid who played youth football for Sam also became like one of his own children. "I am just as proud of the kid who is a heavy machinery operator today as I am of Joe," says Sam. "Any of my players who have succeeded and didn't use the challenges of their lives as an excuse—I'm proud of all of them."[114]

Even though they won a lot of hardware, Don Cooley agrees that youth sports for his son, Joe and the rest of this group was less about championships and more about relationships. "They all have super-fond memories of youth sports in Athens and none of it has anything to do with the games."[115]

Like the time Marikay and Tom Vander Ven took ten boys to a late-night showing of "The Simpsons." "We didn't get home until 1:30 in the morning," remembers Marikay. "They all slept on our living room floor and had to get up the next day to go to baseball. They were so wiped out, but then they played great."[116]

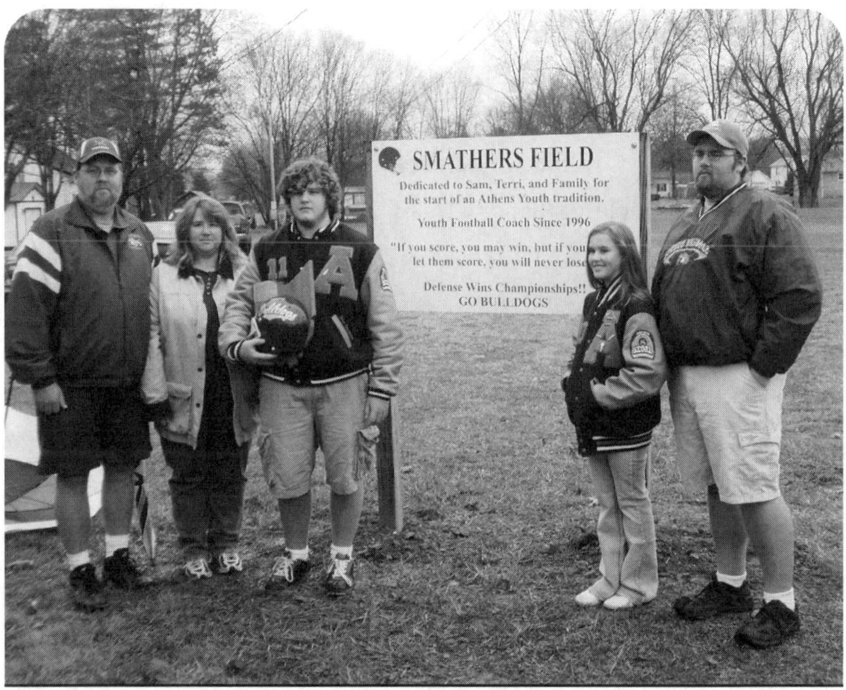

The Athens youth football practice field is renamed Smathers Field. *Left to right:* Sam, Terri, Stanley, Trisha and Alan. *Photo credit: The Smathers family*

"What we remember most are the times when they were just kids being kids," says Tom, who teaches sociology at Ohio University when not coaching youth sports. "We all got really close. We raised our kids together. There was this connection between sports and community and family. It was all kind of one thing that they were raised in. That probably can help us understand how connected Joe becomes to any community he's in. What kind of leader he is. Sports is family to him. Because that's how he got integrated into Athens. Through sports, their family became part of our family."[117]

3

First Love

"From the time he was young, we would stand back and watch other kids just flock to him without saying a word. It was just uncanny. Joe was like this little sports prophet. And he didn't even know it."[118]

—Jeff Skinner
Joe Burrow's high school basketball coach

At the 2019 Southeastern Conference Media Days a confident Joe Burrow discussed the new-look LSU offense heading into his senior season. Not only did he have a year under his belt as the Tiger signal-caller, but head coach Ed Orgeron had recently hired offensive mastermind Joe Brady away from the New Orleans Saints.

Burrow's enthusiasm was palpable. "Last year we had I think nine or ten new starters on offense, so the main thing is we have everybody back.... And there are some new concepts we have that I'm really pretty excited about."[119]

While he didn't give away many secrets, Burrow did discuss spreading the field more and running the shotgun—things he'd been doing all the way back to his days with Sam Smathers. He also talked about throwing the ball to a set of pretty decent up-and-coming young receivers by the name of Ja'Marr Chase, Justin Jefferson and Terrace Marshall.[120]

After the standard football questions, a reporter changed the conversation: "During the summer, did you binge-watch anything on Netflix?" After referencing *Stranger Things*, Joe threw the media a curve ball. "The hurricane knocked my Internet out this weekend and I watched a lot of YouTube videos on my phone about physics. So that's interesting for me."

The curious reporter followed up. "What *exactly* did you learn?"

"Um, I mean, how long do you want to be here?" asked Joe playfully.

After the laughter in the room died down, the LSU quarterback continued, "So, I watched a lot of videos about relativity, quantum mechanics, black holes, worm holes, white holes, electrons, neutrons, neutron stars. So, all that stuff, all the good stuff."[121]

While the SEC media were intrigued by how Burrow passes the time during inclement weather, his high school physics teacher Chad Springer wasn't surprised in the least.

"It wasn't shocking. Joe's different; he likes things like that," says Springer, who once talked to Burrow about becoming an astrophysicist. "When I had him in class, he was just fascinated by this stuff. Joe is an extremely brilliant man. Education was always easy to him, especially in my class."[122]

Springer remembers one particular test day. Teachers were gathered in the hallway as students filed into the classroom. Another teacher asked Joe if he had studied for the physics exam. Matter-of-factly, Joe responded, "No, I didn't study. There's no need for me to study." After Burrow passed by, the teacher said, "Can you believe that?" But Springer understood what Joe was saying. No offense taken. "Either Joe's doing something right in class or I'm doing something right in how I'm teaching it.'"[123]

Probably both.

Joe aced the exam.

And the class.

"Joe is a very curious man when it comes to physics," says Zacciah Saltzman, a high school teammate who remains one of Burrow's closest friends. "Right now, he's really into space. He'll do all-day deep dives into documentaries to learn as much as he can."[124]

As SEC Media Days came to a close, a reporter cornered Joe in the hotel lobby and asked if he would reveal his most recent Google search. A compliant Burrow scrolled through his phone and responded, "Superluminal Time Travel."[125]

Wanted: Gently Used Flux Capacitor

When Joe was growing up, his father would take him to the nearby Athens High School baseball field and throw him batting practice. Longtime Bulldog coach Fred Gibson loved seeing the budding baseball star out there refining his swing night after night.

By the time Joe reached middle school, he was hitting three things: a growth spurt, line drives to all fields, and his father's vulnerable body parts. Gibson recalls getting a call one day from a beaten and battered Jimmy Burrow: "Gibby, I need some protection!"[126]

Long-time Athens High School baseball and basketball coach, Fred Gibson. *Photo credit: Trisha Doudna*

Gibson gladly provided an L-screen. Only one problem: He had to hang around to put the screen away after they finished. Actually, it really wasn't an inconvenience; Gibby loved watching Joe swing the bat.

"I remember sitting in the stands one day and watching Joe

hit when he was an eighth-grader," recalls Gibson. "I thought to myself, 'I have a star.' He was a shortstop and pitcher, but could play anywhere. Ready to start for me on varsity as a freshman."[127]

Disappointment doesn't begin to describe the feeling that washed over Gibson the day the incoming freshman wanted to talk. "Joe said, 'Coach, I hate to do this because I really love baseball, but I think I'm going to be a Division I basketball player,'" recalls Gibson. Joe had decided to give up baseball to focus on his other two sports.

Jimmy, however, was still mulling over options. As good as Joe was in basketball and football, there were people in the community who thought baseball was his best sport. Jimmy asked Gibby if he'd ever had someone play both AAU basketball and baseball at the same time.

"I hesitated to respond because I'd never been asked that before," recalls Gibson. "I mean you can't miss baseball practice and I definitely don't want you missing games to go play AAU basketball."

Then, all of a sudden, Jimmy, the parent, shifted to Jimmy, the coach. "I take it back," said Burrow. "I would hate it if someone came to me with that question."[128]

So it was decided. Joe would finally hang up his cleats and retire from baseball.

But heading into the spring of his senior year, Burrow contemplated coming out of retirement. "Joe comes to me and says I'm thinking about playing baseball this year," recalls Gibby, who was all for it. "I said, 'Come on out!' Joe responded, 'I'm pretty rusty and haven't played for a long time.' I told him there was only one way to find out if he still had it."[129] He assured Joe of a roster spot if he wanted it.

After careful consideration, however, Burrow decided not to play. He explained his logic to Gibby. "You know, coach, if I come out and take someone's spot on the roster then it's not fair to that guy. But if I come out and don't have it anymore, then I'm going to feel bad about myself. Either way, not a good outcome."[130]

Shady's baseball cleats would remain in the closet.

According to Jimmy, all these years later, Joe still wonders if he made the right decision. "If Joe has one regret, it was not playing baseball his senior season in high school. If he could do it over again, he would play."[131]

Now, this is an interesting nugget about Joe Burrow. And it might explain a lot. This is just conjecture, but my theory is Joe has been investing so much time and energy researching Superluminal Time Travel because he's building a Doc Brown DeLorean in his parents' basement. First stop once it's complete? The Athens High School baseball diamond, Spring 2015—to rectify that one regret.

Until Joe finds a flux capacitor, I guess he'll have to settle for throwing out the first pitch at the 2022 Cincinnati Reds Opening Day festivities.[132] When it was announced that Joe would be tossing out the ceremonial pitch, many fans and pundits wondered if he was capable of throwing a baseball. Folks back home in Athens knew the answer to that question. Like Bill Finnearty, who confidently proclaimed on Facebook that Joe would be good for at least three innings if the Reds needed him.[133]

When Burrow's name was announced over the Great American Ball Park public address system, it was Shiesty, not Shady who strolled toward the mound. Wearing an untucked white Reds jersey, shadeless Joe successfully delivered the pitch to Bengals head coach Zac Taylor, even though old pal Ryan Luehrman said, "He threw it like a football."[134]

JoeyB9 Meets JoeyV19

Joe was hoping to take a few rips in the Reds' batting cage to see if he still had his youth baseball mojo. That tantalizing, groovy, "far out" swing that once broke Gibby's heart.

Check that, twice broke Gibby's heart.[135]

The Reds' brass told Burrow that Opening Day was too much of a zoo, but if he came back later in the season, they would let him take a few cuts.[136]

Not getting into the cage was disappointing for Joe, but hearing the chants of Who Dey! Who Dey! Who Dey! from the stands was a thrill for Burrow, Taylor, Tee Higgins and Ja'Marr Chase when the Bengals' quartet was introduced before the game.

The toast of Cincinnati.

Who could have imagined the Queen City faithful cheering louder for the Bengals than for the Reds in Great American Ball Park? On Opening Day, no less. Inconceivable. That is, until the magical 2021–22 run.

While Burrow and Taylor were there for the ceremonial first pitch, Chase was on the field to receive his NFL Rookie of the Year award from Reds second baseman Jonathan India, who had months prior been named Major League Baseball's National League Rookie of the Year. Two young, hip, up-and-coming Cincinnati fan favorites.

But the most intriguing pregame moment came when Joey Burrow met Joey Votto.

Joey B. Franchise meet Joey V. Franchise.

JoeyB9 meet JoeyV19.

Batman meet Superman.[137]

With eavesdropping reporters hanging around, the heavyweight encounter was well-documented. Which, as it turns out, didn't need to be since Votto posted it to social media. Under an Instagram photo, JoeyV19 disclosed the profound, earth-shattering exchange: "This is me asking @joeyb_9 to do a TikTok. He said, aren't you a little old for TikTok? (crying emoji)."[138]

Joey Burrow might be the only person on the face of the planet who could *dis* Joey Votto and get a thank you, sir, may I have another?

While Burrow didn't join Votto in a TikTok dance-off, how can these two men not be BFFs? Gritty. Hard-working. Highly cerebral. Captains.

A Little Sports Prophet

Another thing the two Joeys have in common—they're both ballers. According to those who know, Votto is one of the best basketball players on the Reds.[139] And for Burrow, basketball was his first love.

It would be fun to watch JoeyV19 and JoeyB9 play one-on-one. Or maybe play a game of H-O-R-S-E with Burrow's Mississippi grandparents, Dot and James. "My mom can still get it pretty close to the basket at ninety years old," says Jimmy. "And my dad is ninety-one and just shot his age in a round of golf."[140]

For most people, a game of H-O-R-S-E (and golf) is a leisurely way to pass the time or carry on a friendly conversation. For the Burrow family? Well, you know about the Burrows and competition. Joe Burrow's high school basketball coach Jeff Skinner remembers a time when the varsity team had just finished practice and was winding down with a shooting game called "On the Board."

Coach Jeff Skinner roaming the sidelines at McAfee Gymnasium. *Photo credit: Trisha Doudna*

"Joe was playing with his teammates and everyone was worn out from practice. It was very subdued," remembers Skinner with a playful grin. "Then Jimmy and Joe's brothers, Jamie and Dan, walk in and join the competition. Suddenly, everything changes. Talk about intense. The Burrows are trash talking back and forth. I thought it was going to come to blows!"[141]

Given Joe's competitive juice, it's no surprise that his favorite basketball player is gritty Australian-born Matthew Dellavedova, who played several years for Burrow's childhood NBA team, the Cleveland Cavs. "He's my man," said Burrow in a 2016 Cleveland.com interview. "He hustles. Gets on the floor. My kind of guy."[142]

In 2019, the same Cleveland.com reporter tweeted a video message from Dellavedova back to Burrow wishing him well as he and the Tigers prepared for their NCAA Championship semi-final game against Oklahoma.[143] Who knows? The message from Delly might have given Joe the extra juice he needed to sizzle the Sooners in that Christmas Day basketball shootout.

Competitive fire is one reason Burrow was a four-year starter on the Athens High School basketball team, where he finished his career with 1,426 points—second behind all-time leading scorer Steve Bruning (who was a teammate of mine in 1980).

Burrow mirrored the intensity and hustle of Dellavedova on the hardwood, but he possessed other qualities, as well, including a silky-smooth shot, graceful finesse, and a tenacious nose for the ball. Perhaps, most importantly, he had something you can't teach: a natural ability to lead by example. "It was more about what Joe did than what he said," recalls Skinner, who also teaches at Athens Middle School. "From the time he was young, we would stand back and watch other kids just flock to him without saying a word. It was just uncanny. Joe was like this little sports prophet. And he didn't even know it."[144]

Staying in Athens

When he got to high school it didn't take long for Joe to earn the respect of the upperclassmen, even though his mother had concerns at first. "I remember a basketball game at Marietta the summer before Joe's freshman year," recalls Robin. "Coach Skinner invited Joe to come along with the varsity, which was loaded with seniors. We really didn't know if he was going to get to play or not, and Skinner puts Joe out there on the floor with the starting five. I just sat there and said to myself, 'Oh no. Everybody's going to hate us!'"[145]

Any doubters were soon won over. Burrow led the team in scoring at 11 points per game as the Bulldogs finished second in the Tri-Valley Conference. "Joe started every game as a freshman and was probably our best player," remembers Troy Bolin, who handled color commentary for the AHS radio broadcasts. "Great shooter, 6-foot-3, dunking as a freshman. I thought this kid could be the best basketball player we've ever had. He was playing on the AAU circuit with a team out of Chillicothe against some of the top dogs in the state. That was his thing. No one was thinking about Joe as a football player when he was a freshman."[146]

Before Skinner coached Burrow on the hardwood, he was his seventh- and eighth-grade history teacher. "Joe wouldn't say a word in class, but he was taking it all in," says Skinner. "Joe was the kind of kid who would go home and rewrite his notes every night. Everything he turned in was perfect."[147]

When that relationship transitioned from teacher to coach, Skinner knew what kind of leader he was welcoming into his basketball program. In all his years as a coach, Skinner rarely allowed players to talk in the huddle. Joe was the exception. "He always asked before he spoke. As a coach's son, he understood that," says Skinner. "He had the green light to say what he wanted, to do what he wanted. Every player on the team knew it. Joe was one of those rare players I could completely trust to never lead his teammates astray."[148]

Even as a freshman, Joe had the authority to change plays on the court when the game was on the line. This happened in a tournament game against higher-seeded Logan Elm. With the game tied, and only a few seconds on the clock, the Bulldogs broke the huddle with a play in mind. Then Joe and Skinner's son, Josh, who was a senior, decided to audible. "They spotted something that the coaches hadn't seen," recalls Skinner. "They made an adjustment that left Joe open to throw a touchdown strike to Joshua, who made the layup to win the game."[149] It turned out to be Joe's first varsity touchdown pass. And it took place on the basketball court instead of the football field.

Joe's freshman season was almost his last in Athens. Through the years, Jimmy had a few opportunities to leave, but none as appealing as the chance to return to Iowa State as the defensive backs coach. "We probably would have gone back to Ames, where Joe was born," says Jimmy. "I had interviewed for the position and was waiting to hear back. I got the call in the car before one of his basketball games. After the call was over, I walked past Joe as he was warming up and said, 'I didn't get the job.' He said, 'Good.'"[150]

The Burrows decided then and there that they wouldn't entertain any more job offers.

They were staying in Athens.

Making History

Skinner sure is glad the Burrows stayed. Otherwise, he would have missed out on a pretty cool conversation starter in his current eighth-grade history classroom. On one side of the door there are pictures of all forty-six U.S. presidents. On the other side, there's a large photo of the only Athens High School basketball team to ever win a district title. National history

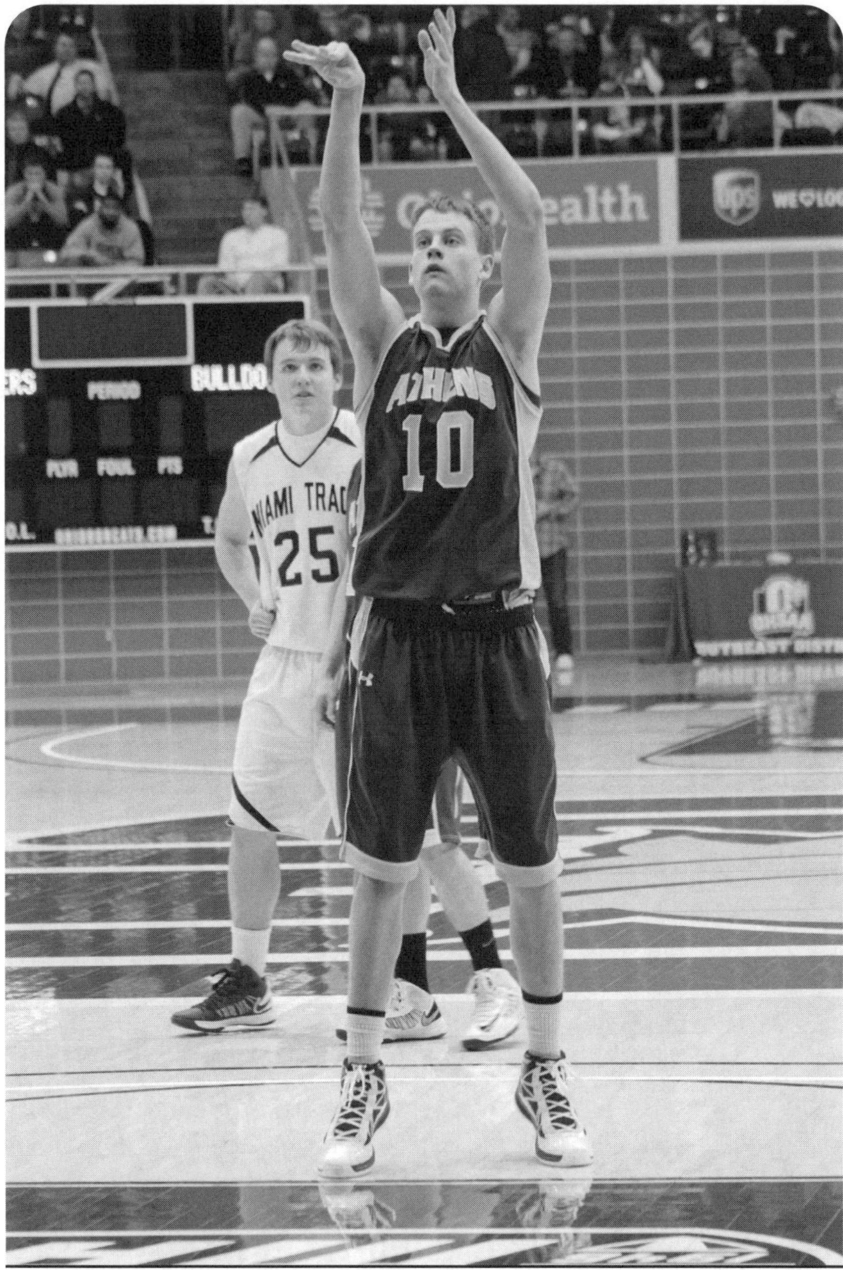

Joe hits a free throw during the Bulldogs' District Championship victory at the Convocation Center. *Photo credit: Trisha Doudna*

on one side. Local history on the other. Not surprisingly, it's the local history that grabs the attention.

"It's amazing how many kids at the beginning of the school year will walk in, point to the picture, and say number 10 looks just like Joe Burrow." Without revealing the secret, Skinner responds, "I know, he gets that all the time!"[151]

When his eighth-grade students arrive in the fall, they don't know anything about Mr. Skinner, the coach. They've only heard about Mr. Skinner, the passionate history teacher, who talks way too much about the Civil War and Ken Burns documentaries.

It's hard to blame the kids. After all, they were in pre-school when Coach Skinner led the Bulldogs to arguably the best run in Athens High School basketball history—a 61–12 record during Burrow's sophomore, junior and senior seasons. "We were loaded," says Skinner. "We didn't lose a conference game for close to three years. We set the single-season school record for wins (22) Joe's final year."[152]

District Champions. *Photo credit: Trisha Doudna*

Ibi Watson slices into the lane for two. *Photo credit: Trisha Doudna*

That one and only district title, however, came when Joe was a sophomore. Pointing nostalgically to the picture, Skinner says, "Look at those guys, they were so young."[153] The baby Bulldogs were led that year by the dynamic duo of Joe Burrow and freshman Ibi Watson. Both averaged 16 points-per-game for a team that went 21–5.

"After they won the district title, I thought we're going to make it to the state tournament at some point before Joe graduates," remembers Bolin. "We were starting three sophomores and two freshmen. Surely, we'll make it to Columbus eventually."[154]

In addition to Joe and Ibi, the Bulldogs had a solid supporting cast led by the Luehrman twins and freshman Zacciah Saltzman, who contributed over 11 points per game.

In what would become a recurring theme during Burrow's prep sports career, many outside the area wondered how Athens would fair against stiffer competition.

Joe's junior year would be the test.

The first challenge came at a Christmas tournament in Florida. Liz Luehrman remembers how the parents found out they were headed south for the holidays. "We were sitting in the stands at a football game and Gibby announces over the loudspeakers that the basketball team is raising money so they can go to Disney," remembers Liz. "We all looked at each other and said, 'What? We're going to Disney World?' So, we decided to run a booth at the fair. It was basically me, Robin, Beth (Cooley), and Marikay (Vander Ven). Robin found a recipe and we fried pickles and snickers bars. We made enough money to make it happen."[155]

"Super moms," says Skinner.[156]

At the ESPN Wide World of Sports Complex, located on the Disney World property, Athens went 2–1, defeating a team from North Miami and splitting with schools from New Jersey. During the tournament, Burrow

Zacciah Saltzman slashes to the basket against New Lexington. *Photo credit: Trisha Doudna*

averaged 17 points and 9 boards per game. In the final contest, Joe and Ibi combined for 51 of the Bulldogs' 68 points.

A few weeks later, Athens traveled to Akron to play highly ranked St. Vincent-St. Mary High School in Lebron James Arena. "It was an amazing atmosphere," recalls Bolin, who still gets goose bumps talking about it. "St. V had Division-I talent across the starting lineup. We had Joe, Ibi, Zacciah and the Luehrman twins. College scouts were in the stands. It was electric."[157] While many expected the Fighting Irish to cruise, Burrow and the Bulldogs hung with Lebron's alma mater, falling 67–57. Joe finished with 15 points and 10 rebounds.

While they didn't win, the Athens Bulldogs earned respect.

"In our big games, Joe just had a different look," remembers Skinner. "When we played really good competition like in the tournament at Disney, St. V and during Columbus summer league games, the faster the competition, the faster he was. The bigger the competition, the bigger he played. Joe just stepped up."[158]

One of Bolin's most memorable games, however, was played on a Saturday night in front of a sparse crowd. The game had little-to-no hype, but turned out to be a thrilling come-from-behind victory over an athletic prep school from Pennsylvania. "A team we'd never heard of wanted to come over and play us," remembers Bolin. "Joe put on a show, scoring 27 points and hitting five 3-pointers down the stretch to win the game."

While only 400 people saw it live, others were captivated by Bolin's impassioned on-air description of the Burrow-led comeback. One listener even called it "the best game I've ever heard on the radio."[159]

I Don't Know, Ask Joe

While the Bulldogs lost in the second round of the tournament Joe's junior year, hopes remained high heading into his final campaign. Then Skinner received two major blows. Starting guard Zacciah Saltzman would miss the season with a back injury and the team's leading scorer Ibi Watson chose to transfer.

"The good ole AAU Circuit got Ibi," says Skinner shaking his head. "He ended up transferring to Pickerington Central. Ibi had a great career, but had he stayed he would have been our school's all-time leading scorer and might have been Mr. Basketball in the state of Ohio. I think we would have had a legitimate chance to win the state championship had Ibi stayed and Zacciah been able to play."[160]

Despite the attrition, the Bulldogs made it to the district championship game. "We still won the most games in school history," says Skinner. "And it was because of Joe."[161]

By the end of his junior year, Burrow had verbally committed to play football at Ohio State. A lot of players would naturally lose interest in other sports. Even Buckeye Head Coach Urban Meyer wanted Burrow to skip his senior basketball season and enroll at Ohio State early. Joe wasn't interested. He never allowed his football success to undermine his commitment to basketball.

Case in point. The summer before Joe's senior year, Skinner took the Bulldogs to Knightstown, Indiana, to play in a summer league game in the storied gymnasium featured in the film, *Hoosiers*. The whole team drove over and spent the night. Except for Joe, who attended an Ohio State prospect's passing camp in Columbus.

"While we're all in Indiana getting ready for our game, Joe is standing out in the heat from 8 a.m. to 2 p.m. throwing who knows how many hundreds of balls," recalls Skinner, shaking his head in amazement. "Then, he and Robin hop in the van and drive two and a half hours to Knightstown. As we're about to tip, he's walking into the gym and lacing up his shoes. He says, 'I'm here coach, I'm here.' I say, 'OK, Joe.' I just stick him in there. No warmup, no nothing. Joe just goes in and lights it up."[162]

According to Skinner, Burrow's senior season on the hardwood was a physical grind. "He had a knee issue, a little tear in the front and it had been lingering for a long time. There were weeks where he might practice only one day. I promised Jimmy I'd protect him. And I did."[163]

Joe went from dunking on a regular basis as a sophomore and junior to playing closer to the ground his senior year. While it was a different style of basketball, Burrow still averaged nearly 20 points per game and earned first-team All-Ohio honors.

Despite the physical challenges, Joe was versatile. He could play any position on the floor. "Joe could bring the ball up the court, play power forward, play center," says Bolin. "His all-around game got better as he gained more muscle in the weight room. Skinner would put him in the post and clear people out. He became a great post player."[164]

The Bulldogs won their first twelve games and were ranked third in the state. The average margin of victory was 30 points. Had they not lost to Warren in game thirteen, the rematch against Akron St. Vincent-St. Mary would have been an unprecedented top-two showdown in The Plains.

"St. V never leaves their home, but they wanted the match-up with Burrow, so Skinner talked them into a home-and-home agreement," remembers Bolin. "After playing in Akron the year before, it was their turn to come to our place. McAfee Gymnasium was completely packed. It was so much fun, so much energy. People from all over Southeastern Ohio were fighting for a ticket."[165]

Like the year before, the game was hotly contested. It went back and forth deep into the fourth quarter until Henry Baddley, who went on to play for Butler, took over down the stretch. As usual, Burrow was at his best when the lights were brightest, scoring 22 points in what turned out to be a 12-point loss.

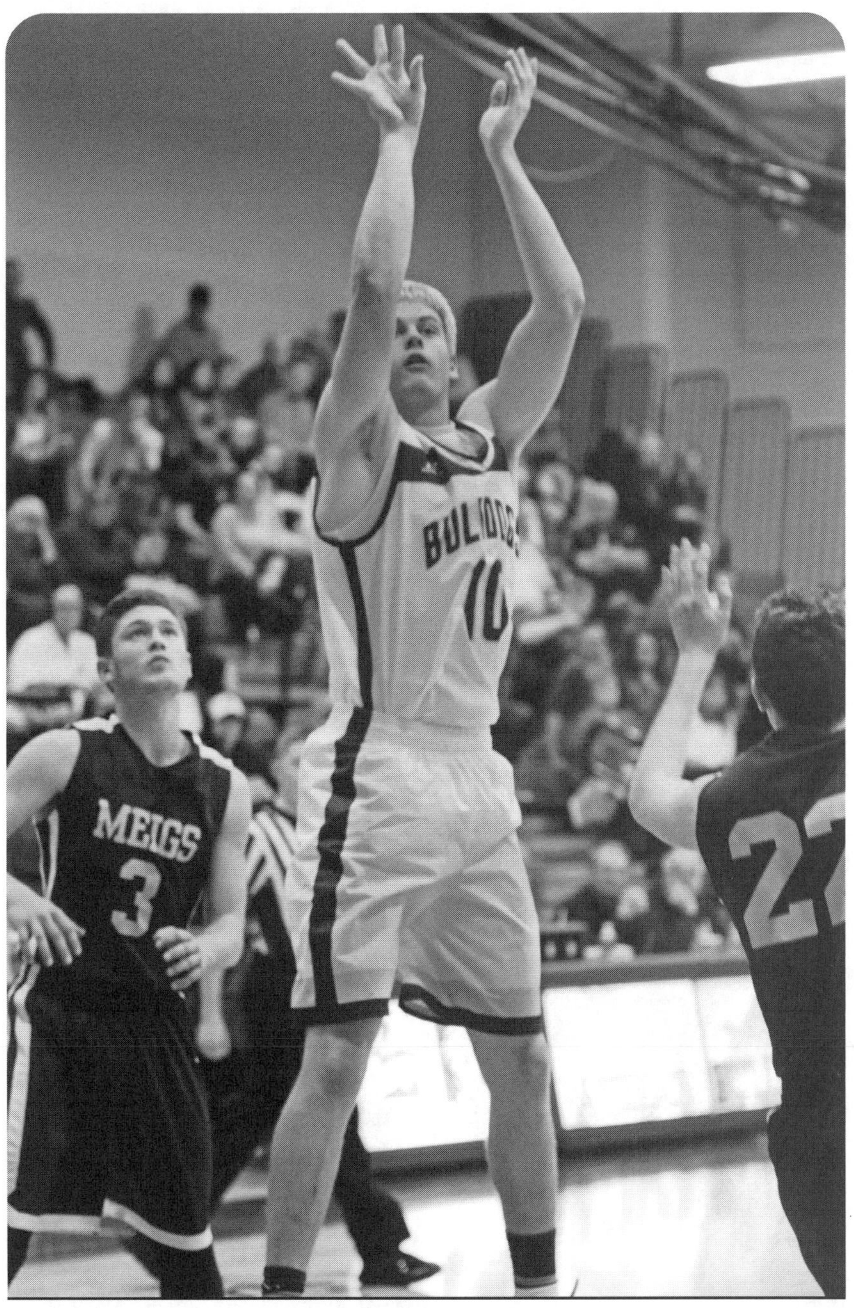

Burrow earned first-team all-state honors his senior year. *Photo credit: Trisha Doudna*

Burrow gathers himself for a jump shot against Akron St. Vincent-St. Mary. *Photo credit: Trisha Doudna*

One of the most memorable wins of the season came against Bishop Watterson, a team that played in the state championship game the year before. In a low-scoring affair, the Bulldogs beat the Eagles 42–27. On this night it wasn't Burrow's high-flying offense that stood out, but rather his defensive acumen.

Due to a lack of depth, Skinner had started playing more zone defense to give his starters a bit of a breather. "Joe played down low on the back right and Ryan (Luehrman) was top left," says Skinner. "I didn't tell him to do this, but Joe started telling the players at the top of the zone to shade right or shade left. So, he started changing our fronts from standing in the back depending on how the other team was lining up. It was the damndest thing I've ever seen. Like a quarterback making audible calls at the line of scrimmage. It got to the point where no one could score on us!"[166]

After the game, the Watterson head coach asked Skinner to explain the impenetrable Bulldog zone defense. With a big grin, Skinner just shook his head and said, "I don't know, ask Joe."[167]

Is it Okay if Joe Burrow Texts Me?

"We just think the world of Coach Skinner," says Robin. "He gave Joe a great opportunity as a freshman to come up and play. I still can't believe he did that. That team had so many upperclassmen. He started Joe over some of his son's friends."[168]

To Skinner, Joe is family. Like many in Athens, he and Joe have a sacred bond. "I will never ask Joe for anything. I will still be the one who helps him if he needs something, not the other way around."[169]

The feeling is mutual. On a trip down south a few years ago, Skinner visited with his former player after an LSU victory. After catching up, Joe embraced his old basketball coach and history teacher and said, "Love you,

Coach." It's a warm memory for Skinner, who admits the encounter fueled him "all the way back to Ohio."[170]

Skinner will occasionally get a text from Joe. It's usually out of the blue and contains inside information. Like during the NCAA basketball tournament. "I'm lying on the couch watching the St. Peter's game and he texts me, 'Oh My God, St. Peter's just ran a push move for a three out of the flex.' And I responded, 'Yeah, I saw that.' Joe sent that text because we used to run the same play for him. When we ran that play, the other coaches would be yelling to their players, 'Here it comes! Here it comes!' Didn't matter. Joe would still hit the shot. He was money, money, money."[171]

Mr. Skinner, the eighth-grade teacher, usually turns off his phone before class starts. It's a class rule. But occasionally he forgets.

"My phone went off in class one time and all the kids yelled, 'Mr. Skinner, your phone dinged! You didn't turn off your phone!' They're eighth graders, that's how they are," explains Skinner with an endearing eye roll. "So, I looked at it and held it up. It read Joe Burrow. So, I said, 'Is it okay if Joe Burrow texts me?' The whole class responds, 'Joe Burrow? Joe Burrow? You know, Joe Burrow? How do you know Joe Burrow?' I just said, 'You guys are clueless.'"[172]

4

Mr. Football

"They were a super close group of guys. They genuinely liked each other. There was a sense that we're not going to let one another down. I want this for me, but I want it more for the guys around me. It would be silly to think Joe wasn't a catalyst for that brotherhood. He's gone on to help create the same chemistry at LSU and with the Bengals."[173]

—Coach Nathan White
Joe Burrow's high school offensive coordinator

While Joe Burrow's first varsity touchdown pass was on the basketball court, the receiver of that pass, Josh Skinner, was quite an accomplished quarterback himself. During his senior season, Josh led the 2011 Bulldog football team to a conference championship and a 10–1 record.

After graduating from high school, Josh pursued a career in architecture, earning a bachelor's degree from the University of Cincinnati and master's from the University of Oregon. When Josh finished his schooling, he landed a job with a local firm.

As Skinner was settling into his new position in Portland, Burrow was building something special in Baton Rouge. After a good junior year with the Tigers, Joe and his teammates took the college football world by storm in 2019. On November 9th, they defeated Alabama in Tuscaloosa and vaulted to the number one spot in the polls. On the strength of that momentous victory, Burrow became the front-runner for the Heisman Trophy.

As usual, the Oregon Ducks were also vying for a spot in the playoff, so many of Skinner's colleagues were paying close attention to the national college football landscape. When Burrow's stock began to rise, they learned that Joe was from Southeast Ohio.

Athens, in fact. Then one day it dawns on one of Joshua's fellow architects: "Hey, you're from Athens, aren't you?"

"Yeah, Athens, Ohio," says Josh.

"Well, you should know this Burrow kid, the quarterback at LSU."

Nonchalantly, Josh replies, "Yeah, I know him. He was my backup."[174]

A Storm Is Brewing

Freshman Year (8–0)

Athens High School Head Football Coach Ryan Adams saw the storm brewing in the distance. He saw it coming all the way back to when Joe and his teammates were playing for Sam Smathers. Back to that conversation between Sam and Ryan in Applebee's when Joe was still in fourth grade.

Still, others remained skeptical.

"You start hearing whispers, this group is going to be really good," says Troy Bolin. "I've heard that before, so you got to show me. But when Coach Adams decided to keep all of those kids together on their own freshman team to develop as a unit, that's when we began to think Ryan must see something special in this group."[175]

Burrow played one game on varsity his first year, but it was at defensive back. All of his signal-calling took place on the freshman team, which didn't lose a game. Bolin points out, "You have to remember; Joe was playing varsity basketball that first year. No eyes were on him as the freshman quarterback."[176]

While outsiders knew little about Burrow the quarterback, his advanced football skillset was not lost on those who saw him practice. Jeff

Skinner recalls Josh coming home and saying, "You should have seen what that skinny freshman did today. Joe's the best quarterback we've got in the program."[177]

Burrow's football IQ was off the charts for a high school freshman, due in no small part to years of watching his father break down film. "It's a blessing to be the son of a Division I defensive coordinator," says Bolin. "I'm sure they had conversations about defenses that a typical eighth or ninth grader just wouldn't have. Joe had an advantage, but he still had to listen and learn. Many kids would have said, 'Sure, Dad,' then gone out and played with their buddies. Joe didn't. He absorbed that information."[178]

Joe also loved studying his favorite NFL quarterbacks. Growing up, he gravitated less to teams and more to players he admired. The Saints' Drew Brees topped the list. Joe liked his intelligence, precision and clutch play.

But when it came to toughness and resilience, one Tom Brady scramble took the cake. The date was December 16, 2001. Burrow was five years old; Brady was twenty-four. The two quarterbacks recently discussed the play on the "Let's Go" podcast.

"My earliest memory of something like that from a quarterback was when Tom, I think you were playing the Bills or maybe the Titans, and you were running to the right, and you slid, and somebody just knocked your head off. Your helmet goes flying."

Brady interjects, "Nate Clements."

Burrow continues, "You got up so fast. And I saw that, and I was like, 'I want to be like that. I'm going to do that.'"[179]

Bill Finnearty, who ran the game clock at all Athens home games, recalls plenty of times when Joe popped right up after getting hit. "There were teams that went after Joe, but nothing ever fazed him."[180]

"Joe wants to make sure his teammates know he's not just a quarterback," says Nathan White, who served as the AHS varsity quarterbacks coach when Burrow was a freshman. "He sees himself as a football player just like the rest of the guys. He's going to work as hard. He's going to get hit. No big deal. When he gets sacked, Joe's the first to point out the offensive guard got hit sixty-four times in that game."[181]

Toughness and resilience are apt descriptors for not only Joe Burrow, but for those around him, as well. While the freshman team was rarely challenged on the field, that doesn't mean the season lacked drama. Like the time a Bulldog lineman was seriously injured in a game at Philo, about fifty rural miles northeast of Athens.

"Kevin Moberg broke his leg bad, and his parents weren't at the game," recalls Liz Luehrman. "So, several parents, including Robin, hopped in a van and held his leg while Bill (Luehrman) drove through the pouring rain. We were in nowhere land. When we made it to the emergency room, it just hit us all. We were so lucky Kevin didn't go into shock. We would have been sunk."[182]

Toughness and resilience also perfectly describe the whole Athens community that year. Just twelve months earlier, on September 16, 2010, a tornado ripped through The Plains right as a girls' soccer match was getting ready to start. The twister destroyed the football stadium.

"It was quite traumatic," recalls Liz. "My daughter was at the high school and Tom Vander Ven was in the concession stand that night. We were very lucky because people got out of the press box just in time. They could have died."[183]

Sam Smathers was on his front porch as the storm was brewing. He crammed as many people as he could into his basement. "I saw the tornado bounce off the football field," says Sam. "My garage was leaning over, barely standing. We were lucky. No one died, but some people lost their entire homes."[184]

Robin and Jimmy remember having family in town. They were there to watch Ohio University play Ohio State, but on this particular evening, the

Burrows and Pardes were preparing for one of Joe's eighth-grade football games. "I looked out my back door and Tim Albin was pointing at the funnel cloud," says Jimmy, who hightailed it down to the basement with Joe, Dan and Robin's father, Wayne. "Robin and her mother were at Foodland. I couldn't get them on the phone, so after the storm passed, I stupidly drove around power lines trying to find them."[185] All in all, the Burrows incurred $40,000 worth of damage, which included large chunks of a neighbor's roof flying through their living room window.

The damage to R. Basil Rutter Field was extensive. The 2010 season was played at Peden Stadium, thanks to Ohio University. While insurance covered part of the restoration, it was up to Bulldog Blitz, the AHS Football Booster Club, to raise a large portion of the funds necessary to rebuild the stadium. Due to the generosity of many alumni, Bulldog Blitz raised $1.2 million toward the best stadium Athens had ever seen.[186] Just in time for the best team Athens had ever seen. A team that was poised to take the state by storm.

"It was crazy, but if it hadn't been for the tornado, we wouldn't have gotten the new turf on the field," says Liz, who served as the president of the AHS Booster Club for many years. "While you might expect the varsity to be the first ones to play a game in the new stadium, as fate would have it, it was the freshmen who got that honor. In hindsight, there was something poetic about that."[187]

Let the Shredding Begin

Sophomore Year (11–2)

After the 2011 season, Adams elevated White from quarterbacks coach to offensive coordinator. Nathan had a young innovative mind with lots of high-flying ideas. He was a 1999 Athens grad, but had spent time coaching in Georgia and Florida and was ready to bring a taste of the South to The Plains.

"I told Coach Adams I'd really like to do something I do well and would fit our kids," says White. "So, we moved from the I-formation to the spread. At the time, we had a returning quarterback (Michael Germano) who had played three or four games on Friday nights when Josh Skinner got hurt. So, going in I'm thinking Michael's probably our guy. That said, there was certainly going to be a quarterback competition between Michael and Joe."[188]

That was the plan, at least. Until Pete Germano, who was working under Jimmy Burrow as the OU defensive line coach, took a position at Fresno State. "Late in the spring I get the call that Michael is gone. So now it's easy, Joe's our guy."[189]

While Jeff Skinner loved Michael Germano, he's confident Joe would have won that battle. "There is no way Michael would have beat out Joe for the quarterback job. There is no way. Joe just wouldn't have let it happen."[190]

Jimmy was excited to see Joe christened as the starting quarterback, but disappointed to lose a good friend and one of the best coaches he'd worked with. That said, the stars aligned further when Jimmy and Frank Solich hired Jesse Williams, the defensive line coach at New Mexico State, to replace Germano. Not only was Jesse a great addition to the Bobcat coaching staff, but he had a son who was a high school sophomore. Trae would immediately join the Bulldogs as an electric, two-way impact player.

"I tell everybody that Joe's the best player I've ever seen, and Trae is 1-A," says White. "Those are the two best football players I've ever been around. And they stood right next to each other in the backfield for three years. It made calling plays really fun."[191]

As soon as White took over as the offensive coordinator, he got to work. Bolin remembers seeing Nathan sitting in Coach Adams' garage drawing up new plays night after humid night, all summer long.[192]

"It essentially came down to no-huddle, signaling everything in, go as fast as we could go," says White. "We put almost everything on the quarterback and let the other ten guys get their signal and go. This kind of offense needs a quarterback who is a stud mentally and physically. I had no idea at that time when I was planning all of this that I was going to see certainly the best I've ever seen. Maybe the best anyone's ever seen running it."[193]

Athens High School Head Football Coach Ryan Adams. *Photo credit: Trisha Doudna*

White was amazed at how quickly it came together, but this was a group that was used to winning and wasn't thinking about building for the future. "These fifteen-year-old kids wanted to go out and win right now. They had always been successful, so why would they think anything other than snap Joe the ball and let him throw us touchdowns?"[194]

The area didn't need to wait until fall to find out how good these young Bulldogs were. During summer seven-on-seven competitions, Burrow and his receivers were nearly unstoppable. "We just shredded people," remembers White. "I thought to myself, we have a chance to be really good this season."[195]

Fred Gibson was announcing a Legion baseball game in Lancaster when a reporter came into the press box.

Reporter: "You're from Athens, right?"

Gibby: "Yep."

Reporter: "Is your quarterback always that good?"

Gibby: "He's pretty good, why?"

Reporter: "Because I was watching them in seven-on-sevens and he never threw an incompletion the entire time. He was phenomenal."

Gibby: "Yep, you're going to be amazed by him."[196]

Ryan Luehrman recalls a seven-on-seven competition at Capital University in Columbus when Joe offered the other team some friendly advice. "We're destroying this team and Joe just says to them, 'Hey, you need to get out of cover 3 or you'll never stop us.' The kids on the other team were like, 'How do you know that?' Joe just responds, 'Because it's really easy to tell.'"[197]

Despite high expectations, the season began with a 52–34 home loss to Gallia Academy. After heading into halftime with a 28–21 lead, Finnearty remembers the young Bulldogs struggling in the second half with the pace of the new high-tempo offense.[198]

White considers Joe Burrow and Trae Williams the best two players he ever coached. *Photo credit: Trisha Doudna*

Even though the Bulldogs dropped the opener, Bolin was still impressed, "We put up a lot of points and White's new offense was really exciting. We were all like, 'This is different.'"[199]

The loss to Gallia turned out to be the only regular season defeat Burrow and his fellow sophomores would suffer during their three-year varsity careers. Twenty-nine straight regular season games without a loss.

After capturing the Tri-Valley Conference–Ohio title, Athens hosted Circleville in search of its first playoff win in school history. The Bulldogs jumped out quickly to a 14–0 first quarter lead and never looked back, winning 63–28. Burrow accounted for eight touchdowns, split equally be-

Joe's first varsity rushing touchdown. *Photo credit: Trisha Doudna*

tween the air and the ground. Running back Trae Williams added 142 rushing yards.

In the regional semi-finals, Athens went on the road to face Springfield Shawnee, a team that had played for the state championship the year before. In a come-from-behind thriller, the Bulldogs scored the final 14 points to upend the Braves, 36–35, and earn a berth in the regional finals. Burrow rushed for 110 yards, including a 43-yard touchdown scamper that showcased his elusive athleticism. He also threw for three scores, while Ryan Luehrman caught six passes for 100 yards.

"One of my all-time favorite games was that victory over Shawnee," says Bolin. "No one expected Athens to win. We put on a show. Shocked everyone. That game was when everybody realized this team is going to be really special."[200]

Finnearty, whose daughter, Shannon, was on the cheer squad, joined the circle on the field after the game. "I just remember the joy I saw on those kids' faces. You win a game, you're happy, but this was another level. Kevin Schwartzel, who coached these kids in eighth grade, was in tears. He just broke down. We sucked so bad when I played in high school. Who could have ever imagined Athens doing this in football?"[201]

In the regional final, the Bulldogs returned to earth. Top-seeded Thurgood Marshall had crushed Gallia Academy 68–9 the week before. The Cougars continued to roll against the upstart Bulldogs, piling up 617 yards of total offense in a 60–21 victory. It was a tough defeat, but head coach Ryan Adams was encouraged by the hopeful words of his young quarterback after the game. "He shook my hand and gave me a smile, and said, 'We'll be back.'"[202]

When the dust of the season had settled, Joe told his mother, "I think football might be my sport now." Robin responded, "I don't know, Buddy, I think it might still be basketball."[203]

Bolin sided with Joe. "At some point during that sophomore year I realized as much as I love Joe as a basketball player this is too much to ignore. What is this kid doing?"[204]

Another Step Forward

Junior Year (12–1)

2012 was a historic year for the Bulldogs and their young quarterback. As a team, they put 647 points on the scoreboard, which currently ranks among the twenty-five most prolific seasons in Ohio high school history. Burrow was responsible for 60 touchdowns and 4,026 yards of total offense. As a sophomore, he was named second-team All-Ohio and even received votes in the 2012 Ohio Player-of-the-Year balloting, an award that went to Mitch Trubisky.[205]

In the offseason, Joe hit the weights, Wheaties and protein shakes, bulking up from 165 to 190 pounds in an effort to fill out his 6-foot-4 frame. His bench press increased by sixty pounds.[206]

Joe and Zacciah Saltzman, one of the Bulldogs' top receivers, had a daily regimen. "After football or basketball practice, we'd work really, really hard in the weight room," says Saltzman, who was a year behind Joe in school. "We just worked each other to death. Every day. Then we went to the pool, followed by a trip to Sonic. Joe got a lemon slush every time. I'd mix it up a bit."[207]

White had no plans of mixing anything up in 2013. Just more of the same—even faster. "The biggest thing was the offense was already installed and we had so many kids returning," says White. "We went quicker tempo, really cranked it. It was hard to imagine being better statistically, but we were."[208]

The season started on the road against Gallia Academy. Athens made a statement right out of the gate, avenging its only 2012 regular-season loss with a decisive 62–19 victory over the Blue Devils. The Bulldogs showcased their multi-dimensionality. On this particular night, it was the punishing ground game with Trae Williams rushing for 171 yards and five TDs. The defense got in on the scoring as well with Ryan Luehrman and Alex Goldsberry both returning interceptions for touchdowns.

In the first four games, the Bulldogs outscored opponents 206–28. And the starters rarely played in the second half. "That's what's so amazing about the numbers these guys put up," says Sam Smathers. "Joe and the first string might have played a series in the third quarter if it was kind of close, but then they were pulled."[209]

Linebacker Bryce Graves remembers the team's remarkable depth. "Our second-string offense got a lot of reps, and they were good. They would have run the TVC."[210] Smathers agrees, "Easy. Hands down. It might have been a dog fight at times, but they would have won the conference."[211]

Joe leads the Bulldogs onto the field with the hammer. *Photo credit: Trisha Doudna*

When asked what it was like calling these games, Athens radio play-by-play announcer Matt Frazee had one word, "Boring." Frazee clarifies, "I mean the first half was wonderful. But it's really hard finding something creative to talk about when you're up by 50 points every Friday night."[212]

Fred Gibson remembers the Alexander game got especially out of hand. "The coach came out in the paper and said he wasn't going to punt the ball against Athens," says Gibson. "Not only did he not punt, he decided to pass the ball on every down. Incomplete. Clock stops. Incomplete. Clock stops. Incomplete. Clock stops. Incomplete. Clock stops. So, we get the ball on the 30-yard line. One pass, touchdown. Same thing. We get the ball at the 35-yard line. One pass, touchdown. We score 77 in the first half. Joe didn't play the last four minutes of the half. We were in the press box yelling, run the ball! Keep the clock moving!"[213]

Joe eludes a Tri-Valley defender. *Photo credit: Trisha Doudna*

Burrow only threw the ball eleven times against the Spartans. Five were touchdown strikes. Williams ran for 249 yards on eight carries. The final score was 83–14. It could have been worse. A lot worse. Graves admits, "We wanted to score 100, but they put their second-string in immediately when the second half started."[214]

The Bulldog faithful found creative ways to stay engaged when the outcome of games was all but decided after the first quarter. In the press box, Gibson, Finnearty and other workers predicted how many touchdowns Athens was going to score in the final three and a half minutes of the first half.[215] Over in the Dawg Pound, Sam's fifty or so vocal guests would raise their voices every time Athens got the ball. One person would yell, "Two!" Another would shout, "Three!" Still another would boldly say, "One!" Each person predicting how many plays it was going take for Joe's offense to score another touchdown.

It's not clear if any side bets were ever made, but Sam does confirm that his stepmother once won the game-night raffle. It was a thrill when Gibby announced the winning numbers, which were clearly heard over on Sam's porch. $1,500. Not a bad return for a $5 investment.

The Bulldogs were a good bet to run the regular-season table in 2013. The only challenge came in Week 5 on the road against Fairland. Athens won a hard-fought game, 55–46. Burrow threw for 492 yards and eight touchdowns, six to Heath Wiseman—tying a single-game state record.

For Athens, however, what stuck out most was hearing frequent racial slurs hurled at their teammate Trae Williams, one of the few African American players on the field. Gibson remembers, "Coach Adams came out of the locker room at halftime and said if they keep calling Trae names, there's going to be one helluva fight. You better get this stopped."[216]

After the game ended, Joe was in tears. Not tears of joy over a hard-fought, record-breaking victory, but tears of sadness and anger over what his teammate had to endure. "Joe was really upset about how Trae was treated," says Zacciah. "It's one of the few times I've ever seen him cry. He wanted to fight the other team."[217]

Athens hosted Logan Elm in the first round of the playoffs. Burrow threw for 491 yards and six touchdowns. Ryan Luehrman was the primary beneficiary with 171 receiving yards and Trae Williams racked up 351 all-purpose yards as the Bulldogs eliminated the Braves, 74–55, to improve to 11–0 on the year. The two teams combined for 129 points—the most ever scored in an Ohio high school playoff game.

The regional semi-final encounter with Tri-Valley was an instant classic and proved to be one of Joe's all-time favorite games. The Bulldogs trailed 21–7 in the second quarter when Burrow broke free for a 56-yard dash. On the next snap, he scored on a one-yard keeper.

With time running down in the first half, Joe found Adam Luehrman in the end zone for a 25-yard touchdown. It was something Bulldog fans had come to expect. "Ryan Luehrman was our main guy," says Gibson, "but Adam would catch a touchdown right at the end of the half almost every night."[218]

The Bulldogs tied the game on an electric 90-yard Trae Williams kickoff return to open the second half. After a back-and-forth struggle, regulation ended with the score tied at 49 points.

The Scotties opened overtime with a field goal. When the Bulldogs got their turn, Joe wasted no time. On a designed quarterback keeper out of the shotgun, a determined Burrow weaved 20 yards through the defense for the game-winning score and a berth in the regional finals.

Burrow ended the night with six touchdowns, four through the air and two on the ground. For the first time all season, Joe played every snap on both sides of the ball. After the game Ryan Adams praised Burrow's will to win. "It all boils down to the same thing…he's a fierce competitor. He hates to lose. He always seems to just find a way to get it done."[219]

An exhausted and ecstatic Burrow ranked the moment above the Shawnee victory: "I'm honestly more excited. Overtime, game-winning touchdown in the second round of the playoffs. Who wouldn't love that?"[220]

The elation, however, was short-lived. For the second year in a row, the Bulldogs lost in the regional finals. This time against a powerful Marion-Franklin team, 38–7. The Red Devils were bigger (averaging seventy pounds more per player across the line); older (fifteen senior starters versus three senior starters for Athens); and more experienced (fourth regional championship game appearance in five years).

On a cold, foggy, and windy night, the Bulldogs' perfect season came to an end. Yet, as *Athens Messenger* reporter Jason Arkley aptly put it, "The Bulldogs lost a game Friday night. But they weren't defeated."[221]

The Horseshoe

Senior Year (14–1)

After advancing to the regional final in back-to-back seasons, the Bulldogs entered Burrow's senior year with unprecedented expectations. Making it to the regional championship was no longer good enough. The goal was state. "If you make it to the final four, anything can happen," says White.[222]

He knew the Bulldogs were good enough. The entire offense was set to return, led by Burrow, who was named the Ohio Gatorade Player of the Year after piling up 4,321 total yards and accounting for 56 touchdowns (47 passing) as a junior. Athens scored 707 points—a total that ranks seventh in Ohio high school history.

Burrow had verbally committed to Ohio State late in May of his junior year. With the college decision settled, Joe was laser-focused on refining his game. Coach White remembers a big jump the summer before his senior year. "We were watching tape and Joe says, 'Coach, I need to get better in the pocket. I didn't have a very good year last year.' I just smiled at him and

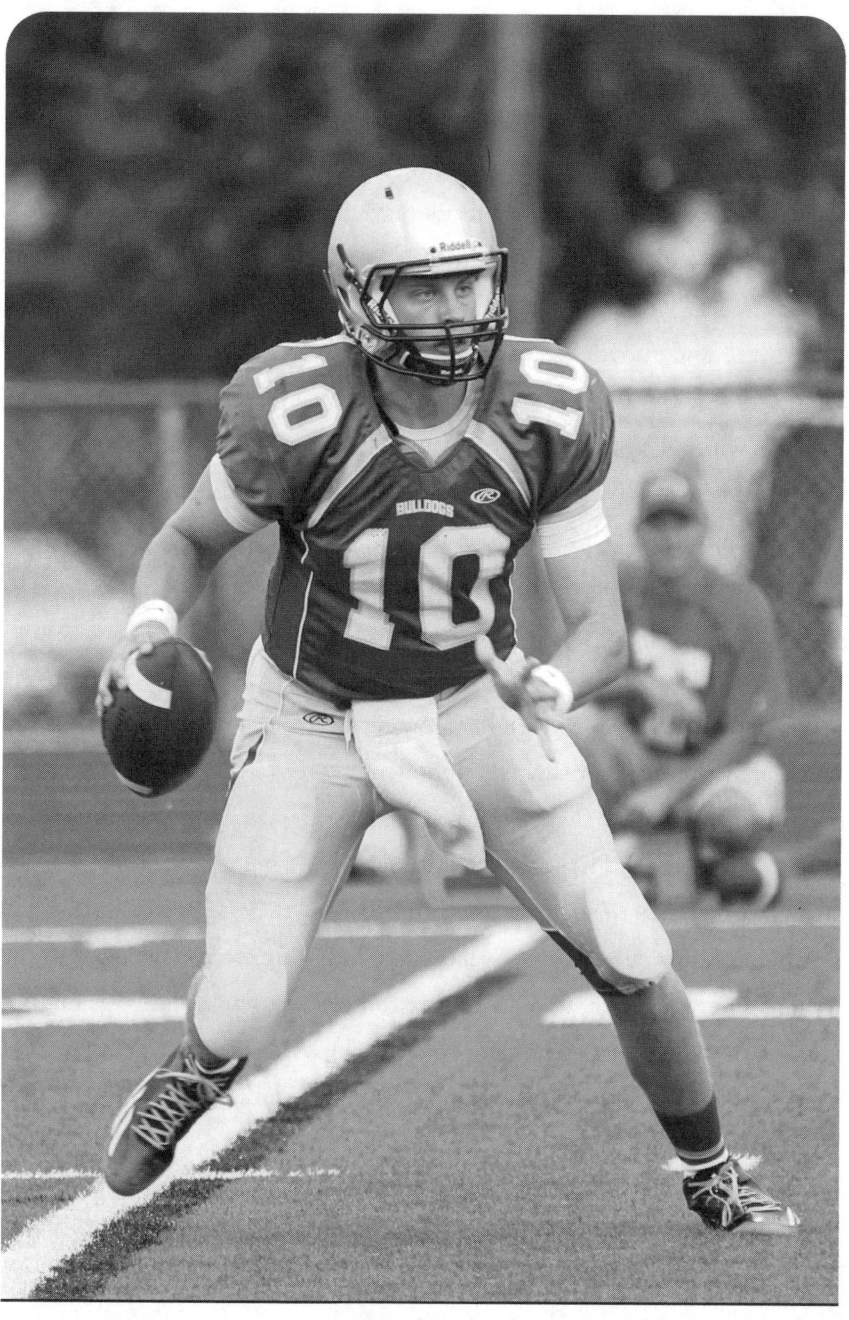

Burrow looks for a receiver in a scrimmage against Trimble. *Photo credit: Trisha Doudna*

said, 'Joe you've already thrown for a hundred touchdowns.' But that's Joe. It's easy to coach a kid who wants to work and get better."[223]

Hard work. It's a trait Joe learned early in the Burrow home and was reinforced during his four years playing for Sam Smathers. Joe was listening when Coach Sam would tell his players, "Boys, it's OK to be happy, but never be satisfied. If you're satisfied, you're saying there's no room for improvement."[224]

White and Burrow went to work every day in the summer. Nathan would run Joe through drills to the point of exhaustion—a merciless thirty minutes without a break. "We're grinding and Joe is ready to puke," recalls White. "He'd say, 'I hate it, but let's keep going.' He almost enjoyed it because it was hard."[225]

But it wasn't just Burrow. The entire team, led by the senior class, locked in on the goal of making it to state. The ball rarely hit the ground during practice. When something was out of sync, Joe and his receivers stayed late until they got it right. They never left the field until they were completely prepared for the next opponent.

"Every single day that year, for fifteen weeks, we had a great practice," says White. "To see forty or fifty kids lock in and get after it for two hours day after day, I've never seen anything like it. They were so smart. They wanted to know our offense. Every single kid. Our receivers wanted to diagnose coverages so they could change routes. The whole team was mature enough to realize that we're not going to reach our goal without having a great day today. And the next day we wake up and have another one and another one."[226]

The Bulldogs seemed poised for a historic season. Only one problem. They would be facing two non-conference games on the road against traditional powerhouses Zanesville and Steubenville. "Nobody wanted to play us," remembers Smathers. "Except for the more successful programs."[227]

When Gibson saw the lineup of games, he was concerned. "I thought, we have the best team in school history and could still miss the playoffs because of the schedule."[228]

As usual, Athens opened with non-conference foe Gallia Academy. The Bulldogs shut out the visiting Blue Devils 52–0, scoring 45 points in the first quarter. Burrow was a perfect 12-for-12 through the air for 307 yards and four touchdowns.

The first big test came the following week against Zanesville. The Blue Devils were 13–1 the previous season with the only loss coming in the state semi-finals. The two schools hadn't met since 2007—Ryan Adams' first season as the Athens head coach. The Blue Devils won that game 74–0 and were still scoring touchdowns deep into the fourth quarter.

As the game kicked off, a sea of fans stretching far into the packed parking lot was streaming into the stadium. Bill Finnearty's sister, Angie Anderson, was at the game. Angie asked someone in the stands, "Is this typical for Zanesville?" The response, "No, they're all coming to see your quarterback."[229]

The Blue Devils marched 73 yards down the field on their opening possession to take a quick 7–0 lead. The Zanesville TV announcer said, "That oughta shut 'em up."[230] The Bulldogs responded by scoring on eight straight possessions and entered intermission with a 52–14 lead.

The rest of the game was played with a running clock. Athens won 66–28.

The Bulldog offense piled up 715 total yards with Trae Williams accounting for 247 on the ground. Burrow was completely on point, throwing five touchdowns to five different receivers, including a strike to Adam Luehrman on the final play of the first half.

At halftime, the Zanesville TV announcer turned to his color man and asked, "Why do you feel Athens had to score that last touchdown when

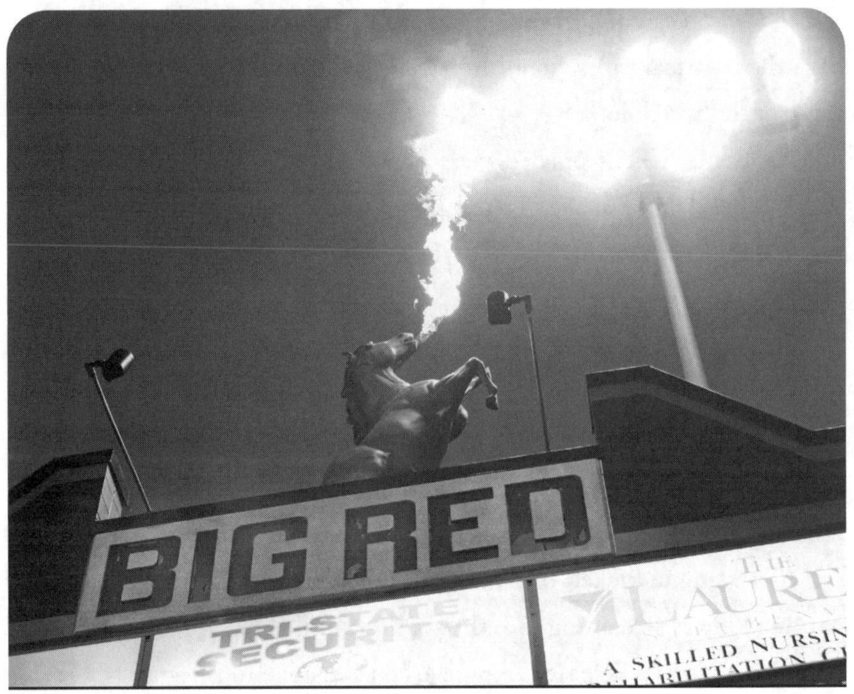

Steubenville's fire-breathing stallion sets the tone for a classic match-up between the Bulldogs and the Big Red. *Photo credit: Trisha Doudna*

they're so far ahead?" His partner responded, "You might not remember that 74–0 beat down, but Coach Adams does."[231]

In the next three games, the Bulldogs outscored their opponents 185–29 and were riding a 24-game regular-season winning streak heading into the showdown with one of the state's perennial powerhouses, the Steubenville Big Red. Steubenville had advanced to the state semi-finals the year before and had a reputation for playing especially well at Harding Stadium, affectionately known throughout the region as "Death Valley."

Liz Luehrman remembers driving up to the game with husband, Bill, and Robin. "We were all very nervous because a loss could have really affected our playoff seeding. The discussion was, 'Why did we agree to do this? This is stupid. Playing this team is a huge risk.'"[232]

Coach Adams, however, saw the match-up differently. He knew if his team was going to go deep into the playoffs, they needed the experience of playing a regular-season game in a high-pressure environment. A fire-breathing mechanical stallion and 10,000 rabid fans should do the trick.[233]

"All their fans were on top of us," remembers Bryce Graves. "Our benches were underneath the front of the stands. It was awesome."[234]

Ryan Luehrman said there was a lot of talking going on before and during the game. "Steubenville thought it was going to be a cakewalk. That's why they scheduled us for Homecoming."[235]

The talking wasn't just on the field. Steubenville had just played number-one ranked Massillon Washington the week before and the press-box crew thought Athens was over-rated. "They were saying, 'There's no way you're that good,'" remembers Frazee, who called the game on the radio that

Burrow and the Bulldogs weathered the elements to score the most points against a Steubenville team in fifty years. *Photo credit: Trisha Doudna*

night. "We just don't think you play anybody." Even though the Bulldog first-string offense had scored touchdowns on 42 of 45 drives that season, the Athens announcer just politely responded, "OK, we understand what you're saying."[236]

By the end of the rainy night, the Bulldogs had hung 58 points on the Big Red—the most points allowed by a Steubenville team in fifty years.

After struggling with a slippery football early, the Bulldog offense got on track. Burrow completed 20 of 27 passes for 363 yards and four touchdowns—two to Adam Luehrman, who hauled in a team-high 148 receiving yards. Burrow and Williams combined for 234 yards on the ground and four rushing touchdowns.

After the game, a drenched but upbeat Burrow was asked where the 58–42 victory ranks in his list of high school wins. "I would say third behind Springfield Shawnee sophomore year and Tri-Valley last year. Those were nailbiters until the end. We kind of pulled this out earlier in the fourth quarter. We heard the stadium record was 66, but decided to pull it off at the end."[237]

Troy Bolin says the signature win over Steubenville put the state on notice. "People in our region were already worried about us, but after that win the whole state put us on their watchlist."[238]

As Frazee was leaving the press box, one of the members of the home crew said, "I've seen some great ones, but I've never seen anybody that good." Frazee calmly responded, "Well, we weren't going to walk in here talking smack, but we could have told you that."[239]

Athens cruised in the next four games to capture the TVC-Ohio title and post a perfect 10–0 regular-season record. The final regular-season home game for Joe and his teammates was senior night and Sam Smathers joined his former players on the field for the festivities.

Fourteen of the Bulldog seniors began their football careers under the tutelage of Coach Sam, who, along with Terri, hosted two senior dinners at the Dawg Pound during the 2014 season. "Sam has the best hot wings around," says Ryan Luehrman, whose father owns the local Kentucky Fried Chicken franchise.[240]

"I just love that guy," says Sam Vander Ven. "Now that I'm a high school coach, I'm just in awe of how effortless it was for Sam, his sons and his staff to coach youth football. He was so good and so passionate. He laid the groundwork for the success we had in high school."[241]

"Sam was a great coach," says linebacker Ryan Mack, "He was friendly and nurturing. He let us have fun."[242] Bryce Graves agrees, "It was awesome playing for Coach Sam. We worked hard in our practices, but we had fun."[243]

If it weren't for Sam, Athens might never have had one of their most productive receivers, Adam Luehrman. "At first I didn't like football," says Adam. "I just sat over there on the sideline and Coach Sam convinced me to keep trying."[244] Smathers remembers young third-grade Adam ready to give up. "He wasn't a football player at that time, but I could see it in him. I just loved him and told him I can't let you quit. You've got skills you don't even know you have yet."[245]

Adam and his brother, Ryan, put their skills to good use during their final regular season, combining for 1,236 receiving yards and 23 touchdowns in ten games. They would be even more productive in the playoffs.

In the first round, Granville was overwhelmed by an Athens team firing on all cylinders. The Bulldogs jumped out to a 48–14 halftime lead and put it in cruise control, winning 65–14. Williams ran for 266 yards and Burrow spread the ball around to six receivers. Saltzman hauled in a team-high seven passes for 115 yards.

The win set up a rematch with undefeated Tri-Valley in the regional semi-finals. But this game wasn't nearly as dramatic as the year before. The Scotties were no match on either side of the ball, as the Bulldogs posted a

41–20 victory. Williams ground out 134 yards on 23 carries, while Burrow tossed three touchdowns—two to Saltzman and one to Adam Luehrman. Burrow made an impact on the defensive side of the ball, as well, snagging a key second-half interception. "Joe's pick was the nail in the coffin," says Ryan Luehrman.[246]

For the third year in a row, Athens advanced to the regional championship game. This time against perennial contender Columbus St. Francis DeSales. The goal all season was to capture the regional title and advance to state. The Burrow-led Bulldogs would not be denied. Joe threw for 319 yards and five touchdowns, including one to himself after a defender deflected the ball into the air. Burrow also led all Bulldog ball-carriers with 135 yards and two rushing touchdowns. The 52–20 final score was the worst playoff defeat in St. Francis DeSales history.

After the game a jubilant Joe celebrated the long-awaited, hard-earned accomplishment. "This year, our motto was, we broke to 'Regional Championship' after every time we lifted, every time we left the field. And we finally got it done."[247]

Added Adams, "Typical Joe. The bigger the stage, the bigger the challenge, the more the kid digs into his bag of tricks."[248]

Athens High School was heading to the Ohio state high school final four for the first time in school history. Only one team stood between the Bulldogs and the dream of playing in the Horseshoe—two-time defending state champion Akron St. Vincent-St. Mary (SVSM).

It wasn't the first time an Athens County football team had advanced to state. Trimble High School had lost in the Division VII state title game the year before and was set to play in the state semi-finals in 2014, as well. Troy Bolin remembers the whole county was on fire for football. "Trimble's football success ran parallel with Athens. It was so fun. We did the radio broadcast for the Athens-SVSM game on Friday night, then came back home to get a little sleep before driving to Mount Vernon to broadcast the Trimble semi-final game the next night. It was a blast!"[249]

The Athens-SVSM game was played on a bitterly cold night in New Philadelphia High School's Woody Hayes Quaker Stadium. Rumor has it Lebron James watched his alma mater from a secluded section of the press box.[250] The game started out well for Lebron and the SVSM faithful as the Fighting Irish turned two Bulldog fumbles into early touchdowns. For the first time all year Athens trailed 17–7 at the intermission.

The second half was a different story. The Athens offense would rack up 485 total yards, 303 in the second stanza.

The Irish scored a touchdown with 7:56 remaining in the game to take a 10-point lead. Not exactly Sam Smathers and his coaching staff drawing up a play in the Nelsonville dirt, but the same players were involved.

It was the Burrow to Luehrman show.

The offense went into high gear, firing on all cylinders. Joe engineered a frenetic six-play, 86-yard touchdown drive shaving hardly a minute off

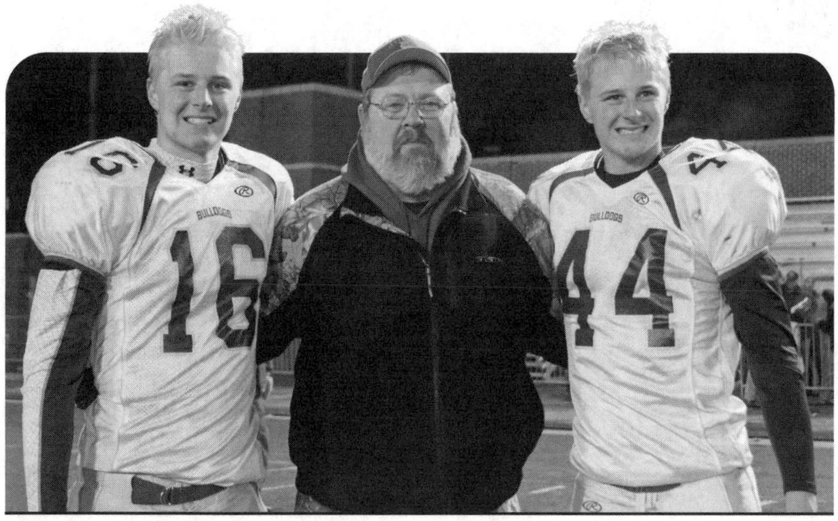

Sam Smathers poses with the "Twin Towers," Ryan and Adam Luehrman. *Photo credit: Trisha Doudna*

Joe proudly talks to the media after defeating St. Vincent–St. Mary. *Photo credit: Trisha Doudna*

the clock. Adam caught a 33-yard strike, while Ryan hauled in two passes, including an eight-yard TD toss to cut the Irish lead to three.

After one of the biggest defensive stands of the season, SVSM punted the ball back to Athens. The Bulldog offense started on its own 22-yard line. Joe proceeded to orchestrate a 78-yard drive that included two third-down connections to Adam. The final pass was a 12-yard toss to Saltzman in the corner of the end zone with 1:51 left on the clock.

The Irish still had time to score, but Trae Williams sealed the game by recovering a fumble and intercepting a pass in the closing seconds to preserve a historic 34–31 victory.

The Bulldogs were going to the Division III state championship game.

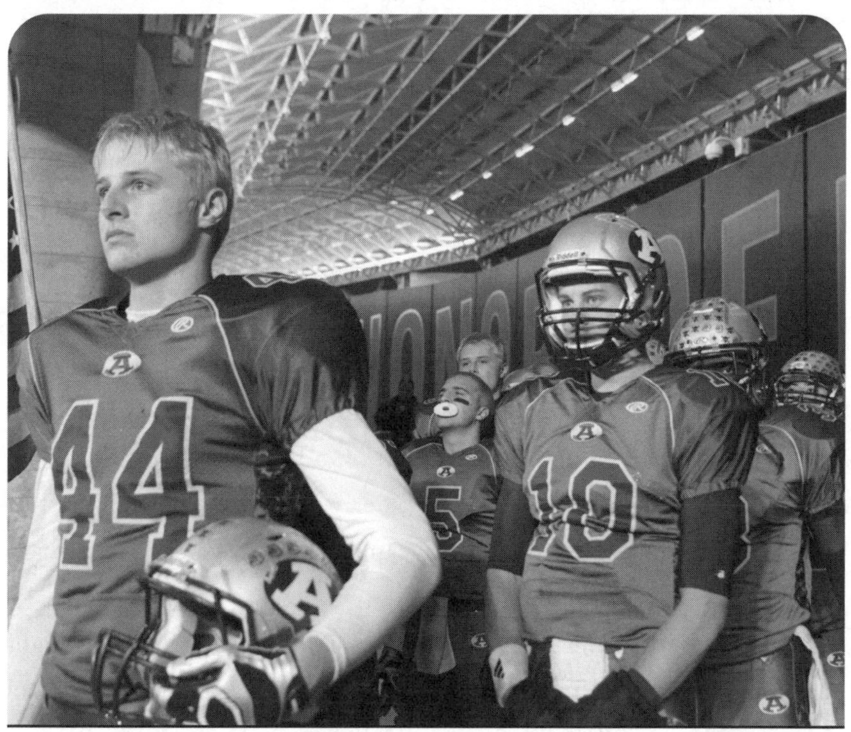

Adam Luehrman and Joe Burrow prepare to lead the Bulldogs into the Shoe.
Photo credit: Trisha Doudna

Burrow finished the night with four touchdowns and 322 passing yards—231 to the Luehrmans. Joe was flying high after the game. "When we got that last stop there was no doubt in my mind we were going to go down and score. Our guys fought so hard. We fought hard all year. Now we've got one more to go."[251]

Bolin, who also blogged for the Southeast Ohio Preps website, remembers there were a lot of naysayers around the area. "People all over the region doubted this team. They'd say, 'You can't beat anyone outside the district. You're still Athens. But when we made it to the state championship game, a bunch of people jumped on the bandwagon. We had a lot of support from Southeastern Ohio when the boys went to Columbus."[252]

The Athens High School charter buses drove down Johnson Road, past the Dawg Pound on the right and Smathers Field on the left then turned onto OH-682 North. Sam Vander Ven, who played wide receiver and safety, remembers feeling the support from the community and even the rest of Southeastern Ohio on the trip up to the Shoe.

"My biggest memory was turning right onto 682 and all our fans were lined up on that mile stretch of road," says Vander Ven. "I'm getting chills just thinking about it." Vander Ven also remembers about thirty minutes up Route 33 passing under a bridge with a banner that read, "Let's Go Athens—from Logan." Another twenty minutes up the road near Lancaster a guy got out of his car to hold up a "Let's Go Bulldogs!" sign. "We tried to make it a normal gameday," adds Vander Ven, "but when you have stuff like that happening, you look to your teammate beside you and say, 'That's pretty damn cool, right there.'"[253]

Bill Finnearty remembers walking around Ohio Stadium that night and seeing the support from Athens rivals, as well. "I remember high school kids and adults from Trimble, Nelsonville York, and Alexander showing up to support us at that game. It really galvanized the county."[254]

In many ways, the game was the football version of *Hoosiers*—a storyline Joe was familiar with having played summer hoops a few months earlier in the historic Hickory gym. Only this time it was Goliath who would get the storybook ending.

When the opposing teams ran through their drills prior to kickoff that night, Toledo Central Catholic had two state titles on their resume and twice as many players suited up for the game. Nathan White gazed across the block O in the center of the field and thought, "It looked like a Big Ten pregame."[255]

TCC was loaded with talent, but just days prior it was the Bulldogs' quarterback who was selected Mr. Football by the state's sports writers.

It didn't take long for the Fighting Irish, and the 10,713 fans in attendance, to find out why. Four minutes into the game the pocket collapsed around Burrow on an all-out blitz. He was dead to rights, but found a way to not only escape but break free for a 49-yard scamper to the Irish one-yard line.

Emotions spill over after the Bulldogs lose a heart-breaker to Toledo Central Catholic. *Photo credit: Trisha Doudna*

Any TCC sideline trash-talk was silenced when Trae Williams broke the plane for the first score of the evening. The Irish responded with back-to-back touchdowns before Joe found Ryan Luehrman for a 54-yard score at the end of the first quarter. Unfortunately for the Bulldogs, the extra point was blocked. Athens would try to recoup that point all evening, but failed on all three two-point conversion attempts.

After the Irish tacked on a second-quarter touchdown, Burrow connected on an eight-yard strike to Adam Luehrman to pull the Bulldogs to within two points heading into the break.

The second half was like a toe-to-toe 15-round heavy weight fight. Both teams refused to give in with the lead changing ten times during the final two quarters.

With 3:00 remaining in the third quarter, Athens had a three-point lead and the ball. Burrow made one of his few mistakes on the evening, throwing only his second interception of the season. On the next play, TCC took the lead on a 40-yard run to the end zone as the quarter came to a close.

Burrow immediately bounced back, distributing the ball to four different receivers. The drive culminated with a 10-yard touchdown strike to Heath Wiseman. After the lead switched hands three more times, Williams crossed the goal line with 2:52 remaining to give the Bulldogs a 52-49 lead.

Bill Finnearty was at the game with his father. "We just looked at each other and both of us said, 'We scored too soon.'"[256]

They were right.

TCC mounted a memorable drive that included three fourth-down conversions and a controversial touchdown with just fifteen seconds remaining.

Even TCC quarterback Marcus Winters admitted a penalty flag should have been thrown on the winning touchdown. The Irish backfield had two players in motion. "I was like, damn, people were moving before the snap."[257]

Fred Gibson remembers Kevin Schwartzel, an experienced Big Ten referee, telling him that he contacted the official who was in position to make the call that night. Schwartzel asked, "Why didn't you throw the flag on that illegal motion play?" The official said, "I reached for my flag and it got stuck in my pocket. Then I figured it was too late to throw it."[258]

Still, there were other moments in the game that could have decided the outcome in Athens' favor. Bulldog players and coaches refused to make excuses in the postgame press conference. After Burrow made his "worst day of my life" comments, a reporter asked what he will remember most about the game. "The pick. First and foremost. That will be the only thing I will be thinking about for a while."[259]

Following the presentation of the second-place trophy and medals, the Bulldogs eventually made it back to the hotel where they spent several sleepless hours. Bryce Graves remembers hearing Ryan Luehrman sitting in the bathtub just moaning for hours on end. "I was just so exhausted and distraught," recalls Luehrman.[260]

The next day they went back to the Shoe and watched the Division II championship game. On the way home to The Plains, the team stopped at Dave & Buster's. "Dave & Buster's helped a lot," remembers Graves. "We just got to hang out as friends, just like we always had."[261]

All these years later, Coach White remembers their remarkable talent. After all, the 2014 team still holds the state single-season record for points scored (861). But above all he is amazed by how tight knit that team was. Ultimately it boiled down to relationships. Just kids playing football with their friends.

"They were a super close group," says White. "They genuinely liked each other. There was a sense that we're not going to let one another down.

I want this for me, but I want it more for the guys around me. It would be silly to think Joe wasn't a catalyst for that brotherhood. He's gone on to help create the same chemistry at LSU and with the Bengals."[262]

That miraculous run to the state title game will long be remembered fondly throughout Southeastern Ohio. *Athens Messenger* reporter Jason Arkley concluded his championship game article with the following hopeful words: "A week from now, a month from now, a year, ten years…what everyone will remember isn't the [Burrow] interception. It's the fact that the Bulldogs gave their town one hell of a ride. Eventually, even Joe Burrow himself will realize that."[263]

5

The Shoe Doesn't Fit

"You made the biggest mistake on your quarterback three years ago. Now, you've made the same mistake again. Write this name down: Joe Burrow. He's going to win the Heisman Trophy."[264]

—Don Cooley

Joe Burrow's youth baseball and basketball coach

The most memorable reception in Joe Burrow's high school football career was the five-yard touchdown pass he threw to himself in the 2014 regional championship game.

A close second came a few months later on a ball that spiraled through the Athens High School hallway straight into his hands. With the following words on it: "You'd be a real catch. Prom?"[265] To sweeten the deal, Karli Davis gave Joe a large bag of Charms caramel apple suckers.[266]

It was an offer too good to refuse.

When Karli planned the prom proposal, she knew about at least one of Joe's quirky pregame rituals.

"So, I eat a caramel apple sucker before every game on the bus and I always wear one sock inside out and the other one right side in," said Joe at a 2018 LSU press conference. "So, those are the two kind of weird things that I do."

Joe accepts Karli Davis' prom request in the AHS hallway. *Photo credit: Kevin Davis*

Burrow went on to explain that the sock thing happened by accident one game in high school and he "just kept going with it."[267] There's no particular significance.

As for the other ritual, neighbor Mary Ann Welsh gladly takes responsibility for Joe's strange sucker addiction.

"The hangout was my house," says Mary Ann, who used to be Robin's early morning running partner. "They were a large friend group of boys and girls. Couple dozen. Really got along well. Mostly athletes. They'd kick off their shoes and go straight to the basement. Sing, dance and goof off."[268]

The crew in Mary Ann Welsh's basement: *Front row (from left):* Olivia Harris, Sami Dixon, Shannon Finnearty, Sydney Marrs, Kaitlin Baker, Olivia Hoon, Cassie Staten, Abby Lawrence and Helena Petrik. *Second row:* Keegan Shaw, Elaina Seyfrang, Evan Berryman, Sara Skinner, Adam Luehrman and Alexis Zatta. *Third row:* Emmett Covington, Ryan Mack, Evan Cooley, Nathan Rickey, Joe Burrow, Ethan Gates, Ryan Luehrman, Kevin Moberg and Sam Vander Ven. *Photo credit: Mary Ann Welsh*

One day, Mary Ann's daughter, Kaitlin, asked if the crew could come over. Mary Ann agreed and hopped in the car to pick up snacks at Dollar General. "I got some chips and pop. Then I noticed Charms caramel apple suckers on the shelf. I remembered having them when I was young, so I bought a couple bags. When the kids arrived, they grabbed the snacks and went to the basement. Wasn't five or ten minutes later, I hear these footsteps coming up the stairs and the door opens. It's Joe. He says, 'These are great. Where did you get them?'"[269]

It was love at first lick. Joe was hooked.

It would take years to kick the habit.

"He stopped doing the sucker thing recently," says Jimmy.[270]

Apparently, he's too healthy now.

But Joe continued the high school ritual all the way through the 2019 National Championship season. While Karli's prom gift carried him for years, once word got out about Joe's sweet tooth, the LSU faithful made sure he would never have to buy another sucker again.

"The LSU folks would just drop them on our front steps," says Robin.[271]

Adds Jimmy, "We still have bags of those things."[272]

The good news is the Burrows never have to buy Halloween candy ever again. It's a very charming thought: Robin and Jimmy opening the front door to little trick-or-treaters dressed as the Bengals quarterback.

"Hope you like suckers. Take as many as you want."

We Demand a Rematch!

The 2015 senior class of Athens student-athletes was special. Arguably, the most accomplished male and female athletic class in school history.[273] "I don't know if there will be another class together like that," says Jimmy.[274] "The senior banquet was crazy," remembers Robin. "There were like twenty-one or twenty-two kids who got college athletic scholarships."[275]

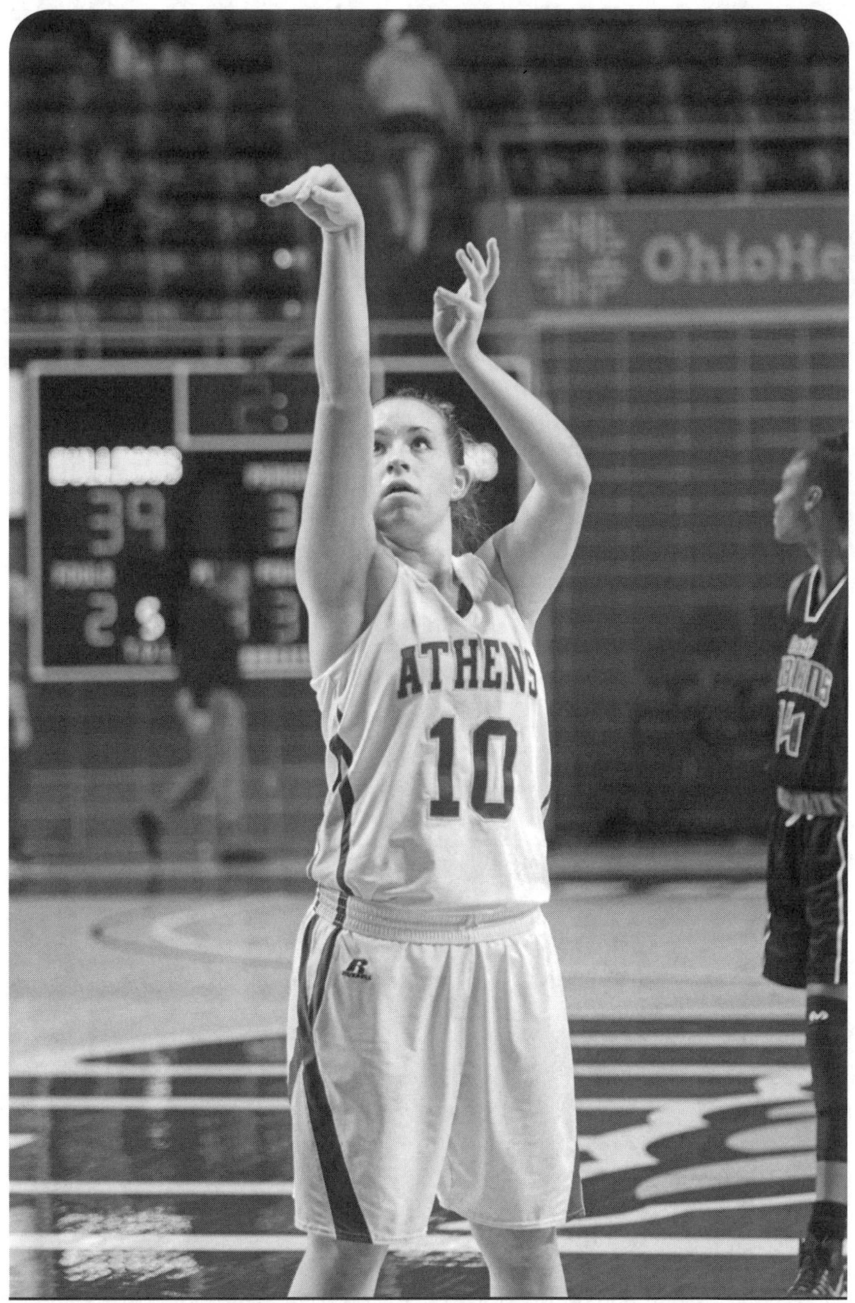

Dominique Doseck displays her perfect shooting form. *Photo credit: Trisha Doudna*

The class was led by Burrow and Dominique Doseck, who were named male and female athletes of the year.[276] Burrow threw for 11,448 yards and 185 touchdowns as the three-year Bulldog quarterback. On the hardwood, Joe and Dominique both scored over 1,000 career points with Doseck finishing her career as the school's all-time leading scorer. Both earned first-team all-Ohio honors in basketball. Dominique played her college ball at Ohio University.

The Luehrman twins joined Doseck as OU student-athletes. Adam and Ryan both played tight end for the Bobcats, while Sam Vander Ven was a student assistant coach. Trae Williams initially was a Bobcat commit before signing with Northwestern, where he played defensive back for the Wildcats.

"They were all just such good friends," remembers Robin.[277] "They went to OU football games and hung out on the hill most of the time," says Jimmy, "and sat pretty high up in the Convo at Bobcat basketball games."[278]

Chad Springer, who is now the AHS principal, doesn't think there will ever be another class like that one. Not only because of their overall athletic

After rooting their friends onto a district title, the boys join the girls in a celebratory photo. *Photo credit: Trisha Doudna*

excellence, but their cohesiveness, as well. "That whole class was unique," recalls Springer. "You'd have Joe sitting at a table with Trae and then you'd also have another kid sitting there who was an all-star soccer athlete. The football players didn't just hang out with the football players. They were just friends with everyone, and they supported each other at their games."[279]

While Dominique focused primarily on hoops in high school, she played volleyball as a senior and helped a talented Bulldog squad win the district crown. Kaitlin, who also played on that championship team, remembers all the boys cheering them on to the title. "I have a picture of them in the crowd going crazy."[280]

While the boys supported the girls the night Athens earned district bragging rights, it was a different story when the genders squared off in a friendly backyard volleyball match.

"So, we're having a party in our backyard," remembers Mary Ann, "and the boys and girls decide to play each other in volleyball. The boys were very competitive and expecting to kick the girls' butts."[281]

Kaitlin recalls the boys growing increasingly frustrated. "One of the Luehrmans or Joe would try to spike it and it would fly out of bounds or go into the net. We had to tell them to stop pulling the net down. We beat them and they got all mad."[282]

When it was over, the boys demanded a rematch.

They all agreed it would take place at Dominique's house. "I have a small court in my backyard, an enclosed gymnasium," says Dominique. "So, we set up the net and played again. They had the height and athleticism, but the girls worked together, which gave us the advantage. I remember them diving all over the place. Didn't matter. We won again. I can verify it: We won both matches. There was a lot of smack talk. But it was all fun and games."[283]

After it was over the boys begged for another rematch.

Never happened.

To this day, the girls have the upper hand. What the boys would give to go back in time and rewrite some backyard volleyball history.

Wait a second. Maybe that's another reason Joe is working on the DeLorean.

Where is that Flux Capacitor?

Incredible Emotional Intelligence

In between discussion of Superluminal Time Travel and the new-look Joe Brady offense, Burrow was asked a more serious question at the 2019 SEC Media Days. This one focused on mental health and the role of sports leaders in speaking out.

Without missing a beat, Burrow responded, "Being manly is expressing your feelings and I think we can see that shifting in our country right now. I think that's a really good thing. As far as being a leader, I think, one, it is important to talk about adversity that you faced and low points in your life to show that it is OK to be depressed. It is OK to be sad and anxious and have anxiety. And I think also as a leader it's important to kind of look out for it with people that might not be as comfortable sharing it. So, I think those are two critical points of being a leader."[284]

Bengals offensive coordinator Brian Callahan believes Burrow possesses "incredible emotional intelligence"—something that was on full display in the above response.[285] Joe's EI is one of the biggest assets of every locker room he's led. From Bulldogs to Bengals.[286]

"Even though he was a sophomore, he was as much of a leader on that team as any senior was," says Tanner Wood, who was a senior linebacker for the Bulldogs in 2012. "He's going to get his foot in the door with people—so to speak—with his actions and his approach. As time goes on and he wins over the locker room, that's when he becomes more vocal."[287]

That said, Joe's elite emotional intelligence didn't emerge magically—he's had to develop it. And like his game on the field, it will always be a work in progress.

"In high school, he was the silent type, very quiet, very calculated in what he said," recalls Principal Springer. "A little socially awkward like many kids at that age, but he obviously has overcome that a lot."[288]

Emotional awareness and sensitivity were modeled in the Burrow home. But Joe's emotional world was also shaped by the music he enjoyed, especially his favorite artist, Kid Cudi. Scott Mescudi is a Cleveland-born hip-hop artist who openly sings about feelings, inner struggles and teen angst—uncommon themes in the machismo world of rap and hip hop.[289]

When not contemplating the conundrums of the cosmos and physics of time travel, one can imagine quiet, impressionable teenage Joe listening to Cudi's 2009 debut album, "Man on the Moon" in his Star Wars-themed bedroom.[290]

Sam Vander Ven, who now lives a few miles away from Cudi's hometown of Shaker Heights, says he kept a Kid Cudi CD in his car all through his teen years. As a high school coach, Cudi remains part of Vander Ven's pregame playlist.

"The 'Man on the Moon' album is a reference to Cudi being so different and embracing his differentness," says Vander Ven. "I think that is how it speaks to a lot of teenagers who are lost and trying to figure out who they are. He provided a mellow narrative about how he was able to overcome his problems instead of allowing them to knock him out."[291]

On a recent trip to watch a UFC Fight in Las Vegas, Joe, Ibi Watson and Zacciah Saltzman reflected on the role Kid Cudi played during their formational years. "When we were in Vegas, we actually had a deep talk about how Kid Cudi shaped so much of our growth," says Saltzman. "We really respect the fact that he put himself out there, because everyone is going through these things, but not everyone wants to talk about it. As a teenager coming into yourself, unsure of who you are, it was great listening to a guy who wasn't afraid to express his emotions."[292]

Cudi gave quiet Joe Burrow permission to express his emotions. To see sensitivity and empathy as manly things. To incorporate emotional awareness into his locker room leadership style. While Joe lives for the bright lights on the field and brotherhood inside the locker room, off the field he finds the spotlight about as appealing as second-place trophies.

"I love playing football, but I don't like everything that comes with it," said Joe on the "Full Send" Podcast. "I hate [the attention]. I get anxiety going out and having to take pictures…I love the fans and I'm very appreciative of everybody, but it's a lot sometimes."[293]

Zacciah says that while "Joe is not always the most social guy, that doesn't mean he isn't feeling things deeply. He has a big heart."[294]

Joe's big heart is something that has never been questioned.

"Every single coach has said Joe is the best kid they've ever coached in their lives," says Troy Bolin. "When every coach says the same thing, it means something."[295]

According to Fred Gibson, you would never have known Joe was the quarterback of the football team when he was walking through the halls. He didn't act like the stereotypical jock or big man on campus. Just a good guy to everyone.[296]

Principal Springer remembers Joe as supremely inclusive. "We had a student with multiple handicaps and Joe made sure he was never left out. He even walked him through the hallways. There wasn't a kid he would turn down or turn away."[297]

Joe's kindness was also on full display the day he, the Luehrman twins, Ryan Mack, and Patrick Thomas presented an autographed football to their former elementary school principal John Gordon, who was fighting cancer at the time. Gordon was a devoted follower of Bulldog athletic teams, but unable to attend football games during the 2013 season. "I had been in the hospital with my condition and they took the time to see me," recalls an appreciative Gordon. Robin, who taught at Morrison when Gordon was principal, said, "It was a memento and their way of showing Mr. Gordon that they were thinking about him and supporting his fight against cancer."[298]

Jeff Skinner remembers that "while Joe was a great friend to everybody, he was also capable of cutting up and having a good time."[299]

Like the time he got trashed. With the whole school watching.

"We were doing senior pranks—nothing too extreme, all fun and games. I think the principal was even watching," says Dominique. "In the middle of the day, football players were racing each other through the hallway in trash cans. I remember Joe in the can and a teammate pushing him. We were supposed to be in class, but everyone was just sprinting around and cheering. He and his teammate wanted to win so bad the can tipped over at the finish line and Joe fell out. It was very entertaining."[300]

Joe could also be entertaining on the stage. At the time, there was a tradition known as Senior Follies—mostly goofy *Saturday Night Live*-style skits. Dominique remembers Joe dressing up like a girl and fully embracing the role. "I can't remember the skit, but I do remember laughing so hard," says Dominique, almost in tears as she recounts the story. "I mean he was not embarrassed at all. Just funny, quirky Joe."[301]

Second Thoughts

Joe Burrow's quirky side was on full display when he returned to The Ohio State University campus a few days after falling short in the Ohio High School Division III championship game. Joe showed up for his official campus visit in ratty tennis shoes and sporting bleach-blonde hair, something many of his Bulldog teammates had vowed to do if they won the regional title.

His host for the Buckeye visit was Stephen Collier, a freshman from Leesburg, Georgia. Collier, who was already a member of the stacked Buckeye quarterback room, saw Ohio's Mr. Football for the first time and said to himself, "What's up with this guy?"[302]

At first, he wasn't sure what to think of Burrow, who was ranked as a four-star recruit by many publications.[303] Over time, however, Collier would grow fond of Joe's cartoon attire, off-beat headbands, and unabashed locker-room dance moves. "The more you got to know him, you realize his quirkiness or being more outside the box was a matter of his confidence in himself and not caring what anybody else thinks about him."[304]

Joe had already verbally committed to Ohio State the previous May after receiving seventeen other scholarship offers, including two from the Southeastern Conference (Kentucky and Vanderbilt), two from the Big Ten (Maryland and Minnesota), two from the Big 12 (Iowa State and West Virginia) and two from the Atlantic Coast Conference (Boston College and Virginia Tech).

The main event of the day was a sit down with head coach Urban Meyer and offensive coordinator/quarterbacks coach Tom Herman, who had just a few days before received the Broyles Award—an honor given to the nation's top assistant.[305]

Herman was the reason Joe was in Columbus.

"I owe a lot to Coach Herman," says Burrow. "He's the only coach from big-time programs that had any faith in me."[306]

Ever since Joe's sophomore season, Herman had seen something in the Bulldog quarterback. Something few other major recruiters noticed. Even when he traveled around the country scouting more highly touted QBs, Herman remained in Joe's corner.

The December meeting with the Burrows took place while the Buckeyes were preparing for the national semi-final matchup against Alabama in the inaugural College Football Playoff. It was a game Ohio State would win, 42–35.

During the sit down, Meyer told Joe he was impressed by his performance in the state title game.

"Do you know what impressed me most?" asked Meyer.

"I don't know, the six touchdowns?" responded Joe.

"No, it was how you handled yourself in the postgame press conference," said Meyer.

Urban certainly appreciated Joe's competitive spirit and no-excuse, team-first attitude.[307]

In the middle of the meeting, Herman ducked out to take a phone call. The Burrows later discovered the University of Houston was on the line. Shortly thereafter, Herman was named the new Cougar head coach.

"That trust and that bond had certainly developed between Herman and Joe," says Jimmy. "You commit to the university, to the school. But yet, in reality, you commit to the person who recruited you. That makes it hard when you know there's a possibility he may leave and that's not the guy that's going to be coaching you."[308]

Within a few days, Joe began to waver. Especially when the new OSU quarterback's coach was announced. It would be Tim Beck, the former University of Nebraska offensive coordinator.

From his earliest days, Joe wanted to play for Nebraska. On the Memorial Field turf is where he learned how to ride a bike. Where Dan, Jamie and Jimmy had donned the Red and White. Some of the most cherished family photos feature young Joe wearing the iconic Big Red helmet.

"That was absolutely our 100 percent dream for him from the time he was born," says Robin. "Even before he was born."[309]

The Burrows had taken an unofficial campus visit to Lincoln when Joe was a sophomore. Joe even had his picture taken with legendary coach Tom Osborne. But head coach Bo Pelini and offensive coordinator Tim Beck showed no interest in the Athens High School prospect.

The Buckeyes beat the Oregon Ducks, 42–20, to win the national championship on Monday, January 12, 2015. Instead of celebrating the Buckeye title, however, Joe was tossing about in a sea of uncertainty.

"Joe began to waver with Tom Herman going to Houston," says Jimmy. "At this point, Oklahoma was showing interest in Joe and Nebraska finally with a new coach had jumped in there, as well. Even Harbaugh from Michigan was calling."[310]

After the national championship win, Meyer checked in with Jimmy.

"He calls me and says, 'What do you think?' I say, 'Joe's having second thoughts.' Coach Meyer asks, 'What do I need to do?' I tell him that he and Tim Beck need to get here to the house as soon as possible."[311]

Meyer was already scheduled to do the *David Letterman Show* in New York City that night, but would take a private jet to Athens the following evening.

While on the Letterman show, Dave asked Urban to simulate a recruiting visit.

Meyer: "Are you fast?"

Letterman: "I'm a linebacker and so fast. I hit like a ton of bricks. Do you call my mom and dad and stop by? How does that work?"

Meyer: "Well, we have nine coaches who identify prospects and once they fit what we are looking for we get into a plane or car and go to their home, visit with the families, tell them about what a great school Ohio State is, how you fit and then try to getcha."

Letterman: "So now I see Urban on my front porch and I'm signing as you walk in."[312]

"Urban's a good recruiter, impressive guy," says Jimmy.[313] But Joe wasn't ready to sign. Not just yet. He had lingering doubts.

Meyer and Beck joined the Burrows in the living room that would one day become famous. The living room in which the world would watch Joe's reaction to hearing his name called as the number-one overall NFL pick during the 2020 pandemic draft.

But that was still five years down the road. Today, there were serious questions to address. "Coach Meyer wanted to hear Joe's thoughts," recalls Jimmy. "Joe looked right at Tim Beck and said 'Coach, you're one of the guys who turned me down at Nebraska and now you're going to be my coach.' There was a lot of scrambling. Coach Beck just went through the process that they had at Nebraska. It was a pretty intense couple hours of conversation."[314]

According to *Huskers Illustrated* writer Michael Kelly, the coaching staff had concerns about Joe's arm strength.[315] In a press conference a few weeks later, Beck said he and head coach Bo Pelini—who was Dan Burrow's defensive coordinator at Nebraska for one season—had already committed to a recruit "which took them out of the race" for another quarterback.[316]

Meyer had heard that Joe's dream school was Nebraska, but didn't know why. He asked Jimmy to explain. "So, we went through the whole history of our family with Nebraska," Jimmy recalls. "I said, if you go downstairs there's no Ohio State stuff it's just all Nebraska. We're getting ready to leave and Coach Meyer says, 'I want to go downstairs.' I said, 'Well, coach, that's where all the Nebraska stuff is,' and he said, 'I want to see it.'"

They descended to the Burrow family basement, chock full of Nebraska memorabilia. Big Red glory as far as the eye could see. Urban looked around the room and after a long pause said, "I didn't get it before, but now I do. I get it." He finally understood what the Nebraska tradition means to the Burrow family and why the snub hurt so much. Meyer and Beck reassured Joe that he was wanted in Columbus and that all would be well.[317]

Backing up Barrett

When Joe made it official on signing day, he became the first Athens High School football player to become a Buckeye since the 1950s.[318] With senior Braxton Miller, junior Cardale Jones and sophomore J.T. Barrett ensconced in the quarterback room, Joe would compete with realistic expectations. He thought, "I'll sit for two years, J.T. will leave for the NFL, then I'll have a great career."[319]

One thing Burrow might not have expected, however, was a name change. In an act of mild hazing, the upperclassmen change the names of the freshmen in the quarterback room. Burrow's name among his teammates would no longer be Joe. He was now "John." When Dwayne Haskins arrived the following year, his name would be changed to "Roy."[320]

As expected, Burrow redshirted his first year. The Buckeyes were ranked number one in the nation for most of the season and favorites to repeat as national champions. But on a rainy November evening, Michigan State shocked the top-ranked Buckeyes, 17–14, in a bitter defeat that left many in the Horseshoe scratching their heads.

Nevertheless, Ohio State finished the season 12–1, defeating Michigan, 42-13, and Notre Dame in the Fiesta Bowl, 44–28, in the last two games. The final Associated Press poll ranked the Buckeyes a disappointing seventh.

After the season, the quarterback room thinned out with Miller and Jones both departing for the NFL. For the time being, this left Burrow and Collier in a battle to backup Barrett.

The 2016 Ohio State spring game would be Joe's first collegiate action in front of a live crowd. But this wasn't your typical scrimmage. Meyer had urged fans to pack the stadium so he could evaluate his young players under pressure. The Scarlet and Gray faithful complied. A record 100,189 people crammed into the Shoe to see Burrow lead the Gray to a 28–17 victory over the Scarlet squad. Joe completed 14 of 23 passes for 196 yards and three touchdowns, including a pair of deep balls to future Washington Commander standout Terry McLaurin.

"Joe Burrow did a great job all day just throwing the ball out there and making plays for our offense and putting us receivers in a good position to make plays," said McLaurin following the game.[321]

The Big Ten Network announcers were equally impressed with Burrow's skillset, especially his ability to throw the ball with precision. "As far as Joe Burrow is concerned, his best attribute is his accuracy," said one broadcaster. Later in the game, the color commentator added, "Another wonderful throw for Burrow, floated it in. This time for Terry McLaurin. Burrow showing nice touch."[322]

Troy Bolin, one of the many Athenians in attendance that day, wasn't surprised by Joe's precision under pressure in front of 100,000 scrutinizing eyes. "That's what I kept telling people. They'd say he's not good enough to go to Ohio State," said the Bulldog radio announcer. "I'd say, yes, he is. He's brilliant, he works harder than anyone I've ever seen and he's accurate. He's like the Greg Maddux of football. Maddux didn't throw 95, but he's one of the best pitchers of all time because of his intelligence and accuracy. Joe's the same way. He's doesn't have a cannon, but he's smart and so accurate."[323]

Burrow also used his feet, displaying agility on a deft spin move that resulted in a 31-yard gain—the longest run of the day by either side. For good measure, Joe gave the OSU faithful a taste of his toughness, bouncing up after six sacks. Toughness would become Burrow's calling card in the Buckeye locker room. Later in his career, when he couldn't get on the field as a quarterback, Joe even asked Meyer if he could play on special teams. To no avail.[324]

After the spring game, ESPN's Austin Ward offered his own commentary: "If it wasn't already safe to put backup QB conversations to bed, Joe

Burrow is showing all the tools this afternoon, even behind a backup OL [offensive line]."[325]

In the postgame press conference, however, Meyer discussed his high expectations for the OSU signal-callers. "If you play quarterback at Ohio State in this offense, you have to be a Heisman candidate—otherwise, we're going to suffer. Joe Burrow has been coming on. He was a guy last year I had my concerns…Just arm strength, release, twitch, ability to run the ball because you have to do that. He's gotten better and better. He's a grinder. He comes from a really good family that are tough people, and you can see him start to grow."[326]

From a hometown perspective, there was much to applaud. "Burrow played well in his true public debut as a Buckeye," observed *Athens Messenger* staff writer Jason Arkley. "He was better than No. 3 quarterback Stephen Collier (4–11, 154 yards, 1 INT) and on this day better than starter J.T. Barrett (13–22, 102 yards, 2 INTs). But he wasn't Heisman candidate good. Not yet."[327]

As usual, Burrow was his own stiffest critic. Instead of focusing on the three touchdowns, Joe mentioned the one interception—just like his comments following the Toledo Central Catholic defeat. "I played OK. Obviously, I had the interception, bad play by me. I still have a long way to go. I took a big step this spring, but I have to take another big one before fall camp."[328]

Fall camp marked the arrival of highly touted Dwayne Haskins, who verbally committed to the University of Maryland before changing his mind and signing with Ohio State. Haskins had offers from several high-profile schools, including LSU, Florida and Penn State. Meyer was captivated by the potential Haskins brought to the Buckeyes.

"As a junior, he was the best prepared quarterback I have ever seen in recruiting," said Meyer. "When I watched him work out and throw the football, at that age, I've never seen anything like it."[329]

Like Burrow, Haskins would redshirt his first year. Unlike Burrow, Haskins came in with a Big Ten ready rifle for an arm. Years later on the "Full Send" Podcast, Burrow disclosed the Meyer methodology when it came to assessing first-year Buckeye quarterbacks. "When a new guy gets there, he's going to put him into the fire to see how he responds," said Burrow matter-of-factly. "He stands right behind the quarterback [in practice] and if you make a bad throw, he's going to let you know it. Some guys can handle it, some guys can't."

One of the podcasters followed up by asking Burrow to identify the most dispiriting thing Meyer ever said to him. Joe said, "He told me I threw like a girl one time."[330]

The Burrow-Haskins battle would eventually turn into an epic competition, but with Haskins redshirting, the backup job belonged to Burrow.

Ohio State posted an 11–2 record in 2016. The only regular-season loss came against Penn State, 24–21, in a Saturday night white-out thriller at Beaver Stadium. Penn State beat Wisconsin in the Big Ten championship game, but in a controversial decision the NCAA Selection Committee passed over the Nittany Lions. Instead, it was Ohio State, a team with fewer losses, that received the nod to play Clemson in one of the national semi-final matchups. Unfortunately for the Scarlet and Gray faithful, it wasn't much of a contest as the Deshawn Watson-led Tigers shut out the Buckeyes, 31–0. Ohio State finished the season ranked sixth in the final AP Poll.

For the first time in recent memory, Ohio State's starting quarterback remained healthy throughout the season. As a result, Joe's playing time was sparse. In five appearances, he completed 22 of 28 passes for 226 yards. Burrow was responsible for three touchdowns, two through the air. On the ground he rushed the ball twelve times for 58 yards. The most memorable appearance was contributing to the 62–3 domination of the Nebraska

Joe warms up in the Horseshoe with Ryan Day and Dwayne Haskins in the foreground. *Photo credit: Troy Bolin*

Cornhuskers. Joe likely felt some measure of vindication, throwing for 62 yards on a perfect six for six. He also ran the ball twice and scored his only touchdown as a Buckeye on a 12-yard dash to the end zone.

Back in The Plains, the Burrows would often head in different directions on Saturdays. Jimmy went 33 E to Peden Stadium, while Robin took 33 W to the Shoe.

"I went to one game with her," said Liz Luehrman, whose sons were both playing for the Bobcats. "But she went to a lot of games alone. And I know it was hard at times."[331]

Robin would also take periodic trips to Columbus to check in on Joe. "I would almost always go up on Sundays," says Robin. "Sometimes during the middle of the week if he needed something. I'd cook him some food, exchange laundry baskets, go get ice cream. Sometimes when he was off at practice, I'd clean that dadgum dorm room. I did that a lot. Ugh."[332]

John Versus Roy

While J.T. Barrett had one more year remaining as the starting Buckeye quarterback, the backup battle between Joe Burrow and Dwayne Haskins, aka John and Roy, officially began to heat up during the spring of 2017.

In the spring game, the two quarterbacks posted similar stat lines. Burrow was 14 of 22 for 262 yards, while Haskins connected on 26 of 37 passes for 293 yards. Both players tossed three touchdowns.

After the scrimmage, Burrow exuded well-earned confidence as the media crowded around his locker. "I know I can play here now," said a bigger and stronger Burrow, who was earning a reputation as a savage in the Ohio State weight room. "Now I need to play at a high level and keep getting better and better. The game's really slowed down for me. I see just about everything that's going on. I know the offense way better. The ins and outs. What's going on up front."[333]

In the postgame press conference Meyer praised all of the Buckeye quarterbacks for their play during the spring. "They've done a very good job. I thought Dwayne and Joe Burrow played well [today]." A reporter followed up by asking if Joe and Dwayne were neck and neck for the backup job. Urban replied, "I know it's very close. But I'm not prepared to say who is two and who is three yet."[334]

In his postgame article, Jason Arkley continued to beat the drum for Joe's climb up the depth chart. "Burrow has been good—great, in fact, over the last thirteen months for OSU," wrote *The Athens Messenger* journalist. "With a pair of spring game appearances, and a handful of mop-up duty games during the regular season in 2016, the former Bulldog has a combined stat line of 50 of 73 passing (68.5 percent) for 684 yards and eight touchdowns."[335]

After Joe's first spring game, Arkley proved almost prescient when he wrote that Burrow "wasn't Heisman good, *not yet*."[336] Following Joe's second spring game, the hometown reporter offered another prophetic word: "As Burrow continues to grow, and evolve as a quarterback the ticking clock becomes more prevalent. There's a belief that it's not IF Burrow can be a great FBS quarterback, but when and where."[337]

During fall camp, the battle for the backup role continued. With a new offensive coordinator, Kevin Wilson, and quarterback's coach, Ryan Day, Burrow was upbeat when the media asked him to assess the offense mid-August.

"I just feel really good about where the offense is right now," said the redshirt sophomore quarterback. "We're all meshing together pretty well, going fast, and I think the offense is really completing itself."[338] A little over a week later, Joe would be undergoing surgery to repair a broken bone in his throwing hand. He'd be sidelined for a month. Urban wouldn't have to make a decision on the backup quarterback. Burrow's injury did that for him.

By the time Burrow returned to the field, Haskins was firmly entrenched in the backup roll and Meyer had no interest in revisiting that question during the season. As the third-string quarterback on the depth chart, Joe saw little playing time. On the season, he completed 7 of 11 passes for 63 total yards.

The 2017 Buckeyes won the Big Ten East and defeated Wisconsin in the Big Ten Championship game to capture the conference title. But two decisive defeats—Oklahoma at home and Iowa on the road—knocked Ohio State out of the playoff picture. The Buckeyes ended the season on a high note by defeating Pac-12 champion USC in the Cotton Bowl, 24–7, and finished the year 12–2 and fifth in the final AP poll.

For many Ohio State fans, however, the most memorable moment of the year came on November 25th in The Big House. With Ohio State trailing 20–14 with 6:07 to go in the third quarter, Dwayne Haskins replaced an injured J.T. Barrett and led the Buckeyes to a come-from-behind 31–20 victory over the Wolverines. It gave Buckeye Nation a foretaste of what a Haskins-at-the-helm future could look like.

"Joe played great during fall camp, so in his mind he was still the backup," says Jimmy. "He was never discouraged until he broke his hand. That allowed

Dwayne to move ahead. In his mind, he still thinks he's the best and doesn't want to transfer. We had one or two meetings with Coach Meyer and Joe was in the room. As parents, we just had to be encouraging and positive."[339]

"When your son or child goes away to college, they still need that unconditional love and support no matter if they are succeeding or not," adds Robin. "I was doing everything I could to show that to Joe in any way that I could. Whether it's through shooting a text message or making a trip to Columbus a couple times a week just to see his face and make sure everything was actually OK. It's worrisome. You hear horror stories of some kids who just can't handle it and you don't want your kid to be that kid."[340]

In a 2022 interview with Chris Simms, Joe opened up about his final year at Ohio State. "I was putting in the same work I've always put in and of course there's self-doubt in that moment," said Burrow. "[When] you're not getting the opportunity to show what you can do it's frustrating and there were times I started updating that résumé. Thinking about being an investment banker or something like that."[341]

Despite the occasional doubts, Joe was far from done with football—whether his career would continue at Ohio State or somewhere else. In 2018, there was no transfer portal. In order to play immediately, transfer student-athletes needed to have their undergraduate degree in hand. So, Joe loaded up his schedule the final few semesters. This would allow him to graduate in three years with a bachelor's degree in Consumer and Family Financial Services.

While Joe was working overtime in the classroom, Jimmy got on the phone with some of his colleagues. "I actually started calling people in January," says Jimmy. "Friends of mine in coaching, just to get the word out that Joe could be available to transfer."[342]

As spring practice approached, the Buckeye coaching staff assured Joe that there would be an open competition for the quarterback job following Barrett's graduation. Not only would he and Haskins compete, but the highly touted Tate Martell would join the battle.

In the 2018 spring game, Meyer split reps between the three quarterbacks. Burrow finished the game 15 of 22 for 230 yards and two touchdowns, including a beautifully thrown 42-yard ball to Damario McCall on the final play of the game. It was a poetic exclamation point. In three spring games, Joe was superb, connecting on 43 of 67 passes for 688 yards and eight touchdowns. Burrow left no questions unanswered. The only question remaining was who would Meyer pick to be his starter.

As Jason Arkley put it, "Your move, Urban."[343]

After the game, Meyer said he and his coaches would evaluate the data the following week and make a decision about the starting quarterback. He made it clear that intangibles and "thirty years of gut" would be part of the process. Meyer also praised Burrow for his development during his time as a Buckeye. "Joe has to be one of the most improved quarterbacks in terms of delivery speed and arm. He's always been a very smart, tough guy and a very good leader, but his improvement is very notable over the last couple years."[344]

Surrounded by a sea of reporters, Burrow answered questions about the battle with Haskins and his future as a Buckeye. "I've heard for three years that you're never going to play here; I'm going to end up transferring, I'm not good enough to play here," said Burrow. "I just sit back, put my nose to the grindstone and work. That's what I've done for three years, and I think I've come a long way."[345]

The following week Burrow learned that Haskins would be the starter. It was a tough decision for the kid from Southeast Ohio, with his undergraduate degree in hand, Joe would take his talents elsewhere. After all, he'd never reach his goal of playing on Sundays if he spent all of his Saturdays on the sidelines.

In an interview with ESPN's Tom Rinaldi, Joe described the conversation with Coach Meyer. "It was pretty emotional. He didn't want me to leave," said Burrow. "And honestly, I didn't want to leave. But I thought it was best for my career. That was my first home. That's where I went to college first. That's where I graduated. That's where I learned to become a man on my own."[346]

The 99-Yard Drive Begins

For Joe, it was time to take the advice of Omaha lawyer Rik Bonness, the Husker All-American center who turned Jimmy's famous goal-line stop in the 1974 Sugar Bowl into an inspirational aphorism: "When it looks like you might lose, make a stand—and start your own 99-yard drive."[347]

When Joe made the decision to transfer, naturally the first school on the list was Nebraska. Maybe the second time would be the charm. After all, the Huskers had just hired a new coach, Scott Frost, who was a Burrow family friend. "Jamie had played one year with Scott, and he also helped us out in a bowl game while I was coaching at Nebraska," says Jimmy. "So, we had a relationship."[348]

The timing, however, wasn't ideal for the new Nebraska coach, who had received a commitment from Adrian Martinez. Frost was high on his recruit and wasn't looking to supplant him with a graduate transfer.

Now, we've all said things we regret. But few words more regrettable and public than those uttered by Frost when asked about the possibility of Burrow transferring to Nebraska. Getting straight to the point, Frost said, "You think he's better than what we've got?"[349]

Within two years, the answer to that question became painfully obvious to Husker Nation.

Joe still had several other options. He considered North Carolina. After all, Mitch Trubisky, another Mr. Ohio had gone from Tar Heel quarterback to second overall pick in the 2017 NFL Draft.

But ultimately it would come down to two schools: Cincinnati and LSU.

When not coaching Athens youth sports, Don Cooley practices as a certified public accountant. He also teaches tax law classes for CPAs and attorneys. Not sure if Rik Bonness was in attendance, but during the time of Joe's transfer process Cooley found himself teaching a continuing education class in Omaha. Don had recently heard from Jimmy that Nebraska turned down Joe for a second time.

As his Omaha students were settling in for the continuing education session, Don introduced himself. "When I mentioned I was from Athens, I started getting questions about OU head coach Frank Solich, because he had previously coached at Nebraska," recalls Cooley. "I said, 'Everybody get out your notebooks. You made the biggest mistake on your quarterback three years ago. Now, you've made the same mistake again. Write this name down: Joe Burrow. He's going to win the Heisman Trophy.'"[350]

6

Goodbye Joe

"Goodbye, Joe, he gotta go, me oh my oh
Jambalaya and crawfish pie and filet gumbo,
Dressed in style, go hog wild, me oh my oh
Son of a gun, we'll have big fun on the Bayou."[351]

—Hank Williams
"Jambalaya"

Two years before Joe Burrow became a Cincinnati Bengal, he nearly became a Cincinnati Bearcat.

On May 8, 2018, less than a month after his final Ohio State spring game, Burrow announced on Twitter his intention to transfer.

"After three weeks of struggling with this decision, I have decided to leave Ohio State and explore other options. My teammates and coaches all know the love I feel for them. I will decide where I will play next year in the coming weeks."[352]

As it turned out, it wouldn't take weeks. The world would know Burrow's decision in twelve days. Joe announced his intention to transfer on Tuesday. By Thursday Joe was in the Queen City meeting with Luke Fickell and the University of Cincinnati coaching staff.

Luke knew Joe well, having served as the defensive coordinator during Burrow's first two years as a Buckeye. Fickell was now in his second season as the UC head coach and laying the foundation for something special. In fact, within five years the Fickell-led Bearcats would play in the College Football Playoff—the first non-power five school to make the final four.

But at the time of the Burrow meeting, the Bearcats were coming off a 4–8 season, including a 2–6 record in the American Athletic Conference. The Bearcats were in desperate need of an offensive spark. Fickell and his staff believed Burrow was the right man for the job.

According to Mike Denbrock, the UC offensive coordinator at the time, Joe's visit was low key. "Normal stuff. We showed him the campus," said Denbrock. "Obviously, from Coach Fickell being with him and his family...we felt like we were in a really good spot."[353]

The Burrows were pleased with the prospect of Cincinnati, as well. "We love Luke Fickell," says Jimmy. "We know his family and other coaches on his staff. We would have supported Joe's decision to go there."[354] Adds Robin, "UC was a strong possibility."[355]

The University of Cincinnati made a lot of sense. In addition to established relationships with the coaching staff, Joe would be handed the keys to the Bearcat offense,[356] an enticing offer after three years of intense quarterback competitions at Ohio State. Staying in Ohio certainly had its benefits, as well. Joe would remain close to family, friends, and his longtime girlfriend, who grew up in Cincinnati and had recently landed a job in the Queen City after graduating from OSU.

Following the meeting, Denbrock was confident "it was over. He was coming to Cincinnati."[357] Only one hurdle remained. Joe would be visiting LSU over the weekend. Denbrock remembers the Burrows were simply doing their due diligence. Nothing to worry about.[358]

As Joe left the Queen City that night, Jimmy remembers his son was leaning "60 to 70 percent toward UC."[359]

But never underestimate the allure of Louisiana. The Oak Ridge Boys wrote a song entitled "Callin' Baton Rouge." But in the case of Joe Burrow, it was Baton Rouge doing the callin.'

A Bathtub of Crawfish

Ed Orgeron had never heard of Joe Burrow. That is until his son Cody called one day.

Cody had just watched the Ohio State spring game and was fired up because he found out that Burrow might be transferring. He encouraged his dad to pursue the Buckeye quarterback.

The wheels started turning. Coach O realized he had a resource on his staff—safeties coach Bill Busch. During Burrow's freshman year at Ohio State, Busch had served as the Buckeyes' defensive quality control coach. As a bonus, Bill had also coached Joe's brother Dan at Nebraska.

Coach O asked Busch what he thought about Burrow. Busch responded, "If we get Joe Burrow, we're going to the College Football Playoff."[360]

"We had a connection with Bill Busch because of Joe and Dan," says Jimmy. "Joe was talking to his brothers about things and Coach O and Busch picked up on that, which is what you do as a recruiter."[361]

Coach O started calling Joe, but didn't get very far. "I don't like talking on the phone," said Joe. "I don't like the recruiting stuff, so Coach O would call my brother Dan every single night."[362]

The strategy paid off. Dan enjoyed talking to Coach O. His respect grew even more when Orgeron appeared on Dan's favorite podcast, "Pardon My Take." "He was already pretty cool on my measuring scale to begin with," said Dan. "That only made him cooler in my eyes."[363]

The Burrows agreed to a visit. On Friday, May 11, Dan took the one-hour flight from Houston. Coach O and Dan were thick as thieves by the time Joe and his parents touched down in Baton Rouge.

Joe had a steak dinner with some of the LSU coaches on Friday night. Coach O remembers "it went okay, but I could tell [Joe] didn't want to be recruited.... The more he tried to dodge all my recruiting tactics, the more I liked him. Knowing Joe now, I realize that was just him. He doesn't let any of the side stuff get in his way. He had a laser focus unlike any that I'd ever seen before."[364]

Robin wasn't surprised by Joe's demeanor that weekend. "I didn't really think Joe would ever open up to Coach O while we were down there. That's just not Joe. He's pretty guarded."[365]

After breakfast the following morning, Joe, Jimmy and Dan met with several of the Tiger coaches. Through the years, LSU has produced some tremendous players, but doesn't exactly have a reputation for cranking out NFL quarterbacks. When asked about the perception of the LSU offense, Joe would later call it "Stone Age."[366]

Coach O wanted to flip the script in Joe's mind.

Orgeron knew this wouldn't be easy, so he asked one of his assistants to splice together LSU footage with some of Joe's OSU spring game and regular-season highlights. He also added some NFL sets that were on the Tiger drafting table. The mash-up reel would be shown during their sit-down with the Burrows.

As the film ran, Joe was in his element. "When we started talking about Joe's plays, his reads, what he was seeing, attacking the coverages, that is when he really lit up," remembers Orgeron. "I have never heard another college player talk about football the way he did."[367]

As Jimmy was watching the highlight reel, he was reminded of how much Joe flashed during OSU scrimmages. "It was crazy. Joe was doing things in the spring games that he went on to do at LSU."[368]

Coach O was most impressed by Joe's command of the room. Like a football savant, he never hesitated. No matter the question thrown at him by the coaches, he had a seamless answer. "That was when I knew he was the smartest guy in the room."[369]

Later that night, Orgeron took the Burrows to Mike Anderson's, a popular seafood restaurant in Baton Rouge. Joe had eaten crawfish before in Columbus, but was anticipating authentic Cajun cuisine. Joe scanned the menu for crawfish. Nothing. He looked again. Nothing. Disappointment set in. "I was looking forward to having crawfish in crawfish country," remembers Joe. "And Coach O says, 'You want some crawfish?' I was like, 'I was hoping to get some.' He says, 'I got it.' He makes a call and twenty minutes later they bring in a bathtub of crawfish."[370]

Coach O knew Joe didn't want to be schmoozed, but he had to take one more crack before the Burrows left town. Outside Mike Anderson's, Orgeron told a crawfish-bloated Burrow he couldn't promise him the job, but if he came to Baton Rouge and did the right things, he would be the quarterback.

Years later on the "Full Send" podcast, Burrow reflected upon that weekend with Orgeron. "When he was recruiting me, he told me something was going to happen, and it happened," says Burrow. "There's not a lot of people like that in this industry. I was very thankful Coach O gave me that opportunity because I knew what I was going to do with it."[371]

Jimmy, Joe and Robin all embrace the LSU decision. *Photo credit: The Burrow Family*

The Burrows flew north, and Dan took the hour-long flight back to Houston. Coach O wasn't sure where he stood, but when he checked with Joe's host for the weekend, Tiger tight end Foster Moreau, Orgeron was pleased to hear that Joe was "70 percent leaning toward LSU."[372]

But with Joe heading back to Ohio, he wasn't taking any chances. Orgeron tried following up with his prized recruit, but no answer. He called Dan and asked what Joe was going to do. Dan told Orgeron that it was up to Joe to make the decision. Coach O wasn't having it.

Dan recalls the conversation: "Coach O just said, 'Dan, you need to man the 'F' up.' So, I sat there, thought about it, wrote some stuff down. Talked to Joe, asked some questions. Because what he always said was, he wanted to play at the highest level, he wanted to win football games. And if that was true, from my perspective, there was only one place that could get done."[373]

Dan also told Joe that leaving Ohio could be "therapeutic." Otherwise, he would always be faced with the inevitable comparisons to Dwayne Haskins, just ninety minutes up I-71 North. Finally, he challenged him to embrace the uncomfortable, something Joe was accustomed to doing—all the way back to his grueling high school workouts with Coach White.[374]

Wise words.

Joe took them to heart.

May 20, 2018, turned out to be a symbolic passing of the torch. That was the day Joe Burrow signed his transfer papers. It was now official. Joe would be sending his love down to Baton Rouge. It was also the day the beloved and iconic Billy Cannon passed away at the age of eighty. Cannon was LSU's only Heisman Trophy winner. That would soon change.

Back in Cincinnati, Fickell and his staff were disappointed. Especially offensive coordinator Mike Denbrock, who was eagerly anticipating the September 22nd match-up between UC and Ohio University. It would have been fun to watch a Joe Burrow-led Bearcat offense against a Jimmy Burrow-led Bobcat defense.

You know about the Burrows and competition.

But Denbrock couldn't blame Joe for heading south. "God bless him. That's the best decision they ever made."[375] Such a good decision that

Denbrock also said yes to Baton Rouge four years later when Brian Kelly became the new Tiger head coach.

As I said, never underestimate the allure of Louisiana.

He's a Ballplayer

It was Joe's decision, but the whole Burrow family wanted him to go south. Liz Luehrman did, too. "We were glad Joe picked LSU," said Liz. "We knew he was destined for bigger things."[376] Adds Jimmy, "Coach O recruiting Joe changed the direction of our lives forever."[377]

That said, the September 22nd game at Nippert Stadium would have been enticing. One can only imagine what it would have been like for the people of Athens if Jimmy's Bobcats squared off against Joe's Bearcats. No doubt the Luehrmans, Vander Vens and Skinners would have been "cheering loud and long for Old OHIO," while at the same time pulling for Joe to score a few touchdowns on his old man.[378]

No one would have been more conflicted than Mrs. Burrow. Right next to Liz, Marikay, and Heather, Robin might have worn a custom-made t-shirt—split down the middle with black and red on the left and green and white on the right, supporting her two favorite men equally. Maybe a tad tacky. But if anyone could pull it off, it would be the fashion merchandizing maven Robin Burrow.

Liz Luehrman, on the right, traveled to support Robin when she could, but most Saturdays she watched her boys play for the OU Bobcats. *Photo credit: The Luehrman Family*

Instead of black and red, the town of Athens would turn purple and gold over the next two years. The gold part was nothing new. After all, the Bulldog colors are green and gold. Purple, that's a different story.

"I can't stand purple," says Sam Smathers, referencing the color of arch-rival Logan. "But now I have a lot of purple in the Dawg Pound. All because of Joe's decision to go to LSU."[379]

Joe arrived in Baton Rouge before the rest of the team that summer. He came ready to bust his rear. "I made it a point to try to work harder than everybody so I could win the team," said Burrow.[380] He would be taking online master's classes, which freed him up to focus on football most of the time. "Kudos to LSU for figuring out how to do that," said Robin.[381] Joe was done with the college life. No parties. No bars. No distractions. He would approach LSU like a post-graduate internship. "When he wasn't doing classwork, he was pretty much at the facility all day," remembers Jimmy.[382]

Linebacker Patrick Queen, who now plays for the Baltimore Ravens, vividly remembers the impression Burrow made on his teammates. "We knew Joe was different from the day he came in. He runs the conditioning test and smokes it, passing some of us up. He had the long hair. People called him 'Sunshine.'"[383]

Burrow had no problem trading "Shady" for "Sunshine," a reference to the transfer quarterback in *Remember the Titans*.

Anything to win his teammates over.

Unlike at UC, Joe wouldn't be handed the keys to the Tiger offense when fall camp began. Coach O had confidence in Joe, but he'd still have to beat out three returning quarterbacks—Myles Brennan, Lowell Narcisse and Justin McMillan. Joe was at a disadvantage. His spring practice was with Ohio State, not LSU. And he was coming into a locker room that had already aligned with McMillan.

The LSU coaches scored everything. "Every situation was given a grade," said Orgeron. "It's marked down on a sheet of paper."[384]

A few weeks following the first scrimmage, offensive coordinator Steve Ensminger met with the quarterbacks. He shared the grades. Burrow and Brennan were at the top. Following that meeting, Narcisse requested a transfer and McMillan quit without telling the coaches.

Realizing his mistake, McMillan asked if he could return. The coaches were hesitant. The team was upset, but didn't know the whole story. Coach O shared the quarterback grades with the team. Some were still resistant, but several defensive leaders trusted Orgeron and were willing to back Joe.[385]

The players had a closed-door meeting. No coaches. Joe understood the sense of loyalty. He knew his teammates at Ohio State would have had his back if something similar took place. "So, I addressed that, and told them that whether I'm the starter or not, whoever is the starter, we've got to rally behind that guy because we have to win games."[386]

It turned out to be another close quarterback battle for Burrow. Only this time, Joe came out on top. His hard work paid off and he was finally the guy.

Zac Al-Khateeb of *The Sporting News* predicted a major breakout season for Burrow and the Bayou Bengals: "He's an X-factor, a playmaker and difference-maker who makes an already talented LSU team a much more viable threat in the [SEC] West. That might sound hyperbolic for a player with few, if any, meaningful reps at Ohio State, but it's true."[387]

That said, Joe hadn't seen the field for three years. It would take time to find his footing and build chemistry with teammates. Coach O remembers the defense was way ahead of the offense during fall camp. "The defense was dominating," recalls Orgeron. "Devin White was chirping the whole time. 'Yeah, that play don't work!' The third time he said something, all of a sudden, Joe yelled back, 'Hey Devin, shut up. Or else I'm going to come over there and beat the f*** out of you!'"[388]

This was new. The Tiger defense wasn't used to anyone on the other side of the ball fighting back. Let alone the quarterback. They were beginning to realize this Burrow kid is different. Really different.

As Coach O puts it, "He's a ballplayer."[389]

Cool as a Cucumber

"That might be the best compliment Coach O can pay somebody," says Burrow. "I think Coach O likes me so much because he always tells me I would have been an All-American linebacker, too. So, I think he loves that part of me."[390]

Nathan White agrees, "I really think if Joe hadn't become a quarterback, he would have found a place to play as a safety in the NFL or he gets huge and plays defensive end. Joe doesn't think of himself as just a quarterback. He's a football player."[391]

One of Jimmy's favorite viral videos is a twenty-one second tire tug of war between Joe and Pete Werner, who would later play linebacker for the New Orleans Saints. Joe not only holds his own with Werner, but ultimately wins the battle—to the sheer delight of his Buckeye teammates. "I love that video," says Jimmy. "It really shows Joe's toughness. That tire war was one of the things that won Coach O over."[392]

Joe's toughness, hard work and competitive fire eventually swayed the Tiger locker room, as well.

While Burrow's toughness would be evident throughout the 2018 season, what stood out most in the opener against the University of Miami was his mental acuity and poise under pressure. On the third series of the game, Burrow called an audible which opened up a lane for running back Nick Brossette to break free for a 50-yard touchdown run.

On the next series, Joe made a check on fourth down. Seven plays later, the Tigers found the end zone again. Under Burrow's direction, the

25th-ranked Tigers would score 30 unanswered points en route to a 33–17 victory over the eighth-ranked Hurricanes.

While Burrow's stat line wasn't eye-popping (11 of 24 for 140 yards), his ability to manage the game was. When asked about Burrow's first start, Orgeron said, "I think he did great. We scored 33 points. He kept his poise, same thing we saw all camp."[393]

The following week the Tigers jumped from 25th to 11th in the Associated Press poll. They cruised to a 31–0 victory over Southeast Louisiana before facing seventh-ranked Auburn on the road. It would be Joe's first trip to The Plains—The Plains, Alabama, that is.[394] It would also be Joe's first taste of Southeastern Conference football.

The Tigers came into sold-out Jordan-Hare Stadium a double-digit underdog. After jumping out to a 10–0 lead midway through the first quarter, Auburn stormed back to take a 14–10 advantage into the intermission. The Plainsmen increased the margin to 21–10 in the third quarter before LSU place kicker Cole Tracy narrowed the lead with a 27-yard field goal.

The biggest play of the evening came with 8:18 remaining on the clock. With four defenders in the vicinity, Burrow threaded a pass across the middle to Derrick Dillon who outran the secondary for a 71-yard touchdown. "It was huge," said Joe. "That play sparked us through the rest of the game."[395]

The Tigers got the ball back and Burrow marched the offense down the field, setting up a game-winning field goal as time expired.

In the postgame press conference, with "Callin' Baton Rouge" blaring in the background, Coach O said, "Joe's as cool as a cucumber. He's not going to fold under pressure."[396]

When asked when he last played with so much on the line, Burrow said, "High school senior year, state championship game. To know I can go out there in a pressure situation and perform really gets my confidence up."[397]

On the strength of two top-10 victories in the first three weeks of the season, LSU climbed to number five in the nation. After defeating Louisiana Tech by two scores the Tigers dismantled Ole Miss, 45–16. On a day when LSU unveiled a statue of Billy Cannon outside of Tiger Stadium, Joe showed flashes of greatness himself, connecting on 18 of 25 passes for 292 yards and three touchdowns. The first TD was a perfectly thrown 21-yard back shoulder fade to true freshman Ja'Marr Chase. Joe also added 96 yards on the ground, including a 35-yard touchdown run.

Following the game, Burrow said, "I think we are really starting to get a feel of each other. Offensive line. Receivers. Me. Running backs. The offense is getting ready to take off."[398]

Hopes were high heading into the Swamp the following week. The fifth-ranked Tigers were favored against the 22nd-ranked Florida Gators. But after marching down the field on the opening possession to take a 7–0 lead, LSU struggled to protect Burrow the rest of the game. He was sacked five times and threw his first two interceptions of the season—one for a pick six. The Tigers fell to the Gators, 27–19.

The SEC gauntlet continued seven days later as the second-ranked and undefeated Georgia Bulldogs came into Death Valley. Unlike the Florida game, however, LSU was the more physical team, dominating the Bulldogs, 36–16. Burrow passed for 200 yards and scored two touchdowns on quarterback keepers.

After the game, Orgeron discussed Burrow's physicality. "Joe's a big strong guy. He could play linebacker. We feel like he can get half a yard."[399] Joe also had a 59-yard scamper, but was pulled down just shy of the goal line. On whether or not he should have scored: "Yeah I got caught by a corner, but I should have scored," said Joe with a sly smile.[400]

Burrow's performance impressed the SEC Network commentators. Former Auburn head coach Gene Chizik said, "Don't look at his numbers, because [Burrow] delivers when the game is on the line." Fellow analyst Chris Doering chimed in, "The guy brings an air of leadership to this team that they haven't had in a while. Not to mention the fact that he is constantly getting them into the right run checks. I can't say enough about Joe Burrow."[401]

When a reporter asked during the postgame presser if this was a signature win, Coach O said, "We're an up-and-coming football team. We still have a long way to go but we want to lead LSU to a championship. Where this takes us we don't know, but hopefully it gives us some confidence that we can play with anybody in the country."[402]

After a 19–3 win over Mississippi State on October 20, the Tigers enjoyed a hard-earned Bye Week before preparing for number one Alabama.

Joe decided to go back home.

So, What's It Like Down There on the B-a-y-o-u?

On his drive up north, Joe will sometimes swing by Amory and visit his grandparents in Mississippi. And, of course, get himself some sliders at Bill's Hamburgers.

"Before he started getting big, he went with us to church…and drew a crowd," says James Burrow. "People, kids coming up for autographs. This town has always been split between Ole Miss and Mississippi State, but now it's an LSU town."[403]

That's Joe. Everywhere he goes, he wins over the crowd.

This includes the folks of Nelsonville—one of Burrow's oldest rivals. Without any fanfare, Joe showed up for the Athens-Nelsonville York Friday night football game during his off week. He casually strolled to the 50-yard line for the coin toss. He wore a cap bearing the numerals "861"—an homage to the point total he and his Bulldog teammates racked up four years earlier. Still a state record.

In a conversation with *Athens Messenger* reporter Jason Arkley, Burrow admitted "it was definitely weird, talking mutually with Nelsonville York as equals and not battling it out on the field." He enjoyed the game quietly (Athens won 49–14), patiently taking photos with fans from both sides of the field.

"It means so much to me when you have the support, not only from the people back in Athens, but the surrounding areas," said Burrow. "People have no idea how much that means to me. When I see that every week it makes my heart warm."[404]

A trip back to Athens wouldn't be complete without heading over to the OU campus and visiting with old friends Sam Vander Ven and the Luehrmans. Ryan asked Joe, "What's the most annoying question you get from people?" In an exaggerated Cajun drawl, Joe responded, "People always ask me, 'What's it like down there on the B-a-y-o-u?" Just then one

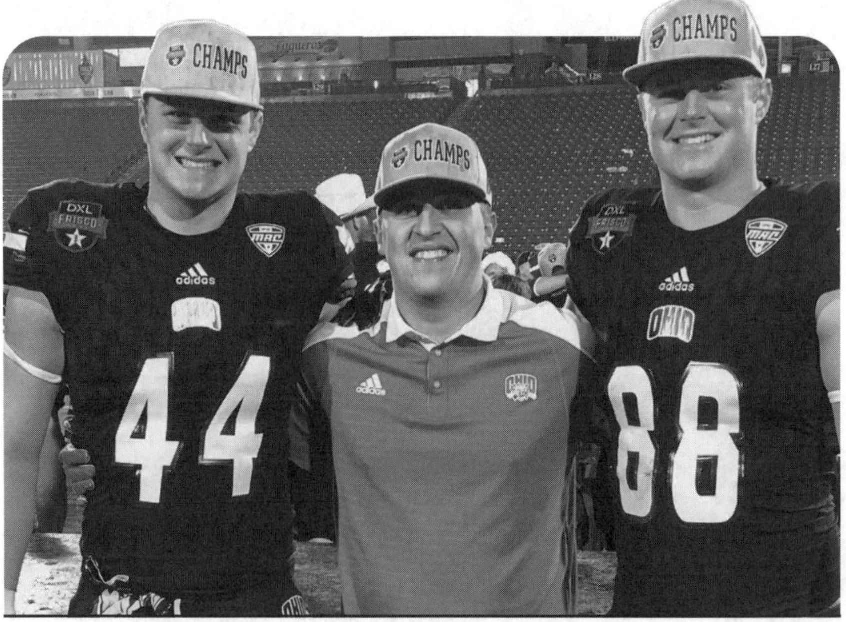

Adam and Ryan Luehrman with Sam Vander Ven after Ohio University's 27–0 victory over the San Diego State Aztecs in the 2018 Frisco Bowl. *Photo credit: The Luehrman Family*

of their roommates entered the room, saw Joe, and without missing a beat asked, "So, what's it like down there on the B-a-y-o-u?" The room erupted in laughter. The roommate asked, "What? What's so funny?"[405]

On Saturday, Joe drove to Columbus to visit with his Buckeye brethren. Just six weeks earlier, as Burrow was leading the comeback against Auburn, his former Ohio State teammates were on the field preparing to play Texas Christian University. Dwayne Haskins remembered the LSU game rolling on the jumbotron and "literally everyone stopped what they were doing during warm-ups to watch Joe play. It was crazy."[406]

"We were all heartbroken when Joe left because we love Joe," says Coach Meyer fondly. "Joe will always have Buckeye blood in him. He's still very close with all of his teammates and all of his coaches."[407] Joe feels the same, "I love Coach Meyer. There's nothing but love there."[408]

To those who think Joe turned his back on Buckeye Nation, Sam Smathers says, "Something a lot of people don't get is Joe didn't transfer from Ohio State. He completed his obligation. He graduated. He's a proud alumnus of Ohio State."[409]

Troy Bolin agrees that Burrow harbors no ill will toward the Scarlet and Gray. "I was talking to someone who thought Joe had hard feelings toward Ohio State," says Bolin. "I pulled up a picture of Joe wearing Athens, Ohio State, and LSU wristbands. If you think he's holding onto a grudge, why is he still wearing an Ohio State wristband?"[410]

The Turning Point

Top-ranked Alabama would be the biggest test of the year for the third-ranked LSU Tigers. The Crimson Tide came to town with a seven-game winning streak over the Bayou Bengals but it was Saturday night in Baton Rouge. The nation's eyes were upon Death Valley, one of the most intimidating venues in all of college football.

Unfortunately for ESPN and the LSU faithful, the game didn't live up to the hype. Burrow and the Tiger offense struggled to get past midfield. The Alabama defense was suffocating, holding LSU to 67 yards in the first half and under 200 total yards for the game.

"I think Alabama overpowered us," said Orgeron after the Tigers were shut out, 29–0. "We tried everything we possibly could, went max protection, just got beat. I do believe we have a good football team, not a great football team. We're nowhere near Alabama, obviously."[411]

Near the end of the press conference a reporter asked if LSU could close the gap on Alabama by next year or if it was going to take longer. "I don't know that," said Orgeron. "I know we have to get bigger, stronger offensive linemen to buck these guys."[412]

While Coach O focused on personnel and execution in the postgame presser, by the following day he was talking with offensive coordinator Steve Ensminger about moving to the spread—something Burrow had been wanting from the beginning. Emptying the backfield and sending out more receivers forces the defense to cover rather than just pinning their ears back and blitzing.

While the lopsided loss to Alabama stung, it was a wakeup call. A pivot point that would lead to LSU 2.0.

After squeaking past Arkansas the next week, the offense started implementing four-receiver sets against Rice. Burrow completed 20 of 28 passes for two touchdowns. It was Joe's first 300-yard passing game as LSU rolled to a 42–10 win.

In the regular-season finale, LSU traveled to College Station to take on Texas A&M. It appeared the Tigers had won the game in regulation, 31–24. In the final minute, an LSU interception led to a Coach O Powerade bath. But the call was overturned. The Aggies were still alive. After another play, the clock wound down to zero. The referees put a second back on the clock. Finally, the home team scored to send the game into overtime.

Seven overtimes later, the Aggies were victorious, 74–72. The game lasted nearly five hours. Both teams left it all on the field, but no one gave more than Joe Burrow. The Tiger quarterback was 25 of 38 for 270 yards and three touchdowns. On the ground, Joe ran for 100 yards and scored three more times.

Years later, Burrow called this game "the real turning point. [It was] when people started to realize I could do it and that our best bet to win a lot of football games was to put the ball in my hands forty to fifty times a game."[413]

Following the game, a severely dehydrated Burrow passed out in the locker room. The team buses idled as the medical staff tended to the LSU quarterback. After cookies, applesauce and IV fluids did their job, the Tiger caravan finally departed from Kyle Field. It was a first for LSU trainer Jack Marucci, who had never seen a player exert that level of "effort, desire and passion," while experiencing such an extreme "state of fatigue."[414]

LSU finished the regular season 9–3 and ranked 11th in the nation. The Tigers accepted an invitation to the Fiesta Bowl to play eighth-ranked Central Florida, a team with twenty-five straight wins. One prognosticator called LSU's offense "pedestrian at best" and went on to predict a possible 13–10 final score.[415]

It didn't quite turn out that way as LSU lit up the scoreboard with 40 points and came away with an eight-point Fiesta Bowl victory.

The Tigers overcame a lot of adversity. With several defensive starters hurt, suspended, or opting to sit out in preparation for the NFL draft, a group of talented, but green, backups would have to answer the bell.

The biggest play of the game came in the first quarter when a UCF defensive lineman rang Burrow's bell. The Tigers were trailing 7–3, but were moving down the field when Derrick Dillon was tugged to the ground on a timing route. A flag wasn't thrown, and the perfect spiral went straight into the arms of a UCF cornerback who took it the length of the field for a touchdown.

As Joe was sprinting toward the ball carrier, he was viciously cold-cocked. To add insult to injury, another UCF player spit on Burrow as he was struggling to catch his breath. A flag was thrown this time for unsportsmanlike conduct.

For a moment, it appeared Burrow might not return. But he quickly composed himself and threw three consecutive touchdown passes, two of them to Justin Jefferson. He ended the game 21 of 34 for a career-high 394 yards and four touchdowns. Ja'Marr Chase led all receivers with six catches for 93 yards.

After the game, ESPN tweeted out the video of Burrow's blindside hit with the caption, "Keep that head on a swivel." Burrow got the last laugh when he retweeted the video with his own caption: "That's lght [alright] I'll take the 4 tds and the dub."[416]

The Twittersphere went crazy.

"The only reason I didn't get up in one second is because I got the wind knocked out of me," said an indignant Burrow after the game. He wanted the world to know why he didn't execute his typical Tom Brady bounce-up move.[417]

Reflecting upon the game, Orgeron later wrote, "Joe took it to another level. I saw something different in that kid. He was the most ultimate competitor I'd ever been around. He doesn't get rattled. When adversity hits, he actually gets better."[418]

How much better, no one ever could have imagined.

7

The Gospel of Jeaux

SENIOR YEAR—FIRST HALF

"Joe came right at the right time. I think he changed our program around. He gave us some stability at the quarterback position. He gave us a leader there. He gave us a coach on the football field. I think we've only just seen the beginning of Joe Burrow, to see what Joe Burrow is really made of. I think he's going to have a great year."[419]

—Ed Orgeron
LSU head coach

Pageantry and tradition are a big part of what makes college football so special. And when it comes to gameday experience, LSU takes a back seat to nobody.

Dr. Charles Coates was the first LSU football coach. When he arrived in Baton Rouge in 1893, he visited a local store on the corner of Third and Main to find colored ribbon for the team's bland uniforms. It was Mardi Gras season, so the store was stocked with purple and gold. Seemed like a good color combination, so he bought out the store's stock.

He also thought LSU now needed a nickname. In a 1937 letter written to the school's alumni, Coates revealed that the mascot was selected to honor a regiment of raucous confederate Cajun soldiers. Coates wrote, "The Louisiana Tigers had represented the state in [the] Civil War and had been known for their hard fighting." Not to mention, "purple and gold seemed Tigerish enough."[420]

For a hundred years, Death Valley has set the standard for intimidating venues. When Tiger Stadium is filled to capacity, the roar of 102,000 rabid fans is deafening. In May 2022, the "Big Game Boomer" podcast ranked the fifty loudest college football stadiums. Six of the top ten were in the Southeastern Conference.

Death Valley was number one.[421]

During games, the Golden Band from Tigerland plays a variety of vintage songs that transport fans back to the Billy Cannon glory days. The fight song, "Fight for LSU," was penned in 1937 and "Hey Fighting Tigers" was played for the first time in 1962 against Texas A&M. Here's a taste:

You've got to go for a touchdown.

Run up the score.

Make Mike the Tiger stand right up and roar.

ROAR![422]

Oh, Mike the Tiger. The first Mike was acquired in 1936. He was named in honor of LSU athletic trainer Mike Chambers, who was instrumental in acquiring a Bengal Tiger from the Little Rock Zoo.[423] The habitat, which has been significantly upgraded through the years, sits between Tiger Stadium and the Pete Maravich Assembly Center. Until as recently as 2016, you could hear Mike ROAR on the sidelines of Saturday night games. Legend has it, LSU will score a touchdown for each Mike-the-Tiger roar on game day.[424]

Mike no longer makes sideline appearances. Some say he prefers watching the broadcast from the comfort of his confines. While Joe Burrow isn't a big fan of caged animals (he still hasn't watched "Tiger King" on Netflix),[425] Mike lives a life of luxury, roaming about his $3.7 million, 15,000-square-foot lush habitat—much to the delight of many adoring fans.[426]

LSU is currently under the reign of Mike VII, who was transferred from a wildlife sanctuary in Florida nine months before Burrow transferred from Ohio State. On January 13, 2020, Mike VII joined Mike III (1958), Mike V (2003) and Mike VI (2007) as the only LSU Bengal Tiger mascots to witness national football championships.[427]

Widespread mourning fills the campus when a reigning Mike the Tiger passes away. Students, faculty and staff eagerly await the selection of the new mascot. When the day finally arrives, white smoke billows out of the Veterinary School—not exactly the Vatican, but for a state with strong Catholic roots, a pretty nice touch.[428]

Mike is a must-see for curious tailgaters. And there are a lot of them on fall days in Baton Rouge. Robin was introduced to the tailgate scene first. "LSU has huge tailgates," says Jimmy. "My sister in Houston has a mobile home. They drove it over and stocked it for all of the games during Joe's first year. So, Robin wasn't alone. She had family there, including Joe's older brothers for a lot of the games."[429]

While Robin loved the pre-game festivities, including the ubiquitous scent of gumbo, jambalaya, shrimp, crawfish, and fried everything wafting through the thick Louisiana air, the experience wasn't complete without her husband.

The Ohio University football schedule limited Jimmy's ability to attend Joe's games. He only saw three in person during Joe's junior year—all on the road.

"Once we hit that point and he had time to sit back and really reflect on the fact that he only had been able to go to three games, it was time to make a hard decision," revealed Robin, in an interview with ESPN's Tom Rinaldi.[430]

While he loved coaching, in 2019 Jimmy decided to retire. "I can't imagine if I'd never seen him play a game in Tiger Stadium," says Jimmy. "The bottom line was just the opportunity to watch Joe play his senior year."[431]

When August rolled around, it would be the first time in fifty-one years that Jimmy wasn't on the practice field as either a player or coach. He was now a full-time dad, husband, fan and avid Tiger tailgater. Jimmy admits that "four-to-five-hour tailgating takes a while to get used to," but he and Robin have embraced it.[432] After all, they aren't exactly novices when it comes to lengthy gregarious gatherings. They had a fair amount of training back in the day with their Athens youth sports tribe, some of whom would join the Burrow tailgates during Joe's magical senior season.

Primal Bonding

What's Joe Burrow's favorite sport?

Football?

Basketball?

Baseball?

Nope.

Try Ultimate Fighting Championship. That's right, UFC.

"During the pandemic, every Saturday was fight night because that was the only sport available," says Zacciah Saltzman. "They were fighting in Abu Dhabi or wherever they had COVID availability. We just got so into it. That's our favorite sport. Joe still thinks he has a shot at becoming a UFC fighter."[433]

According to Saltzman, Joe's obsession with UFC dates back to his days at Ohio State. Looking for ways to "channel his frustration," Joe confidently proclaimed that if he set his heart, soul and mind to it, he could become a UFC heavyweight champion. He started exploring gyms around Columbus and analyzing some of his favorite fighters.[434]

Zacciah and Joe hanging at a UFC event in Las Vegas, Nevada. *Photo credit: Zacciah Saltzman*

Former Bulldog running back Trae Williams says Joe's UFC fixation just randomly pops up when the high school buddies chat sometimes. Like in the middle of "a regular conversation he'll be like, 'I'm pretty sure I could beat all you guys up.'"[435]

"Joe's never been afraid of contact," says Jimmy. "That's just who he is."[436]

Bryce Graves can personally attest to that. One day in practice, when the defense was getting the better of the offense, Joe lowered his shoulder and ran the Bulldog linebacker over. Problem was, tackling the quarterback was forbidden in practice. Graves just looked at the offensive coaches and said, "What the heck? If he's going to do that, then I'm going to lay into him!" The coaches just laughed and replied, "Nope, you can't hit Joe."[437]

Joe would have welcomed a return blow from the Bulldog linebacker. Like Tyler Durden from "Fight Club," Burrow enjoys primal bonding. This might be one reason why the 2019 Fighting Tigers had so many brawls during spring and fall practice, especially one that centered on quarterback and linebacker.

Coach O had hired Joe Brady away from the New Orleans Saints in the off-season and the installation of his new high-octane offense didn't take long. Linebacker Patrick Queen remembers the Tiger defense was "getting toasted. Like every play, offense 50 yards, 40 yards, touchdown, touchdown." The defense wasn't used to the offense dominating. "If we'd get a stop we were talking so much trash. Everybody just wanted to fight."[438]

The final practice before the spring game was especially hot and intense. On one memorable sequence, safety JaCoby Stevens got to Burrow on a blitz around the edge. It wasn't a cheap hit, but Burrow was still recovering from shoulder surgery and felt a twinge of pain. The two players got into a tussle.

Coach O breaks it up. "Hey, don't hit Joe."[439]

On the very next play, Queen slashes through the line and lays into Burrow. Coach O jumps back in and says, "Hey, don't hit Joe. I'm not going to say it no more."

The defense returns to the huddle and decides they're going to do it again. Burrow gets the snap, rolls out and throws the ball away. Queen remembers, "I push him, jump in his face, start talking trash and do a little Cowboy dance. All I see is him reaching back and 'Boom,' he punches me [in the face] with my facemask on. I said [to myself] 'Joe really just hit me.'"[440]

Now it's an all-out melee. Queen has Burrow in a headlock and the star quarterback is punching the star linebacker over and over in the stomach. From 30 yards away JaCoby Stevens comes flying in like a missile and "smokes Joe."

After five minutes of chaos, the coaches finally restore order. A smirking Coach O slowly shifts his gaze back and forth between the offense and the defense. Half pissed, half amused, he finally says, "You dudes are funny. Why you fightin' each other?"[441]

This kind of behavior shouldn't come as a surprise to a coach who likes to "set his jaw" before every game. In other words, punch himself in the face to get himself fired up.[442]

"I freakin' loved seeing how our offense had started standing up to the defense," says Orgeron. "The offense suddenly had an edge to it.... I wanted our guys to get into a froth. We called it 'fire in the hole.'"[443]

According to Orgeron, all the fighting ceased two weeks before the beginning of the season. "We just didn't want anyone breaking a hand in a fight on the practice field."[444] Burrow believes the competition and physicality during the spring and fall practices galvanized the offense and defense into a single unit. "We became super close as a team, on and off the field," says Burrow.[445]

In a matter of months, LSU would cap off one of the most remarkable seasons in college football history with a national title. The two players in the middle of that memorable melee—Joe Burrow and Patrick Queen—would be named offensive and defensive players of the game.

The Summer of 10,000 Catches

At the 2019 SEC Media Days, a reporter asked Orgeron if Joe Burrow might be the most important recruit during his LSU tenure.

Coach O didn't hesitate.

"Joe came right at the right time," said Orgeron. "I think he changed our program around. He gave us some stability at the quarterback position. He gave us a leader there. He gave us a coach on the football field. I think we've only just seen the beginning of Joe Burrow, to see what Joe Burrow is really made of. I think he's going to have a great year."[446]

But for Burrow, Orgeron and the Tigers to reach their goals, LSU's passing efficiency would need to improve. "Last year, we did not catch the ball very, very well," said Orgeron.[447] Without pointing fingers, Burrow agreed: "Drops were kind of an issue for us last year, and that comes with young receivers. We had true freshmen and a true sophomore playing for us."[448]

So, Coach O met with newly hired passing game coordinator Joe Brady and receivers coach Mickey Joseph to make sure the receivers worked on their concentration and ball skills before fall camp.

Enter the Summer of 10,000 Catches.

In the best-selling book *Outliers*, Malcolm Gladwell explores the claim that it takes 10,000 hours to achieve expert status at something.[449] Brady didn't have 10,000 hours, so he did the next best thing. He asked his receivers to catch 10,000 balls before the season began.

But it wasn't just about quantity of catches, it was about efficient practice. Brady wanted his guys to do the right things the right way, over and over and over again until muscle memory kicked in. "We're not looking to put on a show, we're looking to put on a clinic," said Brady.[450]

Brady would improve his players' concentration and reflexes by introducing creative drills. One drill was called "Behind the Door." Receivers stood on one side of a closed door. When the door flew open a ball would already be in the air. They needed to immediately adjust to velocity and trajectory to catch the ball. In another one, receivers wore goggles designed to restrict peripheral vision. This drill was especially effective at helping receivers snag tight-window passes.

Many of these ideas came from the Saints, where one of Joe's best friends, J.T. Barrett, had worked under Brady's tutelage. As soon as Burrow received news of Brady's hiring, he called J.T., who assured his close friend that they were going to love each other.[451]

Burrow was also comforted by the fact that his high school quarterback coach Nathan White and Joe Brady both spent time in South Florida learning the up-tempo, run-pass option (RPO) spread.

This was the offense Burrow was born to run.

When Robin checked in with her son late in the summer, he was upbeat. "Joe said it's really encouraging to see guys showing up for summer workouts on time," remembers Robin. "He sensed the comradery was really building. He said, 'I think we're going to be really good. Really, really good.'"[452]

Cajun Corseaux

The sixth-ranked Fighting Tigers opened the season against Georgia Southern. The first score was a quick slant to Ja'Marr Chase. By the end of the second quarter, Burrow had tossed four more strikes to tie a school record for first-half touchdown passes. "We've come out of the Stone Age with the RPO style offense," Burrow would later say.[453]

With a commanding 42–3 lead, Joe played the initial series of the third quarter then called it a day. He was in total sync with his talented receiving corps, connecting on 23 of 27 passes for 278 yards. On the night Burrow and backup Myles Brennan spread the ball around to fourteen different pass catchers, as LSU racked up 472 yards of total offense while holding the Eagles to 98 yards.

The scheme, productivity and playing time looked remarkably similar to Burrow's days as an Athens Bulldog.

"The 2019 LSU team was almost a mirror image of the 2014 Athens team," observes Troy Bolin. "In 2018, Joe goes down there and he's under center where he's not comfortable. They have a fullback; they have a tailback. Just like Athens in 2011. But it really took off when Brady came in—almost identical to what happened with Nathan White. Both times the offense changed to build around Joe's strengths. It's a spot-on comparison."[454]

After the game, Burrow confirmed Bolin's take. "This is what I've been doing since high school. I hope it lived up to everybody's expectations."[455]

"Joe was on fire," said Orgeron in the postgame presser. "We could have done whatever we wanted tonight. Those guys were phenomenal."[456]

The new look LSU offense was a revelation to the fans and media. So was something else a reporter just happened to witness. "Yeah, I do that before every game," said Burrow. "I put my helmet on and smash it against the wall."[457]

So, it looks like we can add Skull Smashing to the Suckers and Socks pre-game rituals.

The first test of the season would come the following Saturday as the sixth-ranked Tigers traveled to Austin to take on the ninth-ranked Texas Longhorns. ESPN's Gameday crew was in town to promote their featured game of the week.

With a large throng of vocal Longhorn fans in the background, Texas alum and actor Matthew McConaughey served as the guest prognosticator. "It's going to be vicious, there's going to be some grace…but it's going to be a bloody battle," predicted McConaughey, in his smooth, trademark Texan drawl. "And that's what we're here to do tonight. Thank you for coming to our house, Tigers. Tonight, we will send you home 29–27 losers. Hook 'em baby!"

After McConaughey, it was Lee Corso's turn. The old coach mentioned how special Texas is to him because his son is a UT alumnus. The warmth continued as Corso and McConaughey performed a swaying duet of "The Eyes of Texas," accompanied by the Longhorn band.

The vibe then took a turn. The old coach admitted to preferring "Hold that Tiger" while producing an LSU jersey with "Corseaux" stitched across the back. The *coup de grace* came when Corso slipped on the Tiger head, signifying his predicted outcome of the game. In the final seconds, the show degenerated into bedlam as the multi-tasking McConaughey belted out "The Eyes of Texas" while simultaneously wrenching the Tiger head off Corso's shoulders and tossing it into a sea of frenzied fans.[458]

How could the on-field action live up to such pregame pandemonium?

Oh, but it did.

One of the big storylines was the reunion of Joe Burrow and Tom Herman, the former Ohio State coach who recruited the Bulldog quarterback before departing for Houston. Now in his third year as the Texas head coach, Herman offered nothing but respect for Burrow.

"I love Joe," said Herman. "I recruited him, I got to know his family. He's physically, mentally tough. He's uber-competitive. He's a leader amongst leaders."[459]

All of these qualities and more were evident as the country tuned into this early season top-10 showdown.

The first quarter was dominated by the defenses. After kicking a field goal to take a 3–0 lead, LSU mounted two goal-line stands. The second came after Burrow threw an interception to Joseph Ossai, a linebacker who would later become one of Joe's teammates in Cincinnati.

In the second quarter, the Tiger offense got into rhythm. Burrow tossed two touchdown passes to Justin Jefferson and LSU entered the locker room with a 20–7 advantage.

The final thirty minutes turned out to be one of the most entertaining halves of the season. With just under four minutes remaining, and holding a 37–31 lead, Orgeron suggested to Ensminger on the head set that they run their four-minute offense to eat up some clock. But Ensminger and Brady wanted to score again. Orgeron told them to go for it.

An incompletion and sack set up a third down and 17 from their own 39-yard line. Texas sent a heavy blitz. The LSU quarterback flashed fancy footwork as the pocket began to disintegrate. Stepping up and then to his left, Burrow squared his shoulders and held the ball just long enough for Jefferson to stick his foot in the ground and streak across the middle. The pass was right on time. Justin did the rest, outracing the Longhorn defense down the far sideline to the end zone. "That might be the knock-out punch!" said ESPN's Rece Davis.[460] Orgeron later called it "one of the most defining plays of our season, and of my career."[461]

The TV camera caught Robin cheering at the top of her lungs. A jubilant Jimmy was multi-tasking. His right hand held up the "L" for LSU, while his left arm playfully cradled Dan in a Patrick Queen headlock. Earlier in the evening the camera showed the retired coach giving the upside-down Hook 'em Horns sign—a video that went viral. Joe couldn't resist getting in on the action as time wound down, waving goodbye (pageant style) to the rowdy Texas student section.

Final score: LSU 45, Texas 38.

On the night, Burrow completed 31 of 39 passes for 471 yards. For the first time in school history, three Tiger receivers topped 100 yards. Jefferson led the way with 163 yards and three touchdowns.

When asked about Burrow's performance, Orgeron said, "The kid's a ballplayer. He lives for that moment."[462]

After handling Northwestern State 65–14 the following week, the Tigers traveled to Nashville to take on winless Vanderbilt in the SEC opener.

While the nation wasn't paying much attention to this match-up, the folks in Athens were. The September 21st date had been circled on the calendar for months. "As soon as the LSU schedule came out, everybody marked it and got hotel rooms," remembers Sam Smathers. "It was the closest game we were going to get to see Joey. Not sure the exact number of people who went, but someone put up a sign that read, 'Last one out of town, turn out the lights!'"[463]

As expected, Joey was also lights out. He completed 25 of 34 passes and tossed a school record six touchdowns. Four went to Ja'Marr Chase, who finished the day with ten catches and 229 yards.

After the third touchdown, one of the SEC announcers said, "It's just too easy right now for Joe Burrow and this LSU offense."[464]

Following the fourth touchdown, a 51-yard strike to Chase, Burrow could be seen flashing 5–5 to the Vandy sideline. Afterwards, Smathers found out why.

"Early in the game, Vandy tackled Joey hard on their sideline. It got Joe fired up and he told them he was going to hang 55 on them. You don't poke the Bear!"[465]

Jeff and Heather Skinner were among the Athenians who made the nearly seven-hour trek to Nashville. As much as they liked the game, the Burrow tailgate was the high point.

"What I enjoyed most about that day was seeing all the Athens people who don't live in Athens anymore," recalls Jeff. "A lot of my former players whom I hadn't seen in years were there. Jimmy and Robin's tailgate brought us all together. It was terrific. We all love Joe, and we all love to talk about Joe, but our lifelong close friendship with Jimmy and Robin may be the best thing Joe's ever given us."[466]

Tebow Preaches the Gospel of Jeaux

After an off-week, LSU returned to the field against Utah State. The game featured two future first-round quarterbacks—Burrow and Jordan Love. LSU cruised to a 42–6 win behind five Burrow touchdown passes. Joe racked up 344 yards on 27 of 38 completions, becoming the first quarterback in school history to throw for 300-plus yards in four consecutive games. Love only completed half of his attempts (15 of 30) and threw three picks to the suffocating Tiger defense.

The following Saturday night, the fifth-ranked Fighting Tigers hosted the seventh-ranked Florida Gators. After a disappointing loss in the Swamp the previous year, LSU was poised for revenge in Death Valley. It would turn out to be the highest rated and most watched regular-season college football game in two years.[467]

The crowd was deafening. Orgeron was concerned that his players might be too hyped. "Before when we played them, I knew we had to stop the fighting," recalled Orgeron. "The players were almost more concerned with fighting them than beating them."[468]

Later in the season, Burrow would call the 42–28 win over Florida the closest LSU would come to a perfect game.[469] The Tigers won the turnover battle (1-0). They didn't allow a sack. Burrow threw as many touchdowns as incompletions (3). And it only took the quick-strike Tiger offense an average of 4.5 plays to reach paydirt on each of their six scoring drives.

The most impressive thing about the game, however, was the offensive balance—511 total yards, 293 through the air; 218 on the ground. Clyde Edwards-Helaire rushed for 134 yards, while Chase and Jefferson combined for 250 receiving yards. Edwards-Helaire and Chase each scored a pair of touchdowns.

Orgeron was asked in the postgame press conference about the speed with which his offense scored. "That's us. Pedal to the metal. We're going as hard as we possibly can every play. We feel we can score. We feel we have athletes in space and we're not going to stop."[470]

While Burrow felt good about LSU's second Top-10 victory of the season, he invoked the cautionary spirit of Sam Smathers during the locker room celebration: "Don't let good enough get in the way of greatness. Come back to work on Monday ready to go. We still have a lot of room to improve."[471]

The next test would be a road game in Starkville against Mississippi State, Jimmy's boyhood team. "I had a little cowbell in my room growing up," said Joe during the pregame press conference. "So, I know a little bit about them."[472]

On the strength of the Florida win, the 6–0 Tigers moved to number two in the polls. LSU was generating a lot of national attention. A few days before the game in Starkville, on ESPN's "First Take," Stephen A. Smith asked Tim Tebow to name his Heisman frontrunner. "You have a vote right now, who's your Heisman Trophy winner. Jalen Hurts, Tua?" Without missing a beat, Tebow revealed the chosen one: "Joe Burrow." With mouth agape, a shocked and incredulous Smith replied, "Joe Burrow! Joe Burrow?"

With the conviction of an impassioned evangelist, Tebow preached the Gospel of Jeaux: "Right now, he's got the two biggest wins of any quarterback. He went to Austin, and he beat Texas. And he didn't play just OK, he played great. And then again last Saturday night against Florida, a defense that everyone was hyping up, and he carved them up for four quarters. He's had the two biggest games in college football, and he's been consistent all year. Joe Burrow if I had to vote today."[473]

Smith wasn't the only one doubting Tebow. Joe's preseason odds of winning the Heisman were 200 to one. After the 2018 season, many of the prognosticators had Burrow as a mid-to-late-round NFL pick. His meteoric ascent up the draft boards is unprecedented. Six games into the season and Burrow was in the thick of the Heisman conversation.

Joe wasn't listening to the outside noise. The conversation that most interested him was the one he would have with his Mississippi grandparents following the game in Starkville. While James and Dot occasionally traveled north to The Plains to see "Joey" play football and basketball during his high school days, the Mississippi State game would be their first chance to see him play in college.

When tickets went on sale, James called his alma mater to secure a pair of seats. Only one caveat, he wanted to sit in the visitors' section. The ticket office worker was confused until he explained his relationship to the LSU quarterback.[474]

While the Burrow grandparents had yet to see Joe play in person, they watch all his games on TV. Well, James does. Dot gets too nervous to look, but runs in when the Tigers score. She then retreats to the other room until the next big play. What will she do on Saturday? "I don't know," said Dot before the game. "I'll just sit there and take it."[475]

All went well for Dot and the rest of the visitors' section that Saturday in Starkville. The Tigers won the game handily, 36-13. The LSU offense started slowly, kicking three field goals before finally scoring a touchdown with 5:07 remaining in the first half. But once they got going, the Tigers were unstoppable with Burrow throwing for 327 yards and four touchdowns on the day. The final strike sent Burrow into the LSU record books for most touchdowns in a single season. With eight games remaining.

That said, the most memorable moment of the game might have come when Bulldog defensive end Chauncey Rivers inadvertently pulled Burrow's pants down from behind. Reflexively, Joe yanked them backup on his way to the turf.

Joe laughed about the play after the game. "I can honestly say that has never happened before in my life," said a good-natured Burrow. "I heard there's supposed to be a full moon in Starkville tonight." A reporter reminded him about his family in the stands. With a roll of the eyes, Joe added, "Yeah, my grandparents were here for that one. Awesome."[476]

One can only hope Dot wasn't looking.

The following Saturday number-two LSU hosted another top-10 match up when ninth-ranked Auburn came to Death Valley.

The visiting Tigers took a 3–0 lead with 8:39 to go in the first quarter. The high-flying LSU offense was grounded early, as the aggressive Auburn defense sacked Burrow three times. As the game moved into the second quarter, the home team faced a third and 12 inside its own 10-yard-line. With the pocket collapsing, Burrow scrambled to his right. The Tiger quarterback picked up the first down, but took a wicked hit on the Auburn sideline. He immediately executed his patented Tom Brady bounce-up move.

"Holy cow!" exclaimed CBS color commentator Gary Danielson. "This is where Joe can show his toughness. This is how the team fell in love with Joe Burrow against UCF last year, taking a hit like this and popping right backup. That could change the whole tenor of the game."[477]

It did.

Burrow marched his rejuvenated offense down the field, connecting on five of the next six passes. The drive culminated with a 20-yard fade to Terrace Marshall in the end zone. Auburn fought back with a touchdown of its own before LSU added a field goal. The teams entered the break deadlocked at 10.

Early in the third quarter Auburn added another three points and held a 13–10 lead before LSU turned to the ground game. Clyde Edwards-Helaire took over. The Tiger tailback carried the ball four consecutive times for 45 yards and a score. LSU went back on top, 16–13. The Tigers extended the lead to 23–13 early in the fourth quarter on a seven-yard Burrow touchdown run.

The visiting Tigers responded with a final touchdown with 2:32 remaining, but failed to recover the onside kick. LSU held on for a hard-fought, gritty 23–20 victory.

In the postgame press conference, Burrow smiled with satisfaction as he discussed his Tom Brady pop-up move and blue-collar win. "If your quarterback shows toughness like that it can kind of get your team going," said Burrow. "We definitely showed toughness today. It was not a pretty win by any means, [but] SEC games aren't always going to be pretty."[478]

Following the game, Joe celebrated LSU's 8–0 start by visiting his parents' tailgate, something he rarely does. Troy Bolin was one of a dozen or so folks from Athens who made the fifteen-hour trek to Baton Rouge.

Bolin remembers a special moment with Joe.

"In high school, we always wanted Joe to come on the radio either before or after the game, but he was never very talkative," says Bolin. "At

Joe, Troy Bolin and Jimmy pose for a photo after a hard-fought victory over Auburn.
Photo credit: Troy Bolin

the tailgate, I razzed him a little about a past game, but then took the opportunity to be serious for a moment. I told him how proud I was of him; how proud we all were back in Athens County. Not because he could throw a football 60 yards and score touchdowns, but because of how he handled himself off the field, in public and in the classroom. I told him he represented Southeastern Ohio better than any of us could have ever imagined. He looked me dead in the eye and said, 'Wow, thank you, seriously, thanks a lot. That really means a lot to me.' Standing outside of Death Valley that night, I think it was the most words the kid ever said to me. And he was very sincere."[479]

8

Bayou Burreaux

SENIOR YEAR—SECOND HALF

"So many people put so much work into this from athletic trainers, equipment staff, players, coaches, chefs, dining room assistants. It's not just me or Coach O or the O-line, it's everybody inside that building that gets a piece of this."[480]

—Joe Burrow
National Championship trophy presentation
January 13, 2020

Just say "Marty and Joe" and folks in Southern Ohio know who you're talking about, the greatest radio combination in Major League Baseball history—Marty Brennaman and Joe Nuxhall. But say "Marty and Joe" at Gigi's Country Kitchen in The Plains and you'll get a different response.

It all goes back to a conversation between ESPN's Marty Smith and Joe Burrow that aired prior to the 2018 LSU-Auburn football game. Marty asked Joe a question. "So, all a guy wants to do when he gets to camp is eat a salad. Just give me a salad. And the boys won't let you eat a salad. What happened?"

Joe explained that his teammates pressured him into eating fried chicken instead. "Trying to put weight on you," said Marty with a playful grin. "Make sure you don't get beat up too bad in the SEC West."

As the two men talked and walked across the Death Valley turf, the conversation ranged from Joe's transfer and leadership style to pregame rituals (Suckers and Socks), before it returned to the topic of food.

Gigi's Country Kitchen supporting their hometown hero. *Photo credit: Gigi's Country Kitchen*

"I found it cool that they put your name on the Gigi's restaurant marquis," said Marty. "What's it like to have the support of the home folks back there in Athens?"

Without missing a beat, Joe responded, "It's so great. Gigi's is my favorite breakfast place in Athens. Western omelet, double side of hash browns every time I go home."[481]

Boom. Like a bolt of lightning, that's all it took. A couple seconds of airtime and Gigi's became a national sensation with a cult following stretching from The Plains to Baton Rouge.

Visitors from far and wide come to eat the Western omelet (now named "The Burrow"), pay homage to the ever-growing JoeyB9 shrine, and take selfies in front of the famous Gigi's marquis ("Here We Geaux Jeaux!").

Like Burrow to Baton Rouge, Travis Brand is a transplant to The Plains. He grew up in Cincinnati, attended Hocking College, and opened Gigi's in 2011—the year Joe entered Athens High School less than a mile up the road.

Brand doesn't recall the first time he cooked breakfast for Burrow, but he does remember when the Bulldog quarterback initially caught his attention. It was Joe's junior year. The 83–14 win over Alexander. Ever since, he's been a big Burrow fan.

When he opened Gigi's, Brand never imagined national media descending upon his quaint establishment. In an interview with *The Athens Messenger*, Travis expressed his shock and awe. "Someone walks in and says, 'I'm from *The Washington Post*, I'd like to ask you some questions.' OK, great! Today I learned how to fake my way through an interview with *The Washington Post*. Cool."[482]

Fourteen months since Marty and Joe put Gigi's on the map and Burrow was in Baton Rouge preparing for the biggest test of the 2019 season—an SEC West showdown against Alabama. Back in The Plains, Brand received another call. It was CBS Sports this time. They wanted to interview him for a pregame segment. Travis gladly complied. Anything to support the hometown hero.

"It's the Joe Burrow show, and we're just living in it," said Brand. "It's a humbling experience for all of us. It's blown us all away."[483]

The Tuscaloosa Test

Wherever Joe ate breakfast on November 9, 2019, he likely ordered his favorite: a Western omelet with a double side of hash browns. Maybe a triple side on this day. Throw in some fried chicken while you're at it. Joe would need all the strength he could muster for college football's most anticipated game of the year—second-ranked LSU versus third-ranked Alabama.

Thanks to some favorable scheduling, both teams had two weeks to prepare. The Crimson Tide entered the showdown with an eight-game winning streak over the Tigers, including a dominating 29–0 victory in 2018. Ironically, that soul-crushing defeat in Death Valley a year earlier helped birth the new-look LSU offense that was now confounding every opponent on the schedule.

The winner of this heavyweight bout would likely capture the SEC West and be well-positioned for a College Football Playoff (CFP) berth. The game would also feature two Heisman hopefuls—Joe Burrow and Tua Tagovailoa. In eight games, Burrow had already thrown for 2,805 yards and 30 touchdowns (versus four interceptions). His surgical completion rate of 78.8 percent was equally impressive. Tagovailoa entered the game with 2,166 passing yards and 27 touchdowns on the year. His accuracy was also sharp, completing 74.7 percent of his passes with only two picks.

But the jaw-dropping talent on the field extended well beyond the quarterbacks. In total, seventeen future NFL first-round selections suited up.

ESPN Gameday was in town for the festivities. The guest prognosticator was Alabama alumnus and former world number-one golfer Justin Thomas. Much to the delight of the Crimson crowd, Thomas picked the Tide. "I'm going 'Bama first quarter, first half, all game!"

As always, Lee Corso was last to tee off. "Now, this is strictly business because I picked Alabama in the preseason to win it all," said Corso. "That was then. And this is now. Gimme that Tiger head!" After mounting the LSU Tiger head on his shoulders, the old coach produced his "Corseaux" jersey. Following a brief struggle, an animated Thomas ripped the jersey from Corso's clutches and tossed it off the set.[484]

Despite the 2018 debacle in Death Valley, Orgeron was confident. "I told the team that Monday, 'Guys, we are the better team. Now, we've got to practice like it, and prepare like it. Then we've got to play like it. And, I know we will.'"[485]

Alabama received the opening kick and Tua marched the Tide inside the Tiger 10. On third and goal from the eight-yard-line, Tagovailoa scrambled to his right. Without getting hit, the ball squirted out of his hands.

LSU recovered.

And capitalized.

In less than three minutes, Burrow engineered a six-play, length-of-the-field scoring drive that culminated in a 33-yard touchdown pass to Ja'Marr Chase. On its first drive, LSU did something it couldn't do the entire game the previous season—score on Alabama.

The Tigers extended their margin to 10–0 on a Cade York field goal with 4:54 to go in the first quarter. Posting a quick double-digit lead was a way to take the Bryant-Denny crowd out of the game. Allowing a 77-yard punt return to Jaylen Waddle was a guaranteed way of letting them back in.

The second quarter opened with another Burrow touchdown strike. This one a 29-yard pass to Terrace Marshall over the middle. The Alabama defense was so discombobulated, Burrow could have just as easily thrown the ball to Thad Moss for the score.

Six minutes later, with 6:43 left in the half, Tua found DeVonta Smith on a 64-yard Go route to narrow the margin to 16-13.

After LSU added another field goal, Clyde Edwards-Helaire soared over the line to put the Tigers on top 26–13 with twenty-six seconds remaining in the half. On the next offensive play for Alabama, Tagovailoa threw an interception straight into the arms of Patrick Queen, setting up another LSU scoring opportunity. With six seconds on the clock, Burrow hit a wide-open Edwards-Helaire in the end zone for his second touchdown in the span of twenty seconds.

"Joe Burrow putting on a show, Edwards-Helaire putting on a show, Nick Saban doesn't like the show," said CBS announcer Brad Nessler as the Tigers took a commanding 33–13 lead into the locker room.[486]

But the game was far from over.

"We knew they were going to come back," said Burrow. "That's Alabama on the other side. Dynasty. We knew we were going to get their best shot in the second half."[487]

In the third quarter, Tagovailoa found his rhythm, leading the Tide on a 10-play, 95-yard touchdown drive that culminated with a 15-yard back shoulder toss to running back Najee Harris. Five minutes later, as the fourth quarter began, Harris capped off a 78-yard drive with a one-yard dive across the goal line. With more than fourteen minutes still on the clock, Alabama had sliced the LSU lead to six, 33–27.

"There was no panic on the sideline," said Burrow. "We knew we were going to have to go down and score to win the game. Probably have to score twice."[488]

Over the next 4:26, Burrow calmly engineered a 12-play, 75-yard scoring drive that concluded with a five-yard spinning touchdown run from Edwards-Helaire.

After Alabama scored another touchdown to narrow the lead to five with 5:32 remaining, Burrow went to work again. Key passes to Chase and Marshall moved the ball deep into Tide territory. Then, with the ball on the Alabama 25-yard-line, Burrow faked a handoff to Edwards-Helaire and sprinted left on a quarterback keeper. The entire defense followed the fake and Burrow snaked his way down to the six-yard line.

"Joe Burrow! Might be a Heisman moment, right there!" excitedly exclaimed Nessler.[489]

On the next play, Edwards-Helaire powered into the end zone to increase LSU's lead to 46–34. With 1:37 remaining, the game appeared to be over. But on the first play from scrimmage Tua connected on another Go route to DeVonta Smith, who streaked past the Tiger secondary for an 85-yard touchdown.

With the lead narrowed to 46–41, the only hope was an onside kick. But the Tiger good-hands team secured the win as the end-over-end kick settled poetically into the arms of Justin Jefferson. It was the first LSU win over Bama since Jefferson's older brother, Jordan, quarterbacked the Tigers to an epic 9–6 victory in 2011.

The on-field celebration was euphoric. A lineman hoisted Joe onto his shoulders. Coach O was drenched, a mixture of sweat and Powerade. The jubilant LSU faithful filled the lower bowl, while a wave of Crimson slowly receded into the Tuscaloosa night.

"This is why I decided to transfer, I knew I could play on this stage," said Burrow. "Having these guys embrace me the way they have. Just some quarterback from Ohio that came in last June before the season. It means a lot to me that this entire program has embraced me and the whole state, as well."[490]

Burrow was superb, especially when it counted most. He completed 31 of 39 passes for 393 yards and three touchdowns. He also rushed the ball fourteen times for 64 yards, picking up key chunks of turf in the final two drives. While Tagovailoa played well, his numbers were overshadowed by Burrow's clutch play down the stretch. With the win, LSU controlled its own championship destiny. And much to Stephen A. Smith's chagrin, Joe was now the clear Heisman frontrunner.

But Burrow wasn't the only shining star on the night. On the final play of the game, Joe took a knee and handed the game ball to Clyde Edwards-Helaire, who rushed for 103 yards and hauled in nine passes for another 77 yards. The Tiger running back would not be denied, scoring three crucial touchdowns on the day.

"We have a lot of guys on this team that were kind of overlooked," said Burrow in the postgame press conference. "Clyde being 5–8, not everybody wanted him. Justin Jefferson a two-star recruit, Thad Moss a transfer, me a transfer. I think guys like that are mentally tough."[491]

When the team plane touched down in Baton Rouge, hundreds of screaming supporters greeted the triumphant Tigers. An energetic Joe Burrow jogged down the chain-link fence grazing the fingers of several fortunate fans. "I didn't really realize what this meant to Louisiana," said an emotional Burrow. "It was pretty special. I was very surprised to see it. And I just wanted to do anything I could to embrace those people who came out."[492]

Around thirty kids and parents greeted an exhausted Coach Orgeron and his wife when they pulled into their driveway. Purple and gold decorations hung from the exterior of their house. "It was amazing to see the joy on their faces," recalls Orgeron. "They had made a big banner and had me run through it, like I was back on the high school team before a big game. Their reaction was one of the most gratifying moments I've ever had as a coach."[493]

The Closest Thing to Elvis

While LSU faithful claim tailgate supremacy, many college football pundits give the edge to The Grove—a ten-acre scenic stretch in the middle of the Ole Miss campus. Surrounded by mature Magnolia, Oak and Elm trees, this tailgate Mecca comes to life on game days with a sea of tents and thousands of blue and red revelers filling the grounds.[494]

With the 9–0 Tigers in town to take on the 4–6 Rebels, Robin and Jimmy find a place to pitch their itinerant tailgating tent. It's a homecoming of sorts for Jimmy, who started his college career at Ole Miss. It's also where his younger brother, John, played defensive back during the late seventies and early eighties.

In addition to the typical pregame festivities, the trip to Oxford might include a visit with new friend Archie Manning. While both men have deep ties to the state of Mississippi, they had never met until Archie reached out to Jimmy a few months before. A star-struck Burrow remembers the call. "My heart slowed down beating for a while before I was able to speak. I told my family that was the closest thing to Elvis I ever got."[495] The Mannings and Burrows are now good friends, but that won't keep Archie from rooting for a Rebel upset.

The Burrow trip to Oxford, Mississippi, will definitely include a visit with old friends Jeff and Heather Skinner, who have made the long drive from Athens. While not quite Manning or Burrow famous, Joe's high school hoops coach has developed a following of his own.

The LSU radio, TV and newspapers all interviewed Skinner, because they wanted to hear something besides football. "My face became so common that when I was walking through the legendary Grove, LSU fans started yelling at me, 'Hey, Coach Skinner, come have a drink with us!'" Heather just looked at her husband and said, "You're pathetic." To which Jeff playfully replied, "No, I'm not, I'm a celebrity."[496]

On the field that day, the Tigers continued their march toward an SEC title and CFP berth with a 58–37 victory over the feisty Rebels. In an offensive shootout, LSU racked up 714 total yards, while Ole Miss recorded 614 of its own, including 402 on the ground. Burrow was 32 of 42 through the air for 489 yards and five touchdowns. Edwards-Helaire rushed for 172 yards, while Chase hauled in eight passes for 227 yards and three scores.

The final two regular-season games against Arkansas and Texas A&M would be played in Death Valley. Robin and Jimmy always leave their tailgate early to watch the Tiger Walk, a tradition in which the players proceed through a sea of supporters down Victory Hill and into the stadium. Mom and Dad are always the last to greet Joe before he enters the locker room.

The Burrows have become Baton Rouge royalty. On the way to the Tiger Walk, they can't go ten steps without being stopped for a quick chat and photo opp. They are incredibly gracious. For most LSU fans, Robin and Jimmy are the closest thing to Elvis. The parents of rock star Joe Burrow, the undisputed king of college football.

Before the Arkansas game, a young boy asked if they are Joe's parents. They confirmed his suspicion. Pointing toward Tiger Stadium, the youngster told them, "My dad says they're going to put a statue of Joe over there one of these days." The encounter caught the Burrows off guard. "We were somewhat overwhelmed with emotion as we saw the expression on that little boy's face," remembers Jimmy. "It kind of hit us as to what a special place LSU had become for Joe and our family."[497]

On the field that day, LSU had little problem with a 2–9 Razorback team, improving to 11–0 with a 56–20 victory. The Tiger offensive balance was again on full display with 352 yards coming through the air and 260 on the ground. Burrow was efficient as usual, connecting on 23 of 28 passes for three touchdowns. The win secured a spot in the SEC Championship game and LSU became the first school in conference history to claim a

4,000-yard passer, two 1,000-yard receivers (Chase and Jefferson) and a 1,000-yard rusher (Edwards-Helaire).

Honoring Louisiana

When Travis Brand posted his message on Gigi's marquee leading up to the LSU-Alabama game, he had no idea it would cause a stir. He was just showing support for the hometown hero.

PURPLE OUT
HERE SAT
LSU FANS WELCOME
BAMA FANS NOT SO MUCH

But through the magic of social media, the message on the marquee went viral.

"So, one of Joe's brothers shared the photo on Twitter and the LSU football page retweeted it," says Brand. "Then a random LSU fan posts, 'This guy is funny. If we beat Bama, I'm going to fly him down here for a game.' Sure enough, we beat Bama, the phone rings Monday morning, and he's offering me plane tickets, hotels, what have you. It was crazy."[498]

The invitation was for the Texas A&M game. Senior night. Turns out Brand was already planning on going with a high school friend who was originally from Baton Rouge. Travis and his friend chose to drive, but gladly accepted the rest of the red-carpet treatment.

"We ate Thanksgiving dinner, then drove through the night," remembers Brand. "These guys met us in the parking lot of the hotel with coolers of beer. Within an hour, I'm driving an airboat on the Belle River. Check that one off the bucket list."[499]

After a shower, Travis, his high school buddy, and new Cajun friends were eating dinner at one of the town's most beloved establishments, TJ Ribs—which offers not only some of the best barbecue in Louisiana, but is the Louvre of LSU sports memorabilia. With the scent of baby-back ribs wafting through the air, diehard Tiger fans are surrounded by signed artifacts and priceless photos of Pistol Pete Maravich. But the *crème de la crème*, the Mona Lisa of prized possessions, is Billy Cannon's original 1959 Heisman Trophy encased in glass. It's the only Heisman Trophy in LSU history. For a few weeks anyway.

Brand's Baton Rouge buddies have connections at the restaurant (and everywhere else in town). They ate in a special room. First-class treatment all the way. Word got out that the proprietor of Joe Burrow's favorite restaurant was visiting. Next thing Brand knew, it's lights, camera, action. WBRZ was interviewing him for the 11 o'clock news. "Mind you, this is after driving all night, not sleeping, and drinking beer all day," says Brand. No problem. By now, Travis was a pro. Once you've talked to *The Washington Post* and CBS Sports, it's all easy.

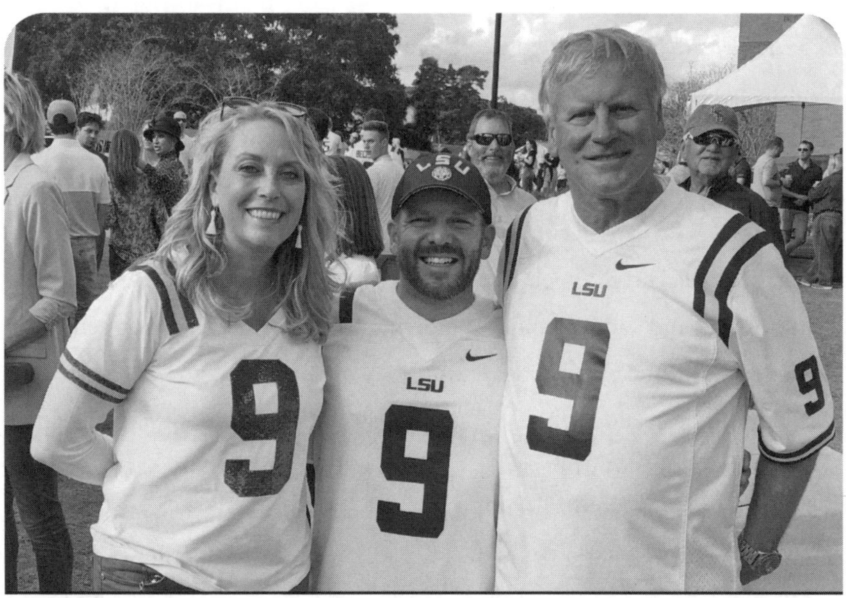

Travis Brand poses with Robin and Jimmy before the LSU-Texas A&M game. *Photo credit: Travis Brand*

Wearing a Burreaux jersey, Travis Brand tours the LSU locker room before Senior Night. *Photo credit: Travis Brand*

After some much-needed sleep, Travis headed over to the tailgate scene. Months before he had ordered a specially made "Burreaux" jersey. It was a hit at the tailgates, especially with Robin and Jimmy. "Dude, that's a cool jersey," said Jimmy. "I wish I had one of those."[500] Unbeknownst to Travis, in a few hours Joe would run onto the Death Valley field for the final time—with "Burreaux" on his back. An LSU videographer followed Burreaux out of the tunnel and caught tender senior-night moments as Joe hugged those closest to him. The already deafening roar of the Cajun crowd reached an ear-popping crescendo when Joe pointed to the specially designed name-plate on his back. Within a few days, the LSU athletic department had plastered the iconic image on billboards all around Baton Rouge.

"It came to me early in the week and I went to our equipment guy to see if we could get it done," said Burrow. "I just thought it would be an awesome tribute to the state and to the university. I think it was great."[501]

After throwing for 352 yards and three touchdowns in a 50–7 victory over Texas A&M, Burrow made a beeline for the student section. "Obviously, I don't go to class, because I take online classes," said Burrow. "So, I don't get to see any of those people. I just wanted to see them for the first time and just thank them for coming to the games and making this the best atmosphere in the country. Saturday night in Death Valley. There's nothing like it. I'm going to miss it with all of my heart."[502]

"The whole atmosphere was insane," said Travis, as he reflected upon the trip to Baton Rouge. "Absolutely nuts. Joe was the ringleader of the biggest circus I've ever seen."[503]

When all the dust settled, Joe autographed Brand's Burreaux jersey. It's proudly displayed in his purple and gold dining room next to the senior-night tickets and game program. Brand's own personal Mona Lisa.

That said, the most precious thing that came out of this whole experience for Travis was the friendships with the generous folks from Louisiana. "They get storms down there; we give them a shout out—see how all the boys are doing," says Travis. "When COVID hit, they called me to see how the restaurant was holding up and if I'd be able to stay open. They asked if I needed to move down there and work with them. I was like, 'You guys are unreal.' Every person you meet down there is the coolest person you've ever met in your life. They are a different breed. The absolute finest."[504]

The SEC Championship Game

Joe and the top-ranked 12–0 Tigers got their revenge against the Aggies on Senior Night. On the first Saturday in December, the fourth-ranked 11-1 Georgia Bulldogs were looking for their own revenge after losing to LSU by nearly three touchdowns the year before.

Some reporters downplayed the conference championship by suggesting that win or lose LSU would be in the four-team College Football

Playoff. Burrow wasn't having it. "We want an SEC Championship as much as a National Championship."[505]

Burrow was laser focused. So focused, in fact, that he wasn't taking his parents' phone calls. When they contacted an assistant coach to find out why, Robin and Jimmy discovered their son's phone had broken. They offered to buy him a new one, but Joe said, "I don't need a phone. I've got a game to play this week."[506]

Yeah, not your typical twenty-two-year-old.

The SEC Championship was held in Atlanta's Mercedes-Benz Stadium. It was nearly a home game for the University of Georgia with Athens barely an hour away. The trip for the folks from Athens, Ohio, however, would take a bit longer. But plenty of hometown supporters made the nine-hour trek to root for Joe and tailgate with his parents.

Those who made the trip were well-rewarded with an unforgettable rendition of the Haka by Vili Fehoko, the father of Tiger defensive lineman Breiden Fehoko. A few weeks earlier a video had gone viral of father and son breaking into a spontaneous Haka in the middle of the Tiger Walk. Today, however, Vili chose to perform the Haka at the Burrow tailgate. It was a way of honoring and thanking Robin and Jimmy for allowing Joe to join the "sacred" LSU family. After firing up the crowd with his flawless (and slightly terrifying) war dance, Vili tenderly embraced Robin and her father, Wayne.[507]

For those who couldn't make the nine-hour drive to see the Haka and high-flying LSU offense in person, there were plenty of purple and gold watch parties back in Southeast Ohio. Take your pick. From backyards to bars to churches, all of Athens County tuned in to watch their favorite son work his magic against the Georgia Bulldogs.

One of the largest gatherings took place at Christ Community Wesleyan Church—the congregation Robin and Jimmy attend when in town. "We've always been supportive of the Burrows," says Rusty Thomas, who serves as vice-chair of the board. "We've got a facility that holds hundreds of people so we thought it would be great to invite church members and the community to watch the game on the big screen."[508]

Around 140 people showed up for the SEC Championship game. With basketball goals pushed to one side and a large Christmas tree flanking the big screen, the purple and gold auditorium pulsated with energy.

Thomas was instrumental in convincing CBS executives to come to town to cover the watch party. Other media soon followed. "CBS had several cameras and even brought in a truck so there was a direct feed to the church," said Thomas. "We also contacted the LSU athletic department, and they sent up a videographer. TV stations from around the area had crews there, as well. It was great."[509]

There was plenty to cheer about as LSU dominated Georgia for the second year in a row and captured the SEC title, 37-10. The loudest cheers of the night, however, might have come when the congregation saw themselves on national TV.[510]

As Jimmy likes to say, "Joe's making us all famous."

In an interview with a local TV station, Teresa Kirkendall focused on the inspiration Joe has provided Southeast Ohio. "He means hope, he means life," said Kirkendall. "There's a lot of people around here that don't have much. He's giving our community hope and showing us that if we have a dream we can achieve that dream."[511]

Joe's dream for a national championship and undefeated season stayed alive on this night as he completed 28 of 38 passes for 349 yards and four touchdowns. Burrow was also the second leading rusher for the Tigers with 41 yards on the ground. Much of that yardage coming on scramble plays.

The most memorable Burrow scramble, however, ended in a 71-yard, off-script pass completion after eluding two future NFL first-round draft picks. With the Tigers leading 20–3 with 3:57 to go in the third quarter, Burrow took the shotgun snap on his own 20-yard-line. The play broke down immediately as Travon Walker blitzed through the line untouched. Joe spun to his left to evade Walker only to find Jordan Davis directly in his face. Like Houdini, Burrow miraculously escaped the clutches of both behemoths, reversing field back to his right. Running toward the sideline he launched the ball 43 yards to Justin Jefferson, who evaded multiple defenders himself before finally succumbing at the Georgia nine-yard-line.

CBS announcer Gary Danielson turned to colleague Brad Nessler and said, "Brad, I want to ask you a question. Can you have two Heisman moments in one year? He had the Heisman play against Alabama with the run and this one is his second."[512]

After the game, Burrow was asked how much of that play was scripted. "It was all improvised," said Joe. "Justin ran a 60-yard hitch route, saw me scrambling and just took off deep. We've got a great feel for each other. I knew exactly where he was going to be when I got out of there."[513]

Sam Smathers proudly watched the play unfold on his Dawg Pound TV. Surrounded by photos of Joe and his Bulldog teammates, Sam's mind immediately went to a similar play from their sixth-grade season. "We were playing Alexander in the playoffs," recalls Burrow's first coach. "The offense was in shotgun, wide double slots. The play was supposed to be a quick slant, but that wasn't open, so Joe scrambled to his right as to take off and run. With his eyes still down field he found an open receiver in the back of the end zone. Who knew that would be Joe's first Heisman moment?"[514]

The Peach Bowl

The College Football Playoff selection committee slotted the 13-0 SEC Champion LSU Tigers in as the number-one overall seed. They would return to Atlanta and play in the Peach Bowl against number-four Oklahoma at the end of the month. In the other semifinal game, second-seeded Ohio State would face number-three Clemson in the Fiesta Bowl.

Before returning to practice, however, some of the top Tigers were back in Atlanta for the College Football Awards Show. Orgeron would later joke that "they should have held it in Baton Rouge, because it was like the LSU show in there…. It was such a proud week for our program."[515]

Meanwhile, back in Athens County, many Burrow supporters were making their plans to return to Atlanta. While Ohio State fans were pleased to be in the playoffs, some were disappointed to discover the Buckeyes would be playing in Arizona instead of Georgia. One Ohio State fan, in particular, had made the mistake of buying Peach Bowl tickets in advance. But instead of reselling the tickets, he googled the phone number for Christ Community Wesleyan Church.

"Somebody in Columbus had purchased six tickets to the game in Atlanta because they thought OSU was going to be there," says Rusty Thomas. "They had seen the story about our LSU watch party on one of the Columbus TV stations and decided to donate the tickets to the church. So, my son and I went with two couples. We tailgated with Robin and Jimmy. The LSU folks were as friendly as can be."[516]

The Tigers were not nearly as hospitable inside Mercedes-Benz Stadium. Turns out, it's a Burrow thing. Joe's brother Jamie had his best game against Oklahoma nearly twenty years earlier when he earned national defensive player of the week honors in a 20–10 Nebraska victory. On this day, younger brother Joe was equally impressive on the other side of the ball, tossing seven first-half touchdowns. The Tigers entered the intermission with a comfortable 49-14 lead and cruised to a 63–28 victory and berth in the national championship game.

Justin Jefferson caught four of Joe's TD passes. The scoring strikes came from 19, 35, 42 and 30 yards out. On the day, Burrow sliced up the Sooner defense for 493 yards through the air and added a three-yard touchdown on the ground.

The Tigers set or tied several college bowl records, including most passing and receiving touchdowns in a CFP game.[517]

The much maligned and banged-up Tiger defense used the time off to get healthy. It showed on the field, allowing only 322 total yards to a Sooner team that came in averaging 554 yards per game.

As usual, in the postgame press conference Burrow credited those around him. "I trust my guys. I trust them enough to throw 50/50 balls up to them and they're going to go make a play for me. I've got great people around me and that's why we've been so successful. We have trust in each other."[518]

Near the end of the presser, one reporter told Burrow Ohio State was leading Clemson. Was Joe hoping for a Buckeye win to set up the perfect storybook ending? With a smile, Joe simply replied, "I'm excited to play for the national title."[519]

Clemson rallied at the end to beat Ohio State, 29–23.

It would be LSU and Clemson for all the marbles.

The excitement surrounding the victory was tempered by a tragedy that occurred earlier in the day. Steve Ensminger's daughter-in-law, Carley McCord, was one of five people killed when a small plane crashed on the way to Atlanta. The devastated offensive coordinator chose to call the plays, as usual, and thought it best to tell the players after the game was over. "Obviously, he was distraught, but he called a great game today," said Orgeron. "Just goes to show you the integrity and the grit and character of the men on our football team."[520]

The National Championship

As the LSU buses departed Baton Rouge for the seventy-five-mile ride to New Orleans, it's easy to imagine Joe Burrow reflecting upon a similar seventy-five-mile ride he took five years earlier from The Plains to Columbus. On that day, he also led a 14–0 team into a championship game. Things didn't go as planned the first time. This was a chance to right that wrong. To finish the season a perfect 15–0. To hoist the golden trophy high above his head. A dream since his youth football days with Sam Smathers.

"Since I was ten years old, this is what I've always wanted to do," said Burrow. "I've said in the past, my goal was never to be the quarterback of an NFL team, I wanted to be a quarterback of a top-ten team playing in the national title game and we have a chance to do that, and this is a dream come true for me."[521]

The last time Joe threw the football in the Super Dome, he was in middle school. Ohio University was preparing to play Troy in the 2010 New Orleans Bowl and Joe was tossing the ball around with older brother, Jamie. Joe was throwing tight spirals 30 to 35 yards down the field. Jamie looks over at his father and says, "Hey, that's not normal is it?" Jimmy responds, "Absolutely not."[522]

"Normal" would be the key word heading into the national championship game. Business as usual for a team that just outscored a pair of top-five opponents 100-38 in the previous two games. For Joe Burrow, normal means routine, doing the same thing every gameday: listening to Lil Uzi and Meek Mill at the hotel, eating a caramel apple sucker on the bus, then chilling with John Mayer and Kid Cudi in the locker room while pulling on one inside-out sock. A winning formula up to this point.[523]

For the Tigers, normal also means a pep talk. Or two. The first was a special treat—Burrow's childhood idol, Saints quarterback Drew Brees. While the talk was inspirational, the highlight was watching his kids run around the facility in Burrow, Chase and Edwards-Helaire jerseys. The second pep talk came from Coach O, who emphasized character, poise and ball security. Then he turned to the final reason LSU was going to win the national championship: Joe Burrow. "Other teams' quarterbacks get hit and they b****," said Orgeron. "Our quarterback gets hit and I'm happy because I know he's pissed off, and he's bringing hell with him."[524]

Back in Athens, LSU watch parties were scheduled throughout the whole county.

Appropriately enough, the *crème da la crème* would take place in The Dawg Pound. While ten to fifteen people typically attended one of Sam's LSU watch parties, this one would attract sixty revelers. Troy Bolin planned to broadcast his radio show from Sam's garage, while WCMH-TV, the NBC affiliate out of Columbus, was on hand to document the whole event.

"It reminds you of when we had the state title run in high school football," said Smathers during an interview with reporter Dan Pearlman. "Everybody's talking football. Everybody's talking Joe Burrow. Everybody's following LSU now and flying the purple and gold in their yard. It's a buzz. It's a great place to be right now."[525]

Sam and his buddies would spare no expense to bring the full Cajun experience to The Dawg Pound. "We're going to do it just like they're doing it in Louisiana, in New Orleans, in Baton Rouge, Slidell, Lafayette," said Steven Shockley, a transplant from Louisiana to Athens County.[526]

"Shockley had the idea to have an original crawfish boil," said Smathers. "He drove seven hours to Elizabethtown, Kentucky, where a boat captain friend from Louisiana shipped seventy pounds of fresh crawfish. He also ordered two king cakes from Baton Rouge, Andouille sausage and fresh Boudin."[527]

When Shockley returned from Elizabethtown, he handled the Cajun cooking. He spread the boiled crustaceans all over the tables and taught everyone in the garage how to properly eat a crawfish. Even the TV reporter got in on the action. "I know why Joe wanted crawfish," says Smathers. "Damn, they're good!"[528]

After all the pregame festivities from Athens to New Orleans, it was time to tee it up. Could LSU unseat the defending national champion Clemson Tigers, winners of twenty-nine straight games? We would soon find out.

Clemson's initial drive stalled, but the punt pinned LSU inside its own 10. Coming into the game, the Bayou Bengals had scored touchdowns on six consecutive opening drives. That streak came to an end as an aggressive Clemson defense forced a three-and-out.

After exchanging punts, Clemson drew first blood on a one-yard keeper by quarterback Trevor Lawrence who scampered around the right edge and into the end zone untouched. LSU finally got on the board with 2:20 remaining in the first quarter when Burrow hit Ja'Marr Chase for a 52-yard touchdown strike. It would be the first of many big plays for Chase on the night.

The Dawg Pound was full of authentic Cajun crawfish on national championship night. *Photo credit: Troy Bolin*

"After the second possession I got back to the sideline and was like they really are playing man to man on Ja'Marr," said Burrow after the game. "So, we started going to him heavy."[529]

Early in the second quarter, Clemson took a 10–7 lead on a 52-yard field goal. The Tigers extended their advantage to 17–7 on a 36-yard reverse by future Burrow teammate Tee Higgins. LSU responded as Burrow and Chase connected again, this time for 56 yards down to the three-yard line. On third and goal, Burrow called his own number, slipping through the Clemson front and into the end zone to cut the lead to three, 17–14.

After the game Burrow would praise Clemson defensive coordinator Brent Venables for having a great gameplan, but the LSU offense was now in rhythm. With 5:19 remaining in the second quarter, Joe capped a six-play, 87-yard drive with a beautifully placed pass to Chase in the corner of the end zone. LSU had its first lead, 21–17.

Following another Clemson punt, the ball was back in Burrow's hands, but with poor field position at the LSU five-yard line. With 3:31 on the clock, a three-and-out would give Trevor Lawrence and the Clemson offense enough time to retake the lead before half.

But Burrow had other plans. Using nearly all of the clock, Joe engineered a masterful 95-yard drive on eleven plays. One of the most critical was a 29-yard quarterback keeper down to the Clemson six. On the next play, Burrow threw a dart to Thaddeus Moss for a touchdown. While LSU increased its lead to 28–17 heading into the intermission, Joe paid the price on the play. Clemson linebacker James Skalski broke through the line untouched and flew into Joe's rib cage just as the ball was released. He would play the rest of the game with torn rib cartilage.

At the beginning of the third quarter, Clemson fought back to cut the lead to three, 28–25, on a Travis Etienne touchdown run at the 10:49 mark. After teams exchanged punts, Burrow orchestrated another drive. On third and 11 from the LSU 41, Venables dialed up a zero-blitz. It was Skalski who got to Burrow again just as the ball was released. The ball spiraled straight into the arms of Ja'Marr Chase, who raced up the LSU sideline for 43 yards to the Clemson 16-yard line. Justin Jefferson hauled in the next pass inside the 10-yard line. Skalski flew through the air and hit Jefferson with the crown of his helmet. He was ejected for targeting. One of Clemson's most active defenders was gone for the game. On the next play,

Burrow found Moss on a four-yard touchdown pass to increase the LSU lead to 35–25.

With 12:08 remaining in the game, Burrow threw the knockout punch—a 24-yard 50/50 ball to Terrace Marshall, who high-pointed it for the touchdown. A jubilant Joe jogged off the field pointing to his left ring finger.

The LSU defense was stout down the stretch, forcing a Clemson punt followed by a fumble in the final minute of the game. The Louisiana State sideline poured onto the field as the scoreboard clock ticked down to zero. Three-hundred forty-six-pound defensive lineman Tyler Shelvin lifted Burrow onto his shoulder and paraded their leader around the field in purple and gold euphoria. Two years from now, Cincinnati Bengals fans would see a very similar sight in Arrowhead Stadium.

But one celebration at a time.

Burrow was named offensive player of the game with 463 passing yards and six touchdowns—five through the air and one on the ground. Patrick Queen was named defensive player of the game after recording eight tackles. A season that began with a headlock and body blows, now came to a perfect conclusion with a heartfelt embrace atop the victory stand.

The national championship trophy belonged to LSU. Burrow had achieved his boyhood dream. Time seemingly stood still as Joe gazed at the golden trophy held high above his head with purple and gold confetti gently swirling around him. When Joe began to speak the camera focused on the Burrows—the proud, beaming father and teary-eyed mother with both hands over her heart. The kid from Southeast Ohio was characteristically selfless.

"So many people put so much work into this from athletic trainers, equipment staff, players, coaches, chefs, dining room assistants. It's not just me or Coach O or the O-line, it's everybody inside that building that gets a piece of this."[530]

Several viral videos captured the party inside the LSU locker room as Joe and his teammates puffed on cigars and flashed their "Get the Gat" dance moves.[531] The party continued on Bourbon Street, where Jimmy had celebrated his own Sugar Bowl victory forty-five years earlier.

For the night, Bourbon Street turned into Burrow Street.

Callin' Baton Rouge

Joe not only brought a national championship to the state of Louisiana and Southeast Ohio, but he broke a family curse. "We call it the Burrow curse," says Jimmy with a smile. "We've lost some championships. All three of my sons lost a state championship in high school. We lost one at Nebraska. I lost a couple Grey cups in the CFL. It's kind of a thing we joke about. Joe finally broke the curse."[532]

When asked about the secret to the success of the 2019–20 LSU Tigers, Jimmy says, "This team had a lot of talent, but what often gets overlooked is they were smart and had a lot of character."[533]

Jimmy's perspective is backed up by the research of longtime LSU athletic trainer Jack Marucci, who also served as a consultant to Coach Orgeron. Over the years, Marucci has done more than guide the Tiger medical team; he has also created a character assessment that includes four traits: academics, off-field behavior, coachability, and interaction with support staff.

According to Marucci, the 2019–20 squad had the highest character rating of any LSU football team in two decades. When it comes to success, Marucci says, "The biggest piece [is] character. Character guys are the ones who, when things don't go quite right, they're not going to complain as much. They're not going to sink the ship. They're not going to point fingers. They can rally the troops better—because you're going to have adversity, it's inevitable."[534]

Marucci's words are a perfect description of Joe Burrow, the leader. A walking billboard for the correlation between character and championship performance.

The pageantry of the Louisiana State Tigers was on full display five days after winning the national title as thousands of fans enjoyed an all-out celebration. The Golden Band from Tiger Land marched down victory hill led by the Golden Girls. The coaches and players floats soon followed with Mardi Gras beads sprinkling the crowd. The celebration culminated in the basketball arena. Just outside, Mike the Tiger basked in the glory of it all.

The adoration for Jimmy and Robin was so intense, LSU officials provided a security detail. "At the celebration, they had to put us in a private area so we could enjoy the parade," says Jimmy. "Then security walked us into the Pete Maravich Center. It got pretty crazy down there."[535]

While Mike the Tiger reigned outside the arena, Tiger King Joe Burrow reigned within. Not surprisingly, when Burrow was introduced he received the loudest ovation. With a backwards hat, Mardi Gras beads, and purple shades, Joe Cool praised the coaches for how they prepared the team week in and week out, but especially for the national championship game. "It was as if we had the answers to the test."[536]

As the little boy told Robin and Jimmy before the Arkansas game, one day Joe's going to have a statue outside of Tiger Stadium. Given the popularity of the Burrows, they might erect a statue of the whole family, especially Dan who, under the influence of Coach O, "manned up" and helped convince Joe to pick LSU over Cincinnati.

When that day comes, all of the Burrows will be in attendance for the unveiling of the statue. Right next to Billy Cannon. The only two Heisman Trophy winners in LSU history. Jimmy and Robin don't get back to Baton Rouge as often as they would like, but they did return in April of 2022 for a Garth Brooks concert. When it comes to musical taste, Joe's parents are less Cudi and more country. In fact, the Burrows are such big Garth fans, they saw him twice in one month.

"We saw him in both Cincinnati and Baton Rouge," says Jimmy. "The Baton Rouge concert was awesome, 115,000 people in Death Valley." The Burrows asked the LSU equipment manager to put a "Burreaux" jersey in Garth's dressing room. He gladly complied.

Jimmy and Robin enjoyed the show on the field. Near the end of the concert, more and more people began to recognize the Burrows and security escorted them away. But not before Garth played fan-favorite "Callin' Baton Rouge," an anthem played at the beginning of every LSU home game.

With everyone at the concert singing along in full voice, the ground-shaking rendition of the hometown favorite registered as a small earthquake on a nearby seismograph.[537] The loudest moment in Tiger Stadium since Joe pointed to the Burreaux on the back of his jersey.

They made a lifetime of memories during Joe's two years in Baton Rouge, especially his senior season. In a touching interview with ESPN's Tom Rinaldi, the Burrows explained, at the end of the day, it's all about family.

"The whole transition of Jimmy retiring has helped Joe understand how important he is to us," said an emotional Robin. "He's everything to us." Added Jimmy, "I made a good decision. I've never sat in the stands with my family to watch a game. It's brought our family together more than ever."[538]

9

Thirty-one Seconds

"Coming from Southeast Ohio, it's a very impoverished area. The poverty rate is almost two times the national average. There's so many people there that don't have a lot. I'm up here for all those kids in Athens and Athens County that go home—not a lot of food on the table, hungry after school. You guys can be up here, too."[539]

—Joe Burrow
Heisman Trophy acceptance speech
December 14, 2019

The day before Joe Burrow played in the high school state championship game, he was named the 28th Associated Press Ohio Mr. Football. He joined an illustrious group of previous award-winners, including 1997 Heisman Trophy recipient Charles Woodson, two-time NFL All-Pro running back Robert Smith, and 2017 NFL second-overall draft selection Mitch Trubisky.

The Buckeye recruiting website, "Eleven Warriors" announced the news: "On the eve of the 2014 state championship game, Burrow has added another major award to his already impressive trophy case."[540] Only one problem. There was no trophy.

"I asked the guy who was interviewing me when do I get the trophy," said a light-hearted Burrow on the "Pardon My Take" podcast years later. "He said, 'Oh, you don't get a trophy.' I said, 'What do you mean?' He said, 'Yeah, you just get the title.'"[541]

A title is nice, but come on. Are you serious? Mr. Football? Best player in the state? No trophy?

No worries. The Burrow family would make one. After all, if Joe could dismantle a trophy piece by piece by piece, surely he could figure out how to build one from scratch. But there was no time for that. So, Robin called a local business—Zonez at the Market on State—and ordered an "Ohio Mr. Football" trophy for their son. When it came, the trophy was placed proudly on the Burrow family mantle.

Johnny Unitas Almost Killed My Dad

Fast forward five years when Joe Burrow was about to turn twenty-three. He was set to have the birthday week of all birthday weeks. In those next seven days, the SEC Offensive Player of the Year would not only get a new phone, but he'd collect every award available to a college quarterback.

Zonez wouldn't be needed this time; Each award came with a trophy.

But the Burrows accepted an offer from Randy Wolfe, one of the most talented carpenters in the region, to build the mother of all trophy cases to display one of the greatest hauls of hardware in college football history.

After Joe's birthday on Tuesday, December 10, the award circuit took him to Baltimore, Atlanta and New York City. He packed four suits, some casual clothes and his Nintendo. Oh, and his laptop. He needed to finish a few final assignments. He was still a student for ten more days. At which time he would collect another award, his master's degree in Liberal Arts.

This trip required a winter coat—a superfluous garment on the Bayou, but a necessity in The Big Apple. All of Joe's heavy coats were at home in The Plains, so he threw on his LSU letter jacket with the requisite hoody underneath. It was a wardrobe choice that generated some playful ribbing from the Twittersphere and one of the "Pardon My Take" hosts.

"Do you realize when you wear that letterman jacket and you have that little curl that comes down in front of your forehead, you are every bully from every movie in the '80s?"[542] Joe laughed. Those who know him, know better.

Upon reflection, the letter jacket seemed perfect for that week. Joe received his first letter jacket and delivered his first speech at the sixth-grade end-of-the-year youth football banquet. "It all started with thank you speeches at youth football," says Robin. "Those boys would get up there, get their jacket and say a few words about the coaches and parents."[543]

Sam Smathers remembered, "Any kid who played four years for me got an Athens letter jacket and a little Bulldog football helmet. It was like their senior year of youth football. I told them if you got something to say, go ahead and say it."[544]

Joe has never been a fan of speeches, but when he speaks, people listen.

There would be a lot of people listening to Joe Burrow that week.

On Wednesday, December 11, Burrow and his parents spent the day in Baltimore with Johnny Unitas Jr., the president of the Golden Arm Foundation. That evening, Joe received the coveted Johnny Unitas Golden Arm

Joe *(far right back row)* and his buddies receive their sixth-grade letter jackets.
Photo credit: The Smathers Family

Award, presented to the top quarterback in the country. It's an award that not only honors the recipient's athletic ability, but also his character, leadership, sportsmanship, teamwork and academic prowess. It's an award that fits Joe Burrow like a glove.

During the day, Burrow examined several artifacts, including the final ball that Johnny Unitas ever threw as a Baltimore Colt. It was a 67-yard touchdown. Tour guide and historian Michael Gibbons painted the picture for the Burrows: "As [Unitas walked off the field] a little bi-plane flew overhead saying, 'Unitas We Stand.' And 60,000 people stood up."[545]

Burrow also slipped on a blue number-19 Johnny Unitas Colts jersey and received an autographed picture of Unitas playing in the 1958 NFL Championship game in Yankee Stadium. It was a cool experience for Joe, but beyond description for his father. If the 71-yard pass to Justin Jefferson in the SEC Championship game was Joe's second Heisman moment, then this was Jimmy's second Elvis moment.

As a kid, Joe heard plenty of stories about Unitas, the greatest quarterback of his era. "He was an idol to my dad. The best player he's ever seen."[546]

A smiling Joe continued during his acceptance speech, "When I handed [the autographed picture] to my dad, I think he almost had a heart attack. You almost killed my dad."[547]

The following night, Thursday, December 12, the award circuit continued at the College Football Hall of Fame in Atlanta. ESPN's College Football Awards show is the equivalent to the Oscar's with multiple categories and the full red-carpet treatment.

Joe traded the letter jacket for a purple pinstripe suit with pocket square. He was barraged with questions on the red carpet. A reporter from Louisiana asked, "What has Baton Rouge meant to you?" Joe responded, "It means the world to me. They've loved me like a true son. And I just try to do everything I can to repay them." The reporter followed up, "What has

Ja'Marr meant to you?" A jovial Joe said, "He's meant about 1,500 yards and 18 touchdowns to me. I think he deserves to win the Biletnikoff tonight. He's a great player and he's going to be a great player for a long time."[548]

It was a big night for the Louisiana State Tigers. Ed Orgeron won the Home Depot Coach-of-the-Year Award, Joe Brady received the Broyles Award for top assistant, Grant Delpit won the Jim Thorpe Award for top defensive back, and Ja'Marr Chase received the Biletnikoff Award for best receiver.

Tom Rinaldi asked Orgeron how his previous coaching experiences have helped him become the coach he is today. "I want to treat all my players like my sons," says Orgeron. "Like my family. Have a family-type atmosphere, where everybody enjoys coming to work, plays together, one team, one heartbeat."[549]

The biggest winner on the night, however, was Joe Burrow. He received the Davy O'Brien Award for nation's best quarterback, as well as the Maxwell and Walter Camp awards for National Player of the Year. The Associated Press also named Burrow the National Player of the Year.

"I wouldn't have changed my journey for anything in the world," said Joe. "I'm grateful for it. I think it's made me better as a person and a player."[550]

Later in the month *The Sporting News* would name Burrow National Player of the Year. Then, at the end of January, Joe, unsurprisingly, received the only honor bestowed after the bowl season concludes—The Manning Award for the nation's top quarterback.

"I'm not sure we've ever seen a quarterback have the high level of sustained and consistent excellence against a very challenging schedule that Joe Burrow had this season," said Archie Manning. "Week-in and week-out, he played elite-level football while leading his team to victory."[551]

Welcome to the LSU Heisman Family

It's not easy being the wife of a college football coach. During the season, your husband's gone seven days a week. In the off-season, there's recruiting and planning for the upcoming year. So, when you finally get a vacation with your spouse, it's kind of a big deal.

That's why Leanne Ponamsky was looking forward to Mother's Day 2018. She and Derek had planned a getaway for the weekend. Then, at the last second, her husband received an "all-hands-on-deck" message from Coach O. There was a graduate transfer recruit from Ohio State coming to town. As the special assistant to Orgeron, Derek's services would be needed.

Vacation cancelled.

Leanne was not pleased. Her message to Derek was direct and to the point: "This guy better win the f-in Heisman!"[552]

Nineteen months later, on Friday, December 13, Joe was on his way to New York City to get Coach Ponamsky "out of the doghouse."[553]

It's not easy being the wife of a Heisman Trophy winner, either. Just ask Dot Cannon. Billy had always longed to impart words of wisdom to the next LSU Heisman recipient. But that opportunity slipped away when Cannon died the same day Burrow signed with the Tigers.

So, Dot and daughter, Bunnie, did the next best thing. They penned a private letter to Joe, which he read in his vintage LSU letter jacket on a small charter plane from Atlanta to New York City. The heartfelt letter was passed slowly from Joe to Robin to Jimmy, who would make sure it was securely preserved for posterity.

The Cannons congratulated Joe for his extraordinary achievements and welcomed him into the LSU Heisman family. They also told him that his life was going to change. Whenever and wherever he appeared in public, adoring fans would pursue him for a picture, autograph or conversation. Everyone would want a piece of the private, introverted Joe Burrow.[554]

Truth is, this was already happening. Burrow's unprecedented senior season had sent his popularity in Louisiana through the roof. He couldn't appear in public without getting smothered. Same story in Athens. If he and his high school buddies quietly slipped into a bar on Court Street on a lazy Wednesday evening, within minutes the place would be flooded with OU students. Soon, every outing would require careful choreography.

As the Burrows flew north for the granddaddy of all trophy presentations, a few chosen Athens residents were also on their way to The Big Apple. A week earlier, Robin and Jimmy had invited some old friends to join them at the Heisman festivities. AHS football coaches Ryan Adams and Nathan White would be there with wives Debra and Sarah. Long-time neighbor and Ohio University coach Tim Albin brought his family—Brooke, Tori and Treyce. Jeff and Heather Skinner, Liz Luehrman, and Tom and Marikay Vander Ven rounded out the Athens contingent.

"I remember Tom and I were going to dinner, and I got a text from Robin," recalls Marikay. "I looked at my phone and said, 'Oh my God, Robin just invited us to go to the Heisman ceremony.' We were so honored. We responded immediately, 'Thank you. Yes, we will make it work!'"[555]

Heather also remembers the text from the Burrows. "Jimmy texted Jeff and it said, 'Hey, Joe wants you to be at the Heisman ceremony. I know it's a big ask, but if you guys could come it would be awesome.' We were like, 'Ok, we're going. We'll figure it out. We'll put it on the credit card.'"[556]

While Joe was making the rounds in the media capital of the world, the folks from Athens were settling into their hotel rooms a few blocks away from Manhattan's PlayStation Theatre in Times Square. After some sightseeing, the Vander Vens picked up their credentials and spent a few minutes with the Burrows at the Marriott Marquis. They saw the Heisman Trophy in a display case. Jimmy introduced Tom to some of the Heisman royalty on hand for the occasion—Paul Hornung, Tony Dorsett and Johnny Rodgers.

Later that night, Jimmy introduced many of his Louisiana friends to his old Athens buddies. He knows how to work a room and make everyone feel good. So does Coach Orgeron, who chatted up Coach Skinner about Joe's basketball days. "I got a picture with Coach O," said Skinner, who admitted to being a bit star-struck. "I tell everybody, he's my new best friend."[557]

Due to space limitations, the Athens delegation watched the ceremony across the street in a large ballroom reserved for LSU boosters and other dignitaries. The LSU folks outnumbered the Athens crowd 5:1.[558]

Tom and Marikay got a taste of Louisiana's fascination with Joe Burrow. Marikay interacted with a few exceptionally enthusiastic LSU supporters.

The first person came up to Marikay and politely asked, "Why are you here?" Marikay said, "My son was really good friends with Joe growing up."

"Oh, my God!"

Another avid LSU supporter wondered, "Did he ever spend the night at your house?" Marikay said, "Oh yes, there were many times I made breakfast for Sam, Joe and whoever else was staying. One summer Joe was there almost every day."

"Oh my God!"[559]

Marikay also got a taste of Louisiana hospitality. After a few minutes of conversation, she was invited to stay at a lady's house when Joe is inducted into the LSU Hall of Fame. As Travis Brand put it, Louisiana folks are "a different breed. The absolute finest."[560]

Not a Dry Eye in the House

About an hour before they were due at the PlayStation Theatre, Robin began to wonder if Joe had written an acceptance speech. It's been a crazy week with so many appearances. "A whirlwind for all of us, let alone him," says Robin.[561]

She asked Jimmy if Joe had organized any thoughts. Jimmy didn't know, so he headed over to their son's room. Inside, Joe was scribbling a few notes on a card. "I'm not sure he ever really looked at those," said Jimmy.[562] After the night was through, Joe gave Jimmy the card. Along with the Cannon letter, it's safely stashed away for posterity.

Inside PlayStation Theatre, there was no doubt who won the big award. When Joe heard his name, he clasped hands and exchanged hugs with the other finalists—Justin Fields, Jalen Hurts and Chase Young. Two from Ohio State. Three of the four, if you included Burrow, with Buckeye blood.

Joe walked over to Robin, tears already welling up in her eyes. They hugged. "Love you. So proud of you," she told her son. "You're the man," said Jimmy. Coach O was next. "I'm proud of you, son." Hugs and hand clasps on down the line. Joe Brady. Steve Ensminger. Other Tiger coaches. At the end of the row, longtime girlfriend, Olivia, got a kiss.

As he made his way backup the row he touched his mother's hand one more time before going across the aisle to embrace Ohio State head coach Ryan Day and strength coach Mickey Marotti. Finally on the platform Chris Fowler said, "Joe, say hello to your new friend for life. Give Mr. Heisman a lift here."

After posing with the trophy for a few seconds, Burrow sauntered over to the podium. With an army of former Heisman winners at his back, Joe began his speech. "The first thing I want to say…" He stopped. Under the weight of the moment, he began to well up. For twenty seconds, Burrow struggled to gather himself. Joe wiped away tears, Ohio State and LSU bands clearly visible on his left wrist.

Joe Burrow won the Heisman balloting by the largest voting margin in history. *Photo credit: The Burrow Family*

He began again, thanking his offensive line first. The best unit in the country. They received the Joe Moore Award to prove it. And, yes, that award came with a trophy. Did it ever. Weighing in at over 800 pounds and standing nearly seven feet high, it's the largest football trophy in the country.

Robin appreciated Joe's O-line, as well. After all, their job was to protect her son. Not only that, but the boys in the trenches rarely got the credit they deserved. That's why when Joe was in high school, she had shirts made up that read, "It all starts with the center." She had the same shirts printed and distributed at LSU.[563]

Joe continued by thanking his receivers. "I've got so many weapons on the outside. Terrace, Ja'Marr, Justin. Those guys have been unbelievable. All my teammates have welcomed me with open arms. A kid from Ohio coming down to the Bayou and welcomed me as brothers."

He thanked the Heisman organizers, his family, and the former Heisman winners. Then he turned to the two universities that prepared him for this moment.

"I'm just so thankful for LSU and Ohio State. Playing at two of the best programs in the country. Great coaches both places. My journey, I wouldn't have traded it for anything in the world."

He honored his fellow Heisman finalists, touching on the fact that three of the four are transfers. Three of the four overcame adversity to make it to this room. After thanking his strength coaches, Joe took a beat. He laughed to break the tension. Cheers of encouragement rang through the theatre.

For the next thirty-one seconds, Joe shifted the spotlight to his hometown. "Coming from Southeast Ohio, it's a very impoverished area. The poverty rate is almost two times the national average. There's so many people there that don't have a lot. I'm up here for all those kids in Athens and Athens County that go home—not a lot of food on the table, hungry after school. You guys can be up here, too."

He thanked the entire state of Louisiana for their support and cuisine. "I've learned to love crawfish and gumbo," said Burrow with a chuckle. "During crawfish season, Coach O makes sure we have pounds and pounds and pounds of crawfish."

Then, Joe addressed Coach O directly. Player and coach both in tears. "Coach O, you have no idea what you mean to my family. I didn't play for three years. You took a chance on me, not knowing if I could play or not. I'm forever grateful for you. Can you imagine a guy like Coach O giving me the keys to his football program? He just means so much to me and my family and to LSU. I sure hope they give him a lifetime contract. He deserves it."

Coach O shook a clinched fist at Joe. A mixture of pride, gratitude and solidarity. With Jimmy's arm around the LSU coach, Robin and Ed exchanged heartfelt "I love yous."

Joe's final line summed up his inspiring acceptance speech: "So when I lift this trophy again, it's for LSU, Ohio State, Southeast Ohio, and all of Louisiana. Thank you."[564]

There wasn't a dry eye in the house.

The Athens Reaction

Joe Burrow had won the Heisman vote by the largest margin in history. But across the street in the LSU hospitality room, that's not what the people from Athens were discussing.

"When he started talking about the kids in Athens County, it kind of threw me for a loop," says Jeff Skinner. "My experience with Joe all those years was he didn't say much. For him to articulate that message just blew us all away."[565]

Heather remembers the Athens folks were just looking at each other in amazement. "We all knew that was not a prepared speech. He spoke from his heart."[566]

The Vander Vens have known the Heisman winner as long as anybody, but this was a different side of Joe. "It was just moving to see him like that because he's so poised and straight-faced," said Tom. "To see that naked emotion was very powerful."[567]

For Marikay, it was even more moving when Joe joined the afterparty, working his way slowly through the crowd. "I just remember seeing him and hugging him," said Marikay. "I think he was touched to see everybody, too."[568] Tom agreed, "It clearly was powerful for him to see the people from Athens there."[569]

Tom and Marikay's son, Sam, watched Joe's acceptance speech from Disney World. He was there for a friend's wedding, but caught the whole ceremony in his hotel room. "I was completely frozen, completely shocked," recalls Sam. "I could not believe that I knew that dude up there. Joe and I watched so many Heisman ceremonies together when we were growing up and he's accepting it right now. It was unreal."[570]

That said, Sam wasn't stunned by Joe's decision to address the problem of food insecurity in Athens County. Nothing Joe said or did ever surprised his friend, but Sam was still touched by his comments. "We had teammates growing up who would walk to practice because their families couldn't get them there," recalls Sam. "They would walk miles to get to practice because being a part of our football team was one of the most positive things in their lives. It was one of the only great things that they had. I definitely thought about it, and I know Joe did, too."[571]

At a media event before the ceremony, Burrow was asked what winning the Heisman would mean to the people in his life. He said, "It would mean a lot to everyone that has helped me along my journey, from youth coaches, middle school, high school, LSU, Ohio State."[572]

It was a proud moment for Joe's first youth coach. In fact, Sam Smathers ranks Heisman night fourth, behind his wedding day and the birth of his three kids. "Still can't believe a boy I coached won the highest honor a collegiate athlete could receive."[573]

Surrounded by JoeyB4, JoeyB10 and JoeyB9 photos and memorabilia, including the latest addition—a one-twelfth replica of the Heisman Trophy with Joe Burrow's name on it—the Smathers clan and a few close friends watched the ceremony on the Dawg Pound TV.

Cheers, laughter and sniffles all around.

By the end of the night, there wasn't a dry eye in the garage.

In fact, not a dry eye in all of The Plains.

A couple miles away in his living room, Troy Bolin was moved by Joe's speech. "That was a little hard for me to be honest," said Troy. "When Joe got emotional, it made me emotional. Especially when he was talking about Coach O with Robin and Jimmy right there. I get choked up just thinking about it."[574]

A short drive from Bolin, Bill Finnearty was glued to the screen with a tear rolling down his cheek. "He had every right to be resentful toward Ohio State," said Bill, a lifelong Buckeye fan. "But he's not. He knows the role they played."[575]

While Coach Skinner was hobnobbing with LSU brass, a former assistant Ron Ricketts watched the ceremony in a packed Cat's Corner—one of Robin and Jimmy's favorite Athens hangouts.

Like most in the crowd, Ricketts was clad in purple and gold. As Joe's middle school basketball coach, Ron has plenty of memories to share with the Cat's Corner patrons. Like when Joe single-handedly won a game with a "one-man press." And the times he volunteered midgame to shut down the other team's star player—holding him scoreless the rest of the way. Story after story of Joe's relentless drive to win.[576] The Ricketts-coached and Burrow-led Bulldogs almost went undefeated, suffering a lone defeat. Ricketts quipped, "They should've fired me for losing that one."[577]

Jeff Skinner poses with "new best friend" Coach O during the Heisman reception.
Photo credit: The Skinner Family

A camera crew from Columbus roamed around the bar, capturing hometown reactions to Burrow's Heisman victory. Deep into Joe's speech, the camera zoomed in on Rickett's weathered face. His moist eyes riveted on Joe, who was sharing his heart with the Tiger head coach. "That part really moved me because I know how much Joe likes Coach O," says Ricketts.[578]

Susan Wolfe sat a few feet away. She recalls the night fondly: "The place was rockin'. When his name was called, I was so thrilled for Joe. His speech gave me chills. It was the best. Ever."[579] Susan's husband, Randy, chose to stand. Like the other Cat's Corner patrons, his eyes glued to the hometown hero.

But Randy was not only reflecting upon Joe's journey, the skilled carpenter was also calculating the size of that massive trophy case he would soon be constructing for the Burrow family basement.

A Christmas Miracle

In Columbus, Athens residents Will Drabold and wife, Katie Kostival, watched the Heisman ceremony from one of their favorite cigar shops, the Tinder Box. As Will was savoring a BS Gold, Joe Burrow stepped to the podium. Drabold asked the shop owner to turn up the TV. Through ribbons of smoke and conversational chatter, Will and Katie locked in.

Drabold was immediately captivated.

"Right out of the gate Joe's emotional," said Will. "I literally remember being drawn to the screen. It was like an out-of-body moment when he first mentioned Southeast Ohio and first started talking about Athens. I was watching it. I started tearing up. I still can't explain where the hell that came from."[580]

Will is no stranger to Joe Burrow. He was a senior at Athens High School when Joe was a freshman. As a journalism student at OU, Drabold wrote a feature about Burrow for the university newspaper. Will knows Joe's story, but like the rest of the world he is only now beginning to see his heart.

Back in Athens, Karin Bright, the President of the Athens County Food Pantry, watched the speech from her living room. "Joe started talking and my eyes are welling up at what he's saying," recalls Karin. "I looked at my husband and said, 'This is incredible. So heartfelt, not your typical Heisman speech. He seems to be a wonderful guy.'"[581] Feeling proud and uplifted the Brights go to bed.

In Brooklyn, New York, sportswriter Peter King and his wife, Ann, were watching Joe's speech. They felt a special connection. Both are Ohio University graduates, married in Athens forty years earlier. After Joe was done speaking, Ann told Peter she wanted to make a donation to the Athens County Food Pantry.[582]

Ann had plenty of options. Thirty-three separate online fundraisers spontaneously sprung up. Gifts came from around the world (three fundraisers originated outside the U.S.), but highly concentrated in Louisiana and Ohio, flooded in.[583]

On Sunday morning, Drabold launched one of those fundraisers on Facebook. He copied and pasted an excerpt from Joe's speech along with a picture of the hometown hero holding the Heisman. He set a modest goal of $1,000, then boarded a plane for Los Angeles.

Bright remembers her day starting out like a typical Sunday. In the early afternoon she took her daughter to an appointment. Her phone would ding. It was a Facebook alert. A fundraiser had been started for the Athens County Food Pantry. "That's cool," she thought. It had been launched by someone in Louisiana. This one eventually raises $10,000 for the pantry. Soon she learned about Will's fundraiser. The day was getting more interesting by the minute.[584]

When his plane touched down at LAX, Drabold's Facebook fundraiser had surpassed the goal. By nearly $50,000. "I kind of knew there was something, I knew there was a moment, I knew nerves had been touched, I just did not know to what degree," said Drabold.[585]

Bright was now communicating with the food pantry treasurer, who was at a personal event in Iowa. They texted back and forth as the donations kept climbing. Finally, after midnight, Karin said, "We need to go to bed. Tomorrow's going to be a very busy day."[586]

Drabold started his day in L.A. His fundraiser had been active for twenty-four hours. The number was now at $80,000—surpassing the food pantry's annual budget. Back in Athens, the pantry phone was going crazy. "We were such a low-budget organization, so mindful of funds that we only had a certain amount of minutes on the pantry phone," says Karin. "We blew through those in about half an hour. If people called and left a message, we'd call them back on our personal phones."[587]

When one reporter contacted Bright, she asked him to call back on her number. "He's like what's going on and I said, 'Well we don't want to burn the pantry minutes.' Later, when he arrived for the interview, he walked through the door and said, 'How the phone minutes lookin' now?' I say, 'I don't think we need to worry about them quite as much as we did two hours ago.'"[588]

Bright continued to field calls from the press. She remembers, "It was crazy. We didn't have time to put together a media plan or talking points. We were as stunned as anybody else."[589]

Karin was scheduled to go on vacation—a surprise birthday present from her daughter. "We were going to Asheville to see the Biltmore Christmas decorations."[590] In preparation for the trip, they stopped by Sam's Club. The phone rang while they were in the checkout line. It was NPR. Karin then conducted an interview with a Baton Rouge radio station while driving back to her house.

That was Monday.

On Tuesday at 10 a.m., the donations had soared to $350,000. The wall where Ohio University students paint messages had a picture of Joe kissing the Heisman. The text read:

CONGRATULATIONS JOE BURROW

THANK YOU FOR FEEDING YOUR ROOTS

Drabold finally spoke to the Burrows for the first time. "They were grateful for the fundraiser, but they also had a concern about eligibility," remembers Will. "Because I had posted the image of Joe kissing the Heisman Trophy on the fundraiser page, they thought there could be an NCAA violation. They wanted me to talk with the LSU compliance office. I remember thinking, 'Oh my God. Did I just kill Joe Burrow's eligibility for the national championship game? I'm going to have to crawl under a rock and die.' Fortunately, everything turned out to be fine."[591]

The Brights were now on their way to Asheville. No phone calls. She wanted to enjoy the vacation that had been so thoughtfully planned. They went through a McDonald's drive through. The phone was ringing. Karin remembered her daughter prompting her to answer it. "I'm not answering it. We're on vacation." Finally, her daughter says, "It's Jimmy Burrow, answer the phone."[592]

Karin and Jimmy talked about media interviews and an upcoming recognition event during an Ohio University basketball game. "That's when I actually met the Burrows face-to-face, at that event in late Febru-

Will Drabold appeared on the "College GameDay" set prior to the national championship game. *Photo credit: Will Drabold*

ary," said Bright. "That was just a couple weeks before the pandemic shut everything down."[593]

By Thursday, Will's fundraiser blossomed to over $400,000. And just five days after the Heisman speech, the Athens City School District Board of Education unanimously voted to change the name of the high school football stadium. Henceforth it would be Joe Burrow Stadium.

"Joe's message was about hunger and kids not having enough food, but the overarching message that I took from that speech was the idea of hope," said Bright. "There's hope. You can do this. I'm up here for you. You can be here too. From what I can tell, that is Joe Burrow's whole outlook on life. What's the next step? What's the next thing we can do? Where do we go next? How do we get better? How do we improve? I think it all links together."[594]

A few days later, Peter King spread the word further in his massively popular "Football Morning in America" column that he writes for NBC Sports. The fundraiser total was nearing $500,000 by this point. King offered a chronological play-by-play of how the inspirational story unfolded, interviewing Will, Jimmy and Karin. Bright told King, "It's a Christmas miracle. Thank God for Joe Burrow."[595]

What began as one of the greatest hardware hauls of all time, the birthday week of all birthday weeks, concluded with the kid from Southeast Ohio giving back way more than he received.

10

Welcome to the Jungle

"If you go back and look at what they did at LSU, like eighty percent of the time, they went five out. Five-man protection, get everybody out, put it in the quarterback's hands, deal the football. Where he thrived was quick decisions, accuracy and decision-making. And that, to me, is exactly how I played the game."[596]

—Kurt Warner
NFL Hall of Fame quarterback

You know you've arrived when restaurants start naming food after you. From Ohio to Louisiana, you can find a variety of cuisine—breakfast, lunch, and dinner—named in honor of the 2019 Heisman Trophy winner.

It all began when Travis Brand changed the Western omelet to "The Burrow" following Joe's shout-out to Gigi's during that Marty and Joe interview. Then Zippy's in Baton Rouge added the "Joey Burriteaux" to the menu after the LSU quarterback came in and ordered a build-your-own tortilla (steak, rice, cheese, corn, grilled onions, guacamole, sour cream and salsa).[597] It comes in either regular or Heisman size.

When Cincinnati selected Joe Burrow number-one overall in the 2020 NFL draft, Izzy's added "The Bengal King" to their menu. Serving the Queen City since 1901, this sandwich is an "overstuffed Reuben with corned beef, fresh sauerkraut, Thousand Island dressing and melted imported Swiss cheese on 'striped' marble rye.'"[598]

But if you're looking for a high-end culinary experience, you can't go wrong with one of Cincinnati's finest dining establishments, Jeff Ruby's Steakhouse. Through the years, guests have enjoyed such offerings as the "Steak Collinsworth," the "Marty and Joe," and "Boomer's Blue Crab Bisque."

While Ruby's restaurants aren't sports bars, the menu honors local athletic icons. "Our guests want that, they like that," said Ruby in an interview with ABC-affiliate WCPO. Ruby says he's had a lot of professional athletes approach him about getting on the menu, but it's tough to make the cut.

The kid from Southeast Ohio never had to ask.

"When I saw the speech he gave while accepting the Heisman Trophy, that moved me," says Ruby, who has a foundation that focuses on childhood poverty.

So, before Joe was ever drafted by the Bengals, the "Steak Burrow" was born. In honor of his jersey number, $9 from every order goes to the Athens County Food Pantry. Ruby says "it's an esoteric process" creating a dish that properly reflects the aura of the athlete. In this case, a fourteen-ounce, blackened strip with creole crawfish sauce. If the picture on the wall is any indication, Joe heartily approves.

Joe samples his namesake steak at Jeff Ruby's. *Photo credit: Jeff Ruby Culinary Entertainment*

You can find the "Steak Burrow" on the menu at each of Ruby's establishments throughout Ohio and Kentucky. Joe's favorite location is the original restaurant, The Precinct. When the hosts of the "Full Send" podcast interviewed him in one of The Precinct's private rooms, they asked if he'd ever eaten there before.

Joe didn't hesitate, "All the time, this is my spot."[599]

The Precinct is not only Joe Burrow's favorite fine-dining destination, Ruby's sizzling steaks and swanky cigars have played a role in one of the most remarkable turnaround stories in NFL history.

Bungle for Burrow

On February 4, 2019, Mike Brown hired Zac Taylor as the Cincinnati Bengals' tenth head coach. He replaced Marvin Lewis, who in sixteen years guided the Bengals to a 131–122–3 record. Lewis's teams won four division titles and advanced to the playoffs seven times, but never won a postseason game. Arguably the most crushing defeat came in 2016 against the Pittsburgh Steelers when a fumble and two penalties snatched defeat from the jaws of victory in the final ninety-six seconds.

Taylor was no stranger to the city of Cincinnati, having worked as the UC offensive coordinator and quarterbacks coach under Tommy Tuberville. The thirty-five-year-old Norman, Oklahoma, native also brought five years of NFL experience—three with the Dolphins (quarterbacks coach and offensive coordinator) and two with the Rams (receivers and quarterbacks coach)—before becoming the second youngest head coach in the National Football League.

The day before accepting the head job with the Bengals, Taylor was standing next to Sean McVay on the sidelines at Super Bowl LIII in Mercedes-Benz Stadium, where in ten months, championship confetti would swirl around Joe Burrow not once, but twice following decisive SEC and Peach Bowl victories.

Like Burrow, Taylor was a quarterback. And like Burrow, he was no stranger to transferring—starting his career at Wake Forest before shifting to Butler Community College and eventually the University of Nebraska. He missed playing with Joe's brother, Dan, by one season when he took over the Cornhusker signal-calling duties in 2005. After an up-and-down junior campaign, Taylor threw for a school-record 3,197 yards and was named the Big 12 Offensive Player of the Year as a senior. He was inducted into the University of Nebraska Football Hall of Fame in 2017.

As the Bengals new boss, Taylor would bring a youthful and innovative offensive mind plucked fresh off the Sean McVay coaching tree. He would also bring a philosophy of drafting and signing talented players with a track record of leadership and character. High performance guys who check the Jack Marucci boxes of intelligence, off-field discipline, coachability, and respect for everybody inside the building. Players who excel in these areas are often team captains, which is where Taylor's coaching staff, the front office and scouting department would focus their search for future talent.

But it would take time.

Taylor's first year was rough. The 2019 Bengals lost their initial eleven games, the worst start in the fifty-one-year history of the franchise. Taylor benched quarterback Andy Dalton in favor of rookie Ryan Finley. After the offense continued to sputter, Dalton regained his starting role in Week 13 and guided Cincinnati to a 22–6 victory over the New York Jets.

The one win did nothing to stymie the "Bungle for Burrow" chants among the Bengal fanbase, which had recently shifted from "Tank for Tua" after Joe outplayed Tagovailoa in the head-to-head matchup in early November. Of course, for folks in Athens County, Burrow was always the guy.

Following back-to-back losses to the Browns and Patriots, the Bengals traveled to Miami to play in "The Burrow Bowl"—just eight days after the Heisman Trophy presentation. The first-overall pick in the 2020 NFL Draft was up for grabs with the loser winning the grand prize.

Only one problem for the Bengals. Andy Dalton didn't get the memo.

The Red Rifle fired for nearly 400 yards and four touchdowns, including three scoring strikes in the last 5:01 of regulation to bring the Bengals back from a 35–12 second-half deficit. Dalton's "heroics" sent the game into overtime, but the Dolphins eventually kicked a game-winning field goal and handed Joe Burrow to the Bengals. Leading up to the draft, the Miami front office would try to take him back by offering three first-round picks.

The Bengals had no interest.[600]

They had their man.

Secret Sauce

After a mind-blowing hardware haul in December and a national championship in January, Joe Burrow was now being compared to a slew of successful pro quarterbacks. Every analyst, scout and GM had their own take in the lead up to April's NFL Draft.

ESPN's Adam Schefter spoke to many front-office executives who likened Burrow to Jared Goff, the Rams' signal-caller who had previously blossomed under Zac Taylor's tutelage: "They say efficient, polished, accurate, pretty good arm.... He's a quick decision-maker. More of your typical drop-back guy."[601]

Schefter's ESPN colleagues Mel Kiper and Todd McShay had their own takes. "He reminds me a lot of Tony Romo with his delivery and the way he manipulates the pocket," said Kiper. Offered McShay, "I see more of Carson Wentz.... a guy who plays the quarterback position like a linebacker."[602]

CBS college football analyst Gary Danielson likened Burrow to Bengal great Kenny Anderson, saying, "Kenny was the best for those years and I think he'd be a great fit for Cincinnati."[603]

Danielson and colleague Rick Neuheisel were among the first to boldly compare Burrow to Tom Brady. NFL Network's Daniel Jeremiah agreed,

"When you watch these guys side by side, Tom Brady mechanically, watch what you see from Brady and tell me this does not look identically the same from Joe Burrow. It is eerie."[604]

Fox Sports' Joel Klatt found the best comparison in Hall-of-Famer Joe Montana. According to Klatt, they are "eerily similar. He's a good basketball player, throws a ridiculously catchable ball, has great footwork." Klatt thought Clemson did a commendable job trying to fluster Burrow, but to no avail. "Guess what happened? No effect whatsoever."[605]

NFL Network analyst Lance Zierlein thought the best comp for Joe was a different Hall-of-Famer—Burrow family friend Kurt Warner. "Burrow is self-assured and plays with competitive toughness that teammates will gravitate toward instantly," wrote Zierlein. "He's a rhythm passer who benefited from tempo and scheme, but his vision, touch and read recognition made the offense special. He buys time for himself inside the pocket, but creates explosive, off-schedule plays outside of it with his arm or legs. He throws with staggering precision and timing."[606]

Jimmy Burrow sees the similarities, as well. "Kurt was a very accurate passer and that's one of Joe's strongest points," says the former Barnstormer assistant coach. "Kurt was very competitive and a good basketball player in high school, too. Like Joe, Kurt wasn't a big yell and scream guy, but the team rallied around him as a leader. There are definitely similarities."[607]

When asked about the comparison, Kurt offered two thumbs up. "If you go back and look at what they did at LSU, like eighty percent of the time, they went five out," said Warner. "Five-man protection, get everybody out, put it in the quarterback's hands, deal the football. Where he thrived was quick decisions, accuracy and decision-making. And that, to me, is exactly how I played the game."[608]

While Joe appreciates many of the above comparisons, ultimately he just wants to be the best version of himself. "Everyone has their own secret sauce," says Burrow. "You can't steal someone else's. If Burger King tried to make Cane's sauce, it would be crap. Everyone has to have their own. You just have to find it."[609]

Inside Information

The NFL Draft has become quite the event. In 2019, 600,000 people flooded Music City USA, but the 2020 Las Vegas draft was primed to blow Nashville out of the water. With players ferried to the red carpet by boat and a stage surrounded by the Bellagio Fountains, it would be an unforgettable weekend.

Ron Ricketts remembers one of his trips to Vegas with great fondness. It was ten months before the 2020 NFL Draft. Right before he was set to leave, Ricketts was drinking a beer with Jimmy Burrow at Cat's Corner. "We were talking and Jimmy asks me what I've been doing," recalls Ricketts. "I told him I was going to Vegas on Monday. He said, 'Do you know you can bet on Joe to win the Heisman out there?' I said, 'No, I didn't know that.' Jimmy said, 'Yeah, he's 150 to 1.' I said, 'Well hell, I'll put $20 on him to win it. In Vegas, that's like throwing $20 in the middle of the street.' Before I got out of the bar, five other guys gave me $20 to do the same thing."[610]

Six months later, Ricketts and his Athens buddies were back in Cat's Corner watching the Heisman announcement. They not only celebrated Joe's victory; they flashed around their winning stubs displaying a $3,020 payout. "After I won the money, someone asked me, 'Why didn't you bet more?' I asked them, 'How much did you bet?'"[611]

Some Athenians did bet more, one winning as much as $30,000. Justice Robert Stewart didn't win that much, but he did place a modest bet. "We were in Vegas that August before Joe's senior year and Bob decided to place $100 on Joe to win the Heisman," says wife, Machelle. "It was such a sweet gesture on

Bob's part. He had so much faith in Joe, having watched him in high school. We Athenians felt like no one else knew what we knew. You guys don't know what he's capable of. It was like we had inside information."[612]

The Pandemic Draft

Joe was a bit relieved when the Pandemic moved the draft from the glitzy Las Vegas strip to Roger Goodell's sanitized basement. Burrow was definitely disappointed about the circumstances, but happy to keep it simple. He wore a white long-sleeve T with an outline of the state of Ohio. The area code 740 ran across the center of his chest.

A camera pointed at Joe and his parents sitting on their living room couch. It's where the Burrows have lived since they moved to The Plains in 2005. Through the years, it was a popular hangout for Joe's large friend group. "The boys would often go over to the Burrows on one corner and the girls would head to Kaitlin Baker's house on the other corner," remembers Heather Skinner, whose daughter, Sara, ran with the group. "Eventually, the boys and girls would end up in the backyard playing something. They spent a lot of time together and that brought the adults together, too."[613]

With memories like these, it's not hard to see why Joe's childhood home has a special place in his heart. So special, that when Robin and Jimmy raised the possibility of selling it to move closer to their son, a surprised Joe asked, "You'd sell our house?" Jimmy replied, "Well, maybe." In response, Joe made his wishes clearly known: "I always want my home to be here so I am able to come back." Adds Robin with a chuckle, "That's what he thinks now. When he's the one who has to go through all that stuff in the basement, I'm not so sure."[614]

Joe's love for his hometown has never been a secret. So, when rumors started circulating that he might not want to play in Cincinnati, less than two-and-a-half hours from his mother's home cooking, Robin told a reporter: "We have no idea where that comes from. It's a story out there that someone's created that doesn't have any substance—from our perspective at least."[615]

A few misconstrued comments and fallacious inferences kept the rumor in the news cycle for weeks. Near the end of February, Burrow cleared things up at the NFL Scouting Combine. "You know the only thing that I've said is that I just didn't want to be presumptuous about the number-one pick so that's why I've been non-committal," said Burrow. "I don't know what's going to happen. They might not pick me. They might fall in love with someone else. So, you guys kind of took that narrative and ran with it, but there's never been anything like that from my end."[616]

In an interview with Cris Collinsworth, Joe would later make it clear that both sides were smitten from the outset. "Being from Ohio, this is where I wanted to be," says Burrow. "And then you sit down with Zac Taylor. I mean Zac's unbelievable. He's going to be great for us for a long time. Me and him have a special relationship. There was chemistry from the very first meeting we had at the combine. So, this is a dream for me to be quarterback of the Bengals."[617]

Burrow to the Bengals was a dream come true for the folks of Athens County, too. While Southeastern Ohio has long been divided between the Bengals, Browns and Steelers, everyone is Team Burrow.

"There are a lot of Browns and Steelers fans in the Athens area," says Jimmy. "But we're starting to convert some of them. You're beginning to see more and more Bengals flags flying in people's yards."[618]

Sam Smathers is a lifetime Browns fan; He's not going to convert. But he will always root for the team Joe is leading. That's why Sam carved the Bengals' "B" logo into his Dawg Pound work bench, but replaced "ENGALS" with "URROWS." "I cheer for the Cincinnati Burrows," says a smiling Sam.[619] It's his subtle attempt to support Joe without betraying the team on the lake.

Kevin Goldsberry is in the same boat. As an avid Browns' fan, he solves his dilemma by attending Bengals' games in LSU attire. Jeff Skinner can't shake his lifelong commitment to the Black and Gold, but always pulls for Joe when Pittsburgh and Cincinnati collide.

But the planets couldn't have aligned more perfectly for Athenians who were pre-existing Bengals fans. Like Joe's high school offensive coordinator Nathan White, who told WCPO in a pre-draft interview, "I have a Boomer Esiason poster on my classroom wall and I'd love to throw a Joe Burrow one right next to it. That'd be pretty neat."[620]

Nobody in Athens was more amped about Joe donning the Stripes than the "Twin Towers," two of Joe's favorite childhood targets. Liz Luehrman confirms her sons' lifelong Bengal fanaticism, which includes dressing up as Carson Palmer for Halloween and wearing Chad and Rudi Johnson jerseys to their first game at Paul Brown Stadium in 2006. "Bill is from Cincinnati, so our kids were naturally Cincinnati sports fans," says Liz. "They've always loved the Bengals."[621]

Joe even gave the Ohio University tight ends a shout-out at the NFL Combine. "Adam and Ryan Luehrman are my best friends from high school and they are big Bengals fans. If it works out with the Bengals they would be very excited."[622]

When Burrow's name was called as the first overall pick in the 2020 draft, he donned a Bengals' cap and hugged his beaming parents.

Heisman Trophy.

National title.

First overall pick.

Yeah, a pretty good four months for the Burrows.

Within minutes, Joe was zooming with ESPN's Suzy Kolber. She asked him how he would have responded a year ago if she had suggested he was going to be the number-one pick in the 2020 draft. "I would have told you, you were crazy," replied Joe. "I knew I was going to have a really good season because I knew we had really good players coming back. I had great coaches. And we were going to work really, really hard to do it, but to jump up to number-one overall is crazy to me, but it's a dream come true."[623]

Kolber then asked about the message behind the 740-area code on his shirt. "740 is the Athens County area," said Joe. "I wanted to get something to represent my home area, my hometown and Nike made this for me. It's been great. I just want to show as much appreciation to this area as I can."[624]

While Joe was all about simplicity and giving a shout out to his hometown, he did add a dash of Vegas glitz on draft night. A silver diamond encrusted #9 necklace hung around his neck, dangling between Toledo and Sandusky near the top of the state of Ohio. The chain was a gift from Baton Rouge rapper Lil Boosie.[625] It provided an interesting juxtaposition. A fashion foretaste of things to come.

Pandemic Preparation

Like a scene out of *Field of Dreams*, a line of headlights slowly snaked through the Burrow's subdivision.

Get drafted number one, and they will come.

Honking horns and shouts of encouragement filled the air outside the Burrow abode, while inside Joe fielded questions from the national media.

"I think the high school organized it," recalls Robin. "The bad thing was that Joe was tied up with interviews so he didn't even get to see it or wave or anything. We couldn't open the door because it was so loud, but Jimmy and I stood at the window and waved."[626]

Earlier in the day, the Sheriff's Department placed a car in front of the Burrow house to keep people from coming to the door. Jimmy also parked Joe's car in Tim Albin's driveway behind the house. Following his media obligations, Joe quietly slipped through the backyard, hopped in the car and drove off to a secluded cabin in the woods, where he celebrated with some high school buddies.

"It was all incognito," says Robin with a grin. "The whole thing was so crazy."[627]

Before escaping through the backyard, Joe spoke with ESPN's Scott Van Pelt. He asked Joe to share what he was pondering when he got the call. "The first thought that went through my mind was I'm ready to get to work," said Burrow in between bites of chicken wings. "That's the way we're going to win a lot of football games. I'm going to get to practice and get to doing what I do best. And that's preparing the best way that I can.... Everything has to be a step faster, a twitch better."[628]

Joe is often asked about the source of his confidence. One of his best responses came in a conversation with Dan Patrick. "It comes from preparation. I win the games on Monday, Tuesday, Wednesday and Thursday. I don't win them on Saturday."[629]

Make that Sunday now.

Like everyone, Joe was affected by the pandemic. But there was no time to pout or sulk. Instead, while living at home in The Plains, Burrow committed to a regimented workout schedule with personal trainer and Ohio University strength and conditioning coach Dak Notestine. A typical week looked like this:

While Joe threw to the Luehrman twins during the pandemic, Zacciah Saltzman (pictured) was his training partner. *Photo credit: Trisha Doudna*

- Monday, Tuesday, Thursday and Friday: Lifting
- Saturday: Light lifting (biceps/triceps)
- Sunday: 7–10-mile bike ride
- Three or four days a week: Throwing[630]

Since A.J. Green, Tyler Boyd and Tee Higgins weren't around, Joe threw to some of his favorite high school targets instead. Pandemic restrictions made it difficult to find a facility. At first they threw on Smathers Field, where Joe's career as a quarterback began. Eventually, they were permitted to throw on Nelsonville York's high school field.

"Joe was throwing to the Luehrmans and me," remembers Zacciah Saltzman, who played at Georgetown University after graduating from AHS. "But I was coming off a broken hand. After catching a few of Joe's passes, it hurt so much I had to stop. So, he'd throw to the Luehrmans, then he and I would condition together. I got in the best shape of my life because we were trying to beat each other out all summer."[631]

Joe spent hours on Zoom calls with his new teammates and coaches, learning the playbook, asking questions, practicing his cadence, calling audibles, and running through a variety of simulations. There was also a memorable phone call with Peyton Manning. "I felt like we were in very similar situations coming in and he felt the same," said Burrow during a July press conference. "He just gave me a lot of different advice when it came to marketing, how to handle the huddle, how to handle coaches, how assertive to be in your first year and how you build upon that."[632]

Once restrictions eased, Joe worked out at Athens High School and discussed schemes with Coach White. While the pandemic added an extra hurdle, White was certain his former quarterback would establish himself as the Bengals' leader in due time.

"By week five or six when he was a sophomore…he was our leader," recalls White. "And very rarely in high school football are leaders not seniors.

And very rarely if they're not, are the seniors OK with that. He's going to go in and work hard and earn their respect first and then slowly become more of a vocal leader. I'll be shocked if he doesn't win over that locker room in the first couple years."[633]

As it turned out, it didn't take years.

Try weeks.

By the end of training camp, his teammates had selected him as a captain. "He's the leader of this locker room," said safety Jessie Bates. "He's going to be the face of this franchise for many years to come."[634]

"It was one of my goals coming in," admitted Burrow. "I didn't expect to be a captain, but I couldn't be happier to represent our team and our offense."[635]

Burrow's leadership was a frequent talking point among his teammates throughout camp, but their faith in him became crystal clear when he was asked to read a statement on racial equality at the National Underground Railroad Freedom Center near the end of August.

Earlier in the summer, in the wake of George Floyd's death and national protests, Joe had tweeted, "The Black community needs our help. They have been unheard for far too long. Open your ears, listen, and speak. This isn't politics. This is human rights."[636]

Joe didn't let anyone know he was going to make the social media post. His parents and marketing representative found out by reading it online. Jimmy said he and Robin have always been proud of their son for caring about various social issues. After the Heisman speech, Joe began to realize the power of his platform. Said Jimmy, "You know if you believe in something, no matter if you're a rookie or a veteran, and you feel you can have an impact…then you put it out there."[637]

Zacciah Saltzman believes Joe's commitment to equality and basic human decency is a product of growing up in Athens, which includes not only Appalachia, but a cosmopolitan community with nearly 120 international countries represented among the Ohio University population.[638] Saltzman says exposure to a broad range of diversity has helped Joe become the leader he is today.

"Joe and I were talking about this one time and he told me some players don't exactly know how to communicate with everybody in the locker room," says Zacciah. "I think one of the reasons why he's so good in the locker room is because he was exposed to so many different people growing up. You think even about the arrival of the LGBTQ movement nationally. We were accepting of folks in that community our whole life. So, when you're exposed to a diverse group of people, from hippies to country folk, you realize all these people are great people. I think growing up in Athens is one reason why he is a really strong leader now."[639]

The First Nine Games

The last time Joe Burrow was on a football field, he led LSU to a national title in front of 77,000 screaming fans. In the first nine games of his NFL career, number nine would play in front of 50,000 fans. Total.

The pandemic presented challenges for every organization, every team, every player, but especially for starting rookie quarterbacks.

Make that starting rookie quarterback.

Singular.

Burrow was the only first-year signal caller who would break camp with the starting gig.

Figuring out NFL defenses is difficult under the best of circumstances, but without the benefit of preseason games, Burrow would need to learn on the fly.

Mistakes were inevitable. After the opening game loss to the Chargers, the Bengal quarterback gave himself a "D" grade. Two second-half miscues stood out in his mind—an overthrown touchdown ball to a wide-open A.J.

Green and an errant shovel-pass that landed in the arms of Charger linebacker Melvin Ingram.[640]

Still, after those two mistakes, a resilient and rhythmic Burrow drove the Bengals 84 yards on 14 plays down to the Charger three-yard-line. If not for a controversial offensive pass interference call, Joe would have emerged triumphant in his first NFL outing.

In the first nine games, number nine connected on 65 percent of his passes for an average of 276 yards per game. Burrow consistently took what the defense gave him, distributing the ball to at least seven different receivers on seven occasions. He connected with nine receivers twice. In weeks two, three and four, Burrow became the first rookie in NFL history to pass for at least 300 yards in three consecutive games. In the final game of that stretch, Burrow notched his first NFL victory as a starting quarterback by defeating Jacksonville, 33–25. Cincinnati racked up 505 total yards, becoming the first Bengal team since 1988 to rush for 200 yards and pass for 300 yards in a single contest.

In the first nine games, number nine showed supreme toughness. He was sacked thirty times, including eight against a relentless Philadelphia Eagle defense. Time and again, Burrow played quarterback like a linebacker. Taking hit after hit, he bounced right backup like Tom Brady.

On one particular play, midway through the second quarter, Burrow scrambled and tossed the ball away. As he was heading out of bounds, defensive tackle Fletcher Cox pushed him late. No flag. Lying flat on his back, Burrow looked up at the referee and said, "Hey that was a little late, don't you think?" Cox said, "You're not getting that call, Rook." A feisty Burrow had the final word, "I'll get that call when I'm the GOAT."[641]

In the first nine games, number nine saw familiar faces on the other side of the ball, including former Buckeye teammates Joey Bosa (Chargers) and Denzel Ward (Browns) and former Tiger teammates K'Lavon Chaisson (Jaguars) and Patrick Queen (Ravens). Burrow's least-favorite reunion came against Baltimore as Queen recorded nine tackles, including a strip sack and fumble recovery for a touchdown. For his efforts, Burrow's former sparring partner was named AFC Defensive Player of the Week. The tables would turn the following year.

In the first nine games, number nine frequently showed why he was the first overall pick. Like when he engineered three quick touchdown drives against the Colts—a week after his offense couldn't cross the goal line against the Ravens. Like when he threw for 722 yards in two narrow losses to the Browns. Like when he led the Bengals to a 31–20 victory over the 5–1 Tennessee Titans without Joe Mixon and four starting offensive linemen.

In the first nine games, despite a 2–6–1 record, number nine was bringing hope to the Bengal fanbase.

Then came Week 11, and a trip to the nation's capital.

No Pouting Here

A few days before Thanksgiving, Joe squared off against the Vander Vens' favorite NFL team—the Washington Commanders (at the time, The Washington Football Team). Raised in the D.C. area, Tom naturally grew up loving his hometown boys. Moving to Indiana and then Ohio later in life did nothing to squelch his allegiance. Tom naturally passed along to Sam his passion for the Burgundy and Gold.

"I've never switched to another team just because I moved to a new area," says Tom, who makes a living studying social factors that shape individuals, families and communities. "It's really not a choice. Your team is your team. It's part of your DNA."[642]

If you don't choose your team, I guess you don't choose your friendships, either. Well, at least not all of them. Some are just meant to be. Like the one the Vander Vens and Burrows forged, going all the way back to the first summer their kids played baseball together for the Athens County All-Stars.

So, what happens when an immovable allegiance meets an unstoppable friendship? If you are Dot Burrow, maybe you just go to the other room and refuse to watch. But for the Vander Vens, turning a blind eye to this game would not be an option.

It was a low-scoring affair in the first half with Cincinnati taking a 9–7 lead into the break. The score, however, didn't reflect Burrow's crisp efficiency. He threw for nearly 200 yards, moving the Bengal offense up and down FedEx Field. But two missed field goals and a fumble at the Washington goal line kept the game close.

There was also cause for concern. In the middle of the second quarter, newly signed offensive guard Quinton Spain was beaten badly by Commander defensive lineman Daron Payne, who made a beeline for Burrow. He not only sacked the Bengals' quarterback, but ripped his helmet clean off his head. While Payne was flagged 15 yards for a facemask penalty, it was a harbinger of things to come.

After both teams exchanged punts at the start of the second half, the Bengals faced a third and two at their own 10-yard line. Burrow took the shotgun snap. The pocket quickly collapsed. As he released the ball, two Washington defenders met at the quarterback—one high, one low. Burrow fell to the ground, grasping his left knee in pain.

Due to the pandemic, Jimmy and Robin didn't make the trip to D.C. They watched from the Burrow homestead in The Plains. "When they said we're not going to show it again on TV, that kind of put us over the edge of any hope that maybe he was going be okay," said Jimmy in an interview with FOX19 TV. Robin went into mother mode, tossing things into a suitcase. "From my point of view, immediately I was like oh my gosh we need to pack our bags. We've got to figure out where we're going."[643]

Before Joe was carted off the field, Bengal teammates clasped hands with their leader and offered words of encouragement. Buckeye brothers Dwayne Haskins and Chase Young came from the opposing sideline to show their support. Just a year earlier, Young and Burrow were sitting two seats apart on Heisman night. When Burrow's name was called, Young was the first person to hear words of warmth and affection from Joe. He now returned those same words to his fallen friend.

When Joe arrived home in Cincinnati, his parents were there ready to assist in any way they could. Jimmy remembers Joe kept steering the conversation back to the game. "Of course, we were wanting to know all about the injury and he just wanted to talk about how well they played in the first half."[644]

On the bus ride out of FedEx Field, Burrow sat next to longtime Bengals athletic trainer Paul Sparling. Through the years, Sparling has not only treated countless aches and breaks, but also has tended to the mental and emotional state of players dealing with devastating injuries. "I try to have empathy and accept the fact that it's going to be hard to deliver them bad news, but I think it's better for them to hear it straight up from the very beginning and not give them false hopes," said Sparling in a conversation with Dan Hoard.[645]

The Bengals trainer allows players twenty-four hours to emotionally process the reality of their situation, then it's time to move forward. According to Sparling, Burrow is the gold standard when it comes to handling bad news. "The guy who really demonstrated that to me was Joe Burrow. When I talked to him and gave him the same story on the bus on the way to the airport, I told him my philosophy of twenty-four hours and he said, 'There's no pouting here. I'm working on getting back.' That spoke volumes to me."[646]

The hit tore Joe's ACL and MCL. He would undergo reconstructive surgery on December 2, eight days before his twenty-fourth birthday. It would be a very different birthday week this year. Instead of traveling the country receiving awards, Burrow would be traveling a different road—the long road to recovery. But if anybody was up for it, it was Joe Burrow.

His tweet, shortly after the injury, summed up the impeccable Burrow resolve: "Thanks for all the love. Can't get rid of me that easy. See ya next year."[647]

11

Why Not Us?

"We've got the pieces, we've got coaches telling us what to do, we've got guys who've been in the system long enough. We just need to go out there and do what we need to do. Why not us? Why not us?"[648]

—C.J. Uzomah

When the 2021 camp opened, Joe Burrow welcomed two old friends to the Bengal organization.

Cincinnati finished the 2020 season with a 4–11–1 record, which granted Mike Brown, Duke Tobin, Zac Taylor and the rest of the Bengal brass the fifth overall pick. Leading up to the draft, national pundits and Bengal Nation were split between best available offensive lineman Penei Sewell and top receiver Ja'Marr Chase.

While Team Sewell appreciated adding another weapon, they argued Burrow would not be able to throw the ball lying flat on his back. Team Chase, on the other hand, understood the importance of strengthening the O-line, but reasoned quick passes to a dynamic playmaker would protect their franchise quarterback while also putting points on the board.

Both sides agreed on one thing: It was good to see Roger Goodell in a public venue instead of his basement. As Goodell strolled to the podium in Cleveland, Bengal fans held their collective breath. "With the fifth pick in the 2021 NFL Draft, the Cincinnati Bengals select Ja'Marr Chase, wide receiver, LSU."

Joe and Ja'Marr were reunited.

The second old friend to reunite with Burrow that spring was fellow Bulldog Evan Cooley. While many of their high school buddies stayed in Athens and attended Ohio University, Joe and Evan were among the few who ventured off upon graduation. Joe to Ohio State; Evan to UC, where he earned a degree in Electronic Media.

Evan graduated in 2019, just before COVID started shutting everything down. He explored jobs in the Cincinnati area. The Bengals were on his list. He texted Joe, who gave him contact information for the Bengals video director Travis Brammer. Because of the pandemic, everything was up in the air. Brammer told Cooley to sit tight. When normalcy returned, Evan was hired to shoot footage for long-time Special Teams Coordinator, Darrin Simmons.

"I don't like to say Joe got me the job, because I had the video experience," says Evan. "But when you're applying for a job with the Bengals, having Joe Burrow's name in the subject line doesn't hurt."[649]

Evan Cooley and Joe winning another trophy. *Photo credit: The Cooley Family.*

Joe and Evan have known each other since second grade. They're like brothers. And while brothers love each other, sometimes they like to punk each other, too. A smiling Ryan Luehrman confirms: "Evan is the one guy in our friend group who really knows how to press Joe's buttons."[650]

Case in point: Growing up, Cooley had two phone numbers he would give to people. When it was someone he wanted to communicate with, he gave his own number. Everybody else got Joe's. "I always know Joe's phone number because if there was ever like 'give your number for a blood drive or give your number for this email list,' I'd just write Joe's number." Evan also worked at the Athena Grand Movie Theater and from time to time a girl would ask for his digits. Since he already had a girlfriend, Evan would say, "Yeah, I got ya." And he'd type in Joe's number instead.

But Joe knows how to play the numbers game as well. When Evan was younger, he wore the number 21 in honor of Reds' first baseman Sean Casey. In middle school, Evan shifted to number 10. But when they got to high school it was Joe's turn to get the last laugh. "Joe made varsity before I did and he stole my number," said Evan, with a hint of playful resentment.[651]

Given their history, it's not surprising that the shenanigans would continue when they started working together. "Darrin is very particular about his practice footage," says Evan. "He doesn't want any of the players blocking his shots." Most of the veterans know to stay out of the way. Occasionally Cooley will politely ask a rookie to move aside if filming an Evan McPherson field goal or Kevin Huber punt.

But one day the Bengals were practicing inside Paul Brown Stadium. Everything was compact, so not much room to spread out. Joe happened to be standing in front of Evan's camera.

"I said, 'Joe do you mind moving over?'" remembers Evan. "He just glares at me and gives me that stupid grin of his. I said, 'Joe, C'mon.' He keeps staring at me and smiling. Finally, I said, 'Dude, get the f*** out of the way!' A lot of guys don't know my relationship with Joe. So, when Stanley Morgan overheard this, he was like, 'Oh, s***! Oh wow!' I just whisper to him, 'It's OK, I know him. We've got some history.'"[652]

Joe Is Just Joe

Stanley Morgan might have been surprised by the special teams videographer barking at the franchise quarterback, but Ryan Luehrman wasn't. "We don't let him get away with anything. He's just the same Joe to us."[653] Nathan White remembers it was always that way, going back to high school. "When they hung out, Joe was just Joe," White says. "Another one of the dudes. They didn't care that he had an Ohio State offer or not, which was really cool."[654]

While a lot of famous people leave their childhood friends behind, that's not Joe. Zacciah Saltzman says success has never gone to his friend's head. "He has no interest in fame," says Zacciah. "He talks with us in group texts every day. Joe has the same friends now that he had growing up. When you stay close to your roots, you're not going to change."[655]

Evan's dad, Don Cooley, says, "Joe loves hanging out with his high school buddies because they don't want anything from him. They treat him the same—as if he had a job at Nationwide Insurance."[656]

Jimmy and Robin remember the large friend group of boys and girls back in high school, but the boys always had designated alone time. "The boys and girls did things together, but then there were times when it was just the boys," recalls Jimmy. "If you had a girlfriend she couldn't come over." [657] Robin agrees: "Girls were not invited. The boys were very protective of their time together. They still are. That's just the way it is. That's the way it has always been."[658]

While Cooley and Burrow usually stay in their own lanes at work, brotherly banter is par for the course after hours. Every Monday is Game Night, which allows the old friends to cut up, give each other a hard time and goof off. Just like when they were hanging out in high school. "Typically, we'll start out with some Grand Theft Auto, then play Star Wars after that," says Evan. "It's called a party, but it's just a big group chat."[659]

While his buddies have the utmost respect for Joe, there's no deference or genuflecting on Game Night. Joe's not in charge. Everything's a group decision. "If Joe is just with our group of friends, no one gives a s*** what he has to say," explains Evan with endearing, but unvarnished candor. "Joe gets what he wants all day. Everyone's always trying to make Joe happy, so I imagine it's actually quite refreshing for him to be just one of the guys."[660]

As a high school quarterbacks coach, it might be tempting for Sam Vander Ven to pick the brain of one of the most accomplished signal callers in the world. But he says the group doesn't talk about football. "Joe is just Joe," says Sam. "We just talk about high school memories. The last thing he wants to talk about is football."[661]

They razz each other about little things that took place a decade ago. Seemingly innocuous moments at the time. But in retrospect, they carry more weight. Each story and memory like a link in a sacred chain that binds their brotherhood together.

Like the time Joe came out to an open baseball practice the summer following his sophomore year. A rusty Burrow walked to the plate. "Joe was talking trash," remembers Vander Ven with a nostalgic grin. "I threw him one pitch and he hit a weak dribbler back to me. We gave him so much grief."[662]

Continues Sam, "We reminisce about old stuff and are absolute fools talking about nothing, but at the end of the day we really just need to be Joe's friends."[663]

For Joe Burrow, Monday Game Nights are a normalizing counterpoint to the glitz, glamour and stratospheric hype of Monday Night Football. But trash talking and goofing around with his old Athens pals is more than a diversion for the Bengals franchise quarterback, it keeps him tethered to his roots. It's where he feels most at home.

The Road Back

Dak Notestine grew up in Northern Ohio, but often traveled to Athens to visit family. He fell in love with the picturesque "fairytale" campus nestled in the foothills of the Appalachian Mountains. So, when it came time to pick a college, the Bellefontaine football star put Ohio University on his short list. Newly hired defensive coordinator Jimmy Burrow got Dak across the goal line.

"[Coach Burrow] was exactly who I thought he was during the recruiting process," said Notestine in an interview with the *Ohio News*. "He always asked about how I was doing. He really did care about us, as players, and you felt it."[664]

Notestine walked on, but by the time he was a senior the defensive end had not only earned a starting gig but the role of team captain. After graduation, Dak spent several years as the Bobcats' strength and conditioning coach. He also worked closely with some of the Athens High School players, including Joe Burrow, Trae Williams and Zacciah Saltzman.

"His workouts were brutal, but we love Dak," says Saltzman. "It gave us a huge advantage."[665]

Joe has formed a strong bond with Dak, who now serves as Burrow's personal trainer. "It just naturally grew to where anytime Joe had a question, concern, or needed insight, that I was kind of somebody in that chain that would be willing to help," says Notestine.[666]

And coming off a devastating ACL/MCL injury, Burrow needed all the help and support he could get. He underwent surgery on December 2—ten days after the injury. Eight days before his twenty-fourth birthday. The projected time for recuperation: 9–12 months. Best case scenario? Joe would be ready to go Week 1 against the Vikings.

Dr. Neal ElAttrache performed the surgery in Southern California, where Joe recuperated until the beginning of February. The early days were especially difficult. Robin and Jimmy stayed with him the first week in

Santa Monica. Joe couldn't dress himself. He needed help getting up and down the stairs and in and out of the shower. Robin waited on Joe "hand and foot." They binge-watched *House*. Jimmy and Joe tossed a football back and forth from chair to couch. Each time, Joe would examine his fingers on the laces, always trying to slightly improve his grip. During the week, Joe hopped onto Zoom with his coaches and teammates.[667]

Calls from other quarterbacks around the league also buoyed his spirits. "It was very emotional to me at the beginning because I really felt the brotherhood in the NFL," said Burrow. "Almost every single quarterback across the league reached out to me, told me they were thinking about me, and hoping my recovery goes well."[668]

By early February, Burrow returned to Cincinnati where the Bengals Director of Rehabilitation Nick Cosgray worked with Notestine to develop a physical therapy plan. Dak was by Joe's side four-to-five days a week for the next several months.

"He's so locked in," says Jimmy. "We got a week down in Florida that we had hoped he would take a day or two off in his rehab, but he just wouldn't do it."[669]

By the end of February, Joe began throwing from a stationary position to Bengals support staff. By May, he was throwing to teammates. Burrow used the time off not only to strengthen his surgically repaired left knee, but to develop his core and hips. The result would be a more explosive pass on medium and deep routes.

Joe Burrow warms up at the 2021 Back Together Saturday.
Photo credit: Scott Burson

By the time training camp rolled around in July, Burrow was physically on schedule, but still needed to gain confidence in his knee.

Doubt Joe Burrow at Your Own Peril

Cincinnati entered the 2021 training camp with optimism. The Burrow-less Bengals closed the 2020 season with wins in two of the final three games. Additionally, the front office signed several free agents on the defensive side of the ball—pass-rushing specialist Trey Hendrickson, cornerbacks Chidobe Awuzie, Mike Hilton and Eli Apple, and defensive tackle Larry Ogunjobi. D.J. Reader would also be returning from a serious quad injury to strengthen the defensive front.

On the offensive side of the ball, free-agent right tackle Riley Reiff solidified a questionable offensive line. The receiving corps got a huge boost with the selection of fifth-overall pick Ja'Marr Chase. Tight end C.J. Uzomah was also returning from a ruptured Achilles tendon that shortened his 2020 campaign. Uzomah would prove to be an inspirational leader in and out of the locker room.

"We've got the pieces, we've got coaches telling us what to do, we've got guys who've been in the system long enough," said Uzomah in an early August press conference. "We just need to go out there and do what we need to do. Why not us? Why not us?"[670]

Uzomah explained that he borrowed the "Why not us?" line from his favorite soccer team. "I'm a huge soccer guy and my team is Chelsea," continued Uzomah. "I was on this 'Blue' podcast and they were saying 'Why not us?' There's a bunch of turnover in the locker room, there's a bunch of new pieces and stuff like that. I view this [Bengals'] team in a similar way. We have a bunch of new pieces, new turnover, a culture shift. I felt like it applied perfectly to this team."[671]

Early in camp, the new-look Bengal defense dominated. Chase struggled to catch the ball. And Burrow looked uncomfortable in the pocket. Joe assured the media that once the lights go on, Ja'Marr would be fine. As for regaining his own psychological comfort, Joe said practice would solve his problems. "I wasn't panicked, just took more reps," said Burrow. "Coming off a bad injury, and I hadn't played for a while. We went out there one day and they started throwing bags at my legs. I was back to normal after that."[672]

With a 17-game schedule in 2021–22, most of the media picked the Bengals to make strides but still finish the season with a losing record. Tyler Dragon of the *Cincinnati Enquirer* had the Bengals winning six games in Taylor's third year.[673] The Vegas oddsmakers had the Bengals winning 6.5 games.[674] Few people expected Taylor's squad to make a playoff push.

That said, in mid-September, Dan Orlovsky offered the following bold pronouncement on ESPN's *First Take*: "You give me Joe Burrow and give Joe Burrow that Pittsburgh Steeler defense, I'm saying he's going to win a Super Bowl this year. He's a Super Bowl contender this year." Doubting Thomas himself, Stephen A. Smith, was stunned by Orlovsky's audacity. "What? What? This year? This year! That's insane! You've got to be kidding me! Oh, stop it!"[675]

Stephen A. Smith should've learned by now. Doubt Joe Burrow at your own peril.

While Burrow wasn't making any Super Bowl predictions during training camp, his confidence was palpable. "We are expecting to win a lot of games, make the playoffs and make a run."[676]

You Can't Zero Me!

Robin Burrow had never missed one of Joe's sporting events. Until the pandemic. But with COVID-19 protocols loosening, the Burrows would not only be attending all of Joe's games in 2021, they were also back in the tailgate business.

The Burrows would set up their tailgate in the Paul Brown Stadium parking lot several hours before kickoff—their jeep packed with beverages and snacks. Many old friends, and a few new, consistently join Robin and Jimmy for the pregame festivities.

It's a melting pot of sorts. A diverse cross-section of supporters. Athens. Chillicothe. Columbus. Cincinnati. Baton Rouge. Omaha. Houston. Representatives from who knows where else. Most have intersected with the Burrows at some point in their lives. All drawn together for the common cause of supporting Joe.

If you don't know the Burrows, their vehicle is the one with a three-foot-long stuffed Tiger on the hood. He travels to away games, too. "The Hubbards had a Mike the Tiger that they would bring to the games," says Jimmy. "Robin always wanted one, so we now have a Mike the Bengal that we put on the front of our jeep."[677]

During each tailgate, Robin and Jimmy break from chatting with family and friends to send Joe a good-luck text. He never responds. Too focused. Maybe after the game. But, like tailgating, it's all part of the pregame ritual.

The season and home opener against the Vikings would be very different from last year's opener against the Chargers. Real-life screaming fans instead of cardboard cut-outs fill the seats. Joe's pumped for the real thing. "I'm excited to see the fans," said Burrow with a beaming smile. "We're going to put a great product out on the field. Be explosive. Be exciting to watch."[678]

A crowd of over 56,000 fans made their presence known early, as Minnesota was flagged for three false starts on the opening drive. Both teams struggled to get into rhythm. With the score locked at 7–7 with thirty-five seconds to go in the half, Burrow connected on a 50-yard strike to Chase for the rookie's first touchdown catch. It was also the first chance for the Cincinnati faithful to see Ja'Marr do the griddy.

Before long, everyone would be doing the griddy.

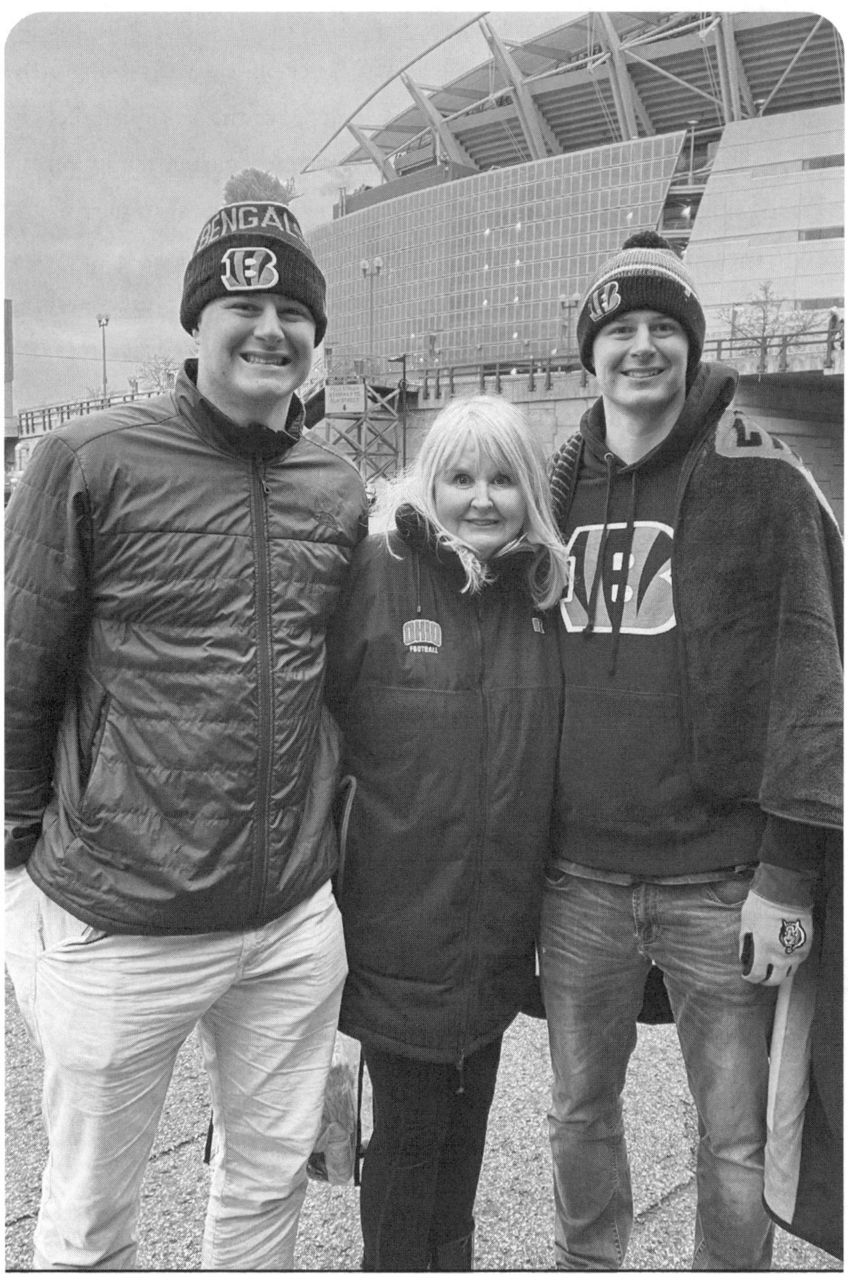

Adam, Liz and Ryan Luehrman in front of Paul Brown Stadium. *Photo credit: The Luehrman Family*

In the third quarter, a two-yard Joe Mixon touchdown run put the Bengals up 21–7 (Mixon did the griddy). After an unsuccessful fourth-down conversion on their own 30, the Bengals gave the Vikings excellent field position. With time running down in the third quarter, Kirk Cousins hit a streaking Adam Thielen for a 24-yard touchdown pass to narrow the lead to seven points.

The Vikings eventually sent the game into overtime and were marching toward a game-winning field goal when Germaine Pratt stripped the ball from Dalvin Cook and recovered it on the Bengals' 38-yard line.

After scratching out nine yards on the next three plays, Burrow hit tight end C.J. Uzomah, who rumbled for 32 yards down to the Viking 20-yard line. The pass set up the first of five game-winning field goals for rookie Evan McPherson. After the kick split the uprights, the former University of Florida kicker was lifted off the ground by fellow rookie Jackson Carmen.

Burrow connected on 20 of 27 passes for 261 yards and two touchdowns. Chase went over 100 receiving yards and Joe Mixon ran for 127 yards—what would be his second-highest total of the season.

In Week 2, the Bengals traveled to Soldier Field to take on the Bears. It was a defensive struggle most of the way. In fact, the Bengals new-look defense only gave up 206 total yards—the lowest total allowed by a Cincinnati defensive unit in seven years.

Trailing 7–3 in the fourth quarter, Burrow threw three interceptions on three consecutive passes. One for a pick six. All of a sudden, the Bears held a commanding 20–3 lead with under five minutes remaining.

But Burrow wouldn't quit. He hit a streaking Ja'Marr Chase for a 42-yard score. Following a Logan Wilson interception, Burrow connected with Tee Higgins on a seven-yard touchdown strike to narrow the margin to 20–17. But the Bengals' offense would not see the ball again. After converting two first downs, rookie quarterback Justin Fields took a knee. The Bengals fell to 1–1.

In Week 3, Cincinnati faced arch-rival Pittsburgh at Heinz Field. The Steelers had revenge on their minds after losing to the Burrow-less Bengals, 27–17, on Monday Night Football the previous December. The Bengal victory not only broke a losing streak of 11 straight games against the Steelers, but also sent a message that this Bengal team, even without Burrow under center, would not be intimidated.

Burrow was now back and the vaunted Steeler defense played without several starters, including all-pro outside linebacker T.J. Watt. For the third week in a row, it was the Burrow-to-Chase show. The Cincinnati quarterback was efficient, connecting on 14 of 18 passes. Two of them went to Chase for touchdowns. Tyler Boyd also caught a TD. The offensive line kept Burrow clean. It was the first time in 75 straight games that the Pittsburgh defense did not sack the opposing quarterback.

On the other side of the ball, Lou Anarumo's defense continued to impress. The Bengal defenders sacked Ben Roethlisberger four times and hit him on three other occasions. Logan Wilson picked off two passes as the Bengals won 24–10.

On September 30, Zac Taylor's 2–1 Bengals returned to the Jungle for a Thursday Night encounter with the Jacksonville Jaguars.

Storylines abounded.

The game featured a rematch between the last two number-one overall picks—second-year signal-caller Joe Burrow and rookie Trevor Lawrence. The two young QBs last squared off in the 2020 national championship game with Burrow getting the better of Lawrence. This primetime encounter would also pit Burrow against former Buckeye head coach Urban Meyer.

Lawrence and Meyer had their way in the first half. The Jags recorded 240 yards of total offense and were inches from taking a commanding three-touchdown lead into the break when Logan Wilson kept Lawrence from scoring on a fourth-and-goal from the one-yard line. Still, the Jaguars took a 14-0 lead into the locker room.

The Cincinnati offense looked like a different team in the second half, scoring on four straight possessions (TD, TD, TD, and FG). Playing without an injured Tee Higgins, the Bengals relied on veteran slot receiver Tyler Boyd, who hauled in nine passes for 118 yards.

The biggest beneficiary, however, was tight end C.J. Uzomah, who caught five passes for 95 yards and two touchdowns. With under a minute remaining, Burrow read the defense. It was a zero blitz. He immediately audibled into a quick screen to Uzomah, who rumbled into field goal range. A mic'd-up and hyped-up Joe jogged over to the sidelines yelling, "You can't zero me! You can't zero me!"

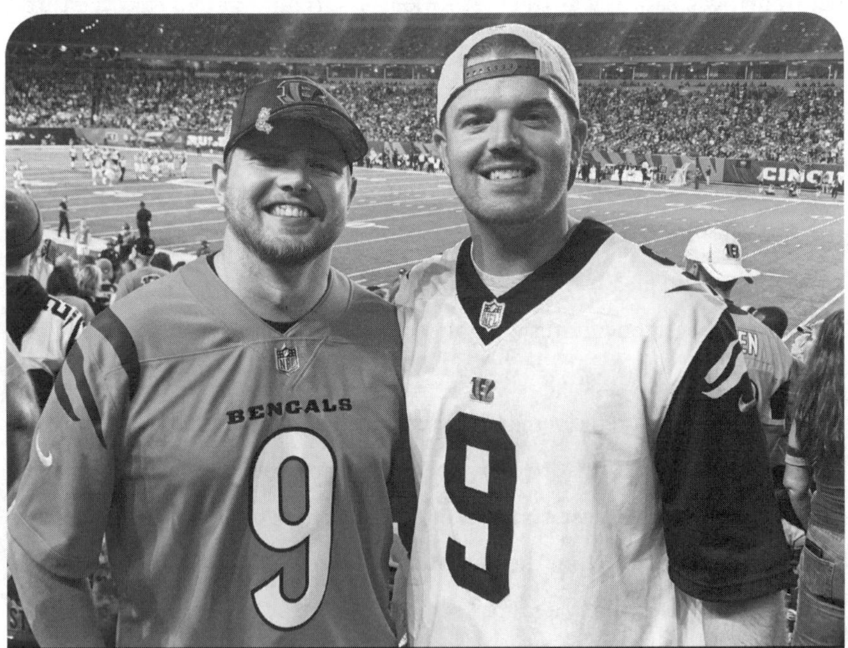

Bryce Graves, a lifelong Bengals fan, attends the Thursday night game against the Jaguars with friend Jarred Merrick. *Photo credit: Bryce Graves*

McPherson sealed the victory from 35 yards to raise the Bengals record to 3–1.

After the game, Uzomah gave all the credit to the Bengals' franchise quarterback. "We had known going in that this coach had come from the Ravens and that's what they like to do," said Uzomah. "They like to zero in critical situations. Franchise is back there just dealing dots.... [Joe's] the smartest person on the field at all times.... He's just Joey Franchise."[679]

If We Can Win This Division, We Can Win It All

In Week 5, the Bengals hosted Aaron Rodgers and the Green Bay Packers. Before a full house of 64,195, it was a game of highs, lows and swirling winds.

Receivers from both sides put on a show. Davante Adams caught 11 balls for 206 yards, while Ja'Marr Chase hauled in six passes for 159 yards. Both quarterbacks threw for two touchdowns.

The big storyline, however, wasn't pitch and catch between elite quarterbacks and receivers. Instead, the game came down to a pair of typically reliable kickers in the face of an unpredictable Ohio River wind. In the final 2:20 of regulation and throughout the overtime period, Mason Crosby and Evan McPherson combined to miss five field goals. With 1:55 remaining in the overtime period, Crosby finally connected from 49 yards to give the Packers a 27–24 victory.

The following week, the 3–2 Bengals defeated the Detroit Lions, 34–11, at Ford Field. It was Cincinnati's largest margin of victory in four seasons. Burrow accounted for three touchdowns and 271 yards through the air. Joe Mixon ran for 94 yards, while adding 59 receiving yards, including a 40-yard touchdown scamper.

The first big road test of the season for Taylor's 4–2 squad came against the 5-1 Baltimore Ravens, who owned a five-game winning streak against the Bengals. Cincinnati held a 13–10 advantage at the half, but Baltimore took the lead early in the third quarter on a 39-yard pass from Lamar Jackson to Marquise Brown.

The Bengals then scored 28 unanswered points. Four different players scored second-half touchdowns: C.J. Uzomah (32-yard pass); Ja'Marr Chase (82-yard pass); Joe Mixon (21-yard run); and Samaje Perine (46-yard run).

It was a historic day. Joe Burrow threw for a career-high 416 yards and three touchdowns. The 41–17 final score was the largest margin of victory over the Ravens in Bengal franchise history. A Bengals team had not scored that many points against the Ravens in sixteen years.

As the game was winding down, a mic'd up Burrow confidently proclaimed to Uzomah and Tee Higgins: "If we can win this division, we can win it all. We can win it all."

It was a signature win for Burrow and the young Bengals. Baltimore in Baltimore, by 24 points. People were now paying attention. "The Bengals [are] 5–2, first place in that division," said Mike Florio on Pro Football Talk. "Who'd have thought they'd be in first place in that division ever this season?"[680]

Now, to avoid a letdown.

The heavily favored Bengals took on a one-win New York Jets squad at MetLife Stadium the following week. The Jets handed the ball to backup quarterback Mike White. First-time starter. Top-10 defense. Didn't look good for White.

But that's why they play the game.

In his first career start, White completed 82 percent of his attempts and tallied 405 passing yards—the second most in NFL history by a quarterback in his initial start.

Burrow had a solid day, completing 21 of 34 passes for 259 yards and three touchdowns. The final strike was a 10-yard pass to Tyler Boyd in the middle of the fourth quarter to give the Bengals an 11-point lead. But the White-led Jets would not be denied as New York scored twice down the stretch to pull out the 34–31 victory.

The 5–3 Bengals returned to Paul Brown Stadium to host in-state rival Cleveland. After driving the Bengals' offense down to the Brown 1-yard line, Burrow targeted Ja'Marr Chase. The Bengals' receiver slipped. The ball went straight into the arms of Denzel Ward, who returned it for a 99-yard pick six.

After that opening left cross to the jaw, Cincinnati never recovered its footing. The stout Bengals' defense had no answers as Nick Chubb ran for 137 yards and two touchdowns. Baker Mayfield also managed the game well, throwing for 218 yards and two scores.

Burrow finished the game 28 of 40 for 282 yards. No touchdowns. Two interceptions.

The Bengals entered the Bye Week beaten, battered, but not defeated. It was time to regroup.

The Stretch Run

The Bengals came out of the Bye with an increased sense of urgency. Seven games remaining. All seven against playoff contenders.

In Las Vegas, the Bengals excelled in all three phases of the game in a 32–13 win over the Raiders. The defense forced two turnovers and only allowed one third-down conversion all day. The offensive line wore down the Raiders defensive front as Joe Mixon ran for 123 yards and two touchdowns. And special teams was led by Evan McPherson, who connected on four field goals—three beyond 50 yards, tying an NFL record.

The 6–4 Bengals returned home with confidence and momentum. The second round of division play began with the Steelers. It wasn't close. The Bengals won 41–10. The 31-point gap was the largest margin of victory for a Bengals' team against the Steelers in thirty-two years.

The defense was suffocating, sacking Roethlisberger three times and picking him off twice. The Steeler offense could only muster 51 yards on the ground. Mixon continued to roll with 165 yards and two touchdowns. Burrow was efficient, completing 20 of 24 passes.

The most significant play of the game, however, might have come on the Bengals' first possession. On the eleventh play of the opening drive, Burrow dropped back to pass. As the pocket collapsed, he instinctively spun left, and without hesitation sprinted toward the end zone. When Burrow got inside the five, he juked a defender and stretched the ball across the goal line for the touchdown. He popped up and pounded his chest three times. If anyone still wondered about Burrow's post-surgery mobility, this play proved the knee and the muscle memory were back.

"Highsmith got some pressure on me and I was able to get outside and had a little boogie right there," said a smiling Burrow after the game. "My knee was feeling good. My knee was feeling great all day. It was exciting."[681]

The Bengals were now 2–0 coming out of the Bye Week. For the second year in a row, the Chargers were in town. This time, the fans would get what they wanted the first time: A Burrow-Herbert showdown.

Cincinnati would play the game without right tackle Riley Reiff, who was sidelined with an ankle injury. As it turned out, the injury would end Reiff's season.

The roller coaster ride continued for the Bengals. Los Angeles jumped out to a quick 24-point lead. Heading into the second quarter it looked like the Chargers were going to run the Bengals out of the Jungle. But an unfazed Burrow calmly orchestrated two touchdowns before the half to cut the lead to 11.

As if the early deficit wasn't a big enough challenge, Burrow dislocated his right pinky finger. Coming out of the break, Joe tried different gloves on his right hand, grimacing each time as he struggled to fit the misshapened digit into the pinky sleeve. Finally, he decided to play without a glove.

A 7-yard touchdown run by Joe Mixon, midway through the third quarter, cut the lead to two points. Then, on a subsequent series, just as the Bengals seemingly were driving to take the lead, the ball squirted out of Mixon's hands. Tevaughn Campbell scooped it up and ran 61 yards for a Charger touchdown. Los Angeles went on to win 41–22.

It was back-to-back Bosas for Burrow. Buddies off the field, but all business between the lines. Joey only had one tackle for the Chargers after leaving the game early with a head injury. The following week Nick would record three tackles, including two sacks when San Francisco invaded the Jungle.

With both teams fighting for their playoff lives, the NFL flexed the game into the highly coveted late afternoon time slot. Two muffed punts put Cincinnati in an early hole.

The Bengals trailed 20–6 entering the fourth quarter. Then Joe Burrow went to work, posting a 151.0 passer rating down the stretch. He found Chase in the end zone twice. The first TD came on a fourth-and-five from the Niner's 17-yard line. Burrow took the snap but was quickly flushed from the pocket. He reversed field and headed toward the far sideline. Chase meanwhile was blanketed in the back of the end zone. But when he saw Joe's improvisation, Ja'Marr reflexively reversed field and tip-toed along the endline as the ball settled safely into his hands.

"It was such a great play by [Ja'Marr]," said Burrow after the game. "I told him that's one of my favorite touchdowns we've thrown together. We were just on the same page. I knew exactly what he was seeing and he knew exactly what I was seeing. He was running left and I threw it right. He put his foot in the ground and went and got it."[682]

In Week 15, the Bengals and Broncos squared off in a high-altitude defensive slugfest. Neither team could find a rhythm in the first half. Rookie

Evan McPherson continued to earn his fifth-round stripes when he booted a team-record 58-yard field goal to send the Bengals into the locker room with 6–3 halftime lead.

The Broncos took a 10–9 advantage late in the third quarter, but two plays later the Bengals regained the lead for good on a 56-yard Burrow to Boyd touchdown strike. The defense then held on for a hard-fought 15–10 win.

On the day after Christmas, Cincinnati hosted Baltimore in a battle for AFC North supremacy. It would turn out to be another record-setting performance for Cincinnati, which won 41–21. It was the second game in a row that the Bengals hung 41 points on the Ravens.

While Baltimore jumped out to an early 7–0 lead, Cincinnati cashed in on its first seven drives—scoring five touchdowns and two field goals. Burrow connected on 37 of 46 passes for a team-record 525 yards. Four passes went for touchdowns. Mixon crossed the goal line twice (one rushing; one receiving) to increase his season total to 16 TDs—one shy of the franchise record. Tee Higgins also turned in a career day, catching 12 balls for 194 yards and two scores. Chase added seven catches for 125 yards.

Earlier in the week, Ravens Defensive Coordinator Don Martindale said that he wasn't ready to give Joe Burrow a gold Hall-of-Fame jacket just yet. Burrow was asked about the statement after the game. "I didn't think it was a necessary comment," said Burrow, who was feeling festive in a Santa hat and red Krusty Krab sweatshirt. Paul Dehner of *The Athletic* followed up by asking if Martindale's slight was on Burrow's mind when he kept throwing at the end of the game. With a smile and tilt of his Kringle-covered head, Burrow said, "Maybe."[683]

The 9-6 Bengals hosted the 11-4 Chiefs on January 2. When Jim Nance and Tony Romo are in town, you know it's a big game. While the Chiefs were playing for playoff seeding, a win would give the Bengals their first division title since 2015.

It was rough sledding for Cincinnati in the early going, as Patrick Mahomes and company showed why they are the two-time defending AFC Champions. Mahomes moved the Chiefs up and down the field at will, tossing touchdown strikes to Demarcus Robinson and Travis Kelce. A 72-yard pass from Burrow to Chase, however, cut the lead in half as the first quarter expired.

In the second quarter, the Chiefs added two Darrel Williams touchdown runs, while Burrow connected with Chase from 18 yards out. McPherson closed the half with a 46-yard field goal and KC entered the break with a 28-17 advantage.

During halftime, Bengals Defensive Coordinator Lou Anarumo, aka "The Mad Scientist," went to work. After giving up 28 points in the first half, the Bengal defense clamped down, allowing a mere field goal the rest of the way.

While the defense was doing its job, Burrow and the offense kept applying pressure. Just three plays into the third quarter the Bengals shaved the lead to four when Burrow moved the Chiefs' defenders with his eyes and connected on a 69-yard touchdown to Chase. With 11:44 remaining in the game, Cincinnati took the lead, 31–28, on a five-yard pass from Burrow to Tyler Boyd.

After the defense held KC to a game-tying field goal, Burrow engineered a masterful 15-play drive that ate up the final 6:01. There would be no last-second Mahomes magic on this day. Instead, McPherson hit his third game-winning field goal of the season. When the ball split the uprights, the party was on.

The Bengals were AFC North champions, and had punched their ticket to the playoffs for the first time in seven years. Courtesy of Joe Mixon, everyone got a victory cigar. The locker room looked and smelled a lot like the 2020 LSU National Championship celebration as Joe puffed on his stogie and broke out his "Get the Gat" moves.

When Chase was told after the game that his total number of receiving yards (266) eclipsed Mahomes' passing yards (259), the incredulous rookie said, "I don't think I did that." When the press corps confirmed the stat, he replied, "I did? Oh s***! Pardon my profanity."[684]

When it was Joe's turn to address the media, he came to the microphone wearing an AFC North divisional championship hat and shirt. "I said it in the preseason," said Burrow. "We were talking about the playoffs and I said we're going to go to the playoffs and the easiest way to do that is to win the division. And everyone kind of laughed at us a little bit, but we knew the kind of team we had and the kind of guys in the locker room we had and we knew we could go out and do it."[685]

With the divisional title in hand, Taylor and his staff decided to sit most of the starters against Cleveland in the final regular-season game. The Browns won 21-16. The Bengals entered the playoffs with a 10-7 record and seeded fourth in the AFC. They would host the fifth-seeded Raiders. It was a chance to win their first playoff game in thirty-one years.

Cincinnati was electric.

So was Athens.

12

It Is Us!

"Burrow has the best shot to force his way into that *Brady-Mahomes-Rodgers* stratosphere for good. He's talented enough to lead these Bengals to Super Bowl LVI in Los Angeles this season and flip perennial losers into winners for good. It's always about timing in the NFL and, right now, we're seeing the emergence of a true star who'll last."[686]

—Tyler Dunne
NFL features writer

To honor the hometown hero, it was determined that the lettering on the back of Joe Burrow Stadium would be illuminated in orange for the duration of the Bengal playoff push. Nearly every building in the Cincinnati area also had an orange hue, from the Florence Water Tower to Newport on the Levee to Great American Ballpark.

Bengal mania gripped the tri-state.

Despite the hype, few dared to predict a deep playoff run. The Bengals hadn't tasted postseason nectar in thirty-one years. Just break the curse. Wishing for more seemed greedy.

That said, there was one person who had the audacity to go big. His name? Tyler Dunne. He runs the football website, "Go Long." The day before the Bengals hosted the Raiders in the Wild Card round, Dunne published an in-depth feature entitled "Joe Burrow is the most dangerous man in football." The subtitle was just as provocative: "No quarterback is hotter right now. This combination of grit and brains—with a touch of swagger—could lift the Cincinnati Bengals to their first Super Bowl appearance since 1988. Here's why."[687]

In the article, Dunne pointed out that over the final four games of the regular season, no quarterback could compare to Burrow's productivity: 107 of 141 (76 percent) for 1,476 yards, 11 touchdowns and no interceptions. "Toughness. Intelligence. Arm strength," wrote Dunne. "He's been the entire package all while getting pinyata'd around for an NFL-high 51 sacks."[688]

The most intriguing aspect of Dunne's article, however, was a conversation with another person unsurprised by Joe's success—Burrow family friend and NFL draft comp Kurt Warner. Dunne found Warner's perspective especially insightful since the two-time MVP and Hall of Fame quarterback sees the game "with a surgical mind."

Warner isn't overly enamored by raw athleticism and/or arm strength. Instead, he believes Super Bowl-winning quarterbacks need "to hit layups with numbing efficiency for one... two... three... four games in a row." They also need to make the intermediate throws with touch and consistency while having enough arm to occasionally connect on the deep ball. Other than Brady, Warner believes Burrow is the quarterback to keep your eye on for years to come.

"Know how to get through your reads and how to get it to the right guy at the right time," says Warner. "That's what Joe does. That's what I always thought separated him. The confidence to believe you can make every play and then the knowledge to know exactly how to do that and to do it quickly and to get your eyes in the right spot."[689]

Another familiar name appeared in Dunne's article—Joe's high school offensive coordinator Nathan White. With the Bengals preparing for a playoff push, White told Dunne, "Nothing will surprise me. The Heisman and the National Championship and everything he did at LSU, I feel like we all watched it before in 2014 when he was here. I'll be shocked if big things *don't* happen.... From an Athens perspective, that's what it feels like: This is what he's always done."[690]

Thirty-one Years

The largest crowd in Paul Brown Stadium history was on hand to witness the Bengals and the Raiders square off in the first AFC Wild Card game. After holding the Raiders to a field goal on their initial possession, the Bengals mounted a 75-yard scoring drive that culminated in a seven-yard Burrow touchdown pass to C.J. Uzomah. The quarter ended with a 31-yard Evan McPherson field goal to extend the lead to 10-3.

With 1:51 remaining in the half, Burrow scrambled toward the near sideline and just before his foot landed out of bounds, he threw a 10-yard touchdown dart to a wide-open Tyler Boyd, increasing the Bengals' margin by 14 points.

But the Raiders refused to roll over. Derek Carr executed the two-minute drill to perfection, guiding the Las Vegas offense 80 yards on 11 plays to score a touchdown right before intermission.

The second half was a defensive struggle. Both teams added a pair of field goals to keep it a one-score game. Thirty-one years of frustration and disappointment hung over Paul Brown Stadium as Carr surgically guided the Raider offense inside the Bengals' 10-yard line.

After spiking the ball on first down and tossing incompletions on the next two plays, the Raiders were down to their final snap. Carr dropped back and fired a beebee into coverage at the goal line. Two Bengal defenders converged and linebacker Germaine Pratt came away with the game-clinching interception.

The game was over. The thirty-one-year curse was broken. The stadium erupted in pandemonium.

Burrow completed 24 of 34 passes for 244 yards and two touchdowns. Chase led all receivers with nine catches for 116 yards. In the postgame press conference, however, Joe wasn't satisfied. "This isn't like the icing on top of the cake or anything. This is the cake, so we're moving on."[691]

On his way home that night, Zac Taylor started a new tradition by dropping off a game ball at a local bar. "I drive past one bar in particular... every day for the last three years," said Taylor, "and Thursday night, Friday night, Saturday night, Sunday night I always see people in there with Bengals gear. And so that's kind of the time when I drive home from work or drive into work where I think those big picture things and [this was] something I had on my mind for a long time to do. It worked out to where we had that opportunity to do that last night."[692]

There would be more game balls delivered to Queen City taverns before the 2021–22 run was over.

The following week, Cincinnati traveled to Tennessee to take on the top-seeded Tennessee Titans in the divisional round. The Bengals suffered the loss of three defensive linemen in the Raiders' game—Larry Ogunjobi, Mike Daniels and Trey Hendrickson. Of the three, only Hendrickson would suit up for Tennessee.

On the opening play from scrimmage, Jessie Bates jumped a route and intercepted a Ryan Tannehill pass. It was the first of three costly picks for the Titans' quarterback.

The Bengals had great field position at the Tennessee 42-yard line, but Mike Vrabel's vaunted defense was prepared. The porous Cincinnati front would allow nine sacks on the day—the most endured by a winning quarterback in NFL postseason history. Despite non-stop pressure, the offense moved the ball into range for their lethal field goal kicker, Evan McPherson. The rookie connected on three first-half kicks and the Bengals took a 9-6 lead into the break.

On the initial possession of the second half, Burrow orchestrated a nine-play, 65-yard drive that culminated with Joe Mixon high-stepping into the end zone. The scoring drive increased the Bengal lead to 16–6. The Titans, however, fought back, scoring 10 points to bring the game even heading down the stretch.

With twenty seconds left on the clock, Tennessee faced a third and five on their own 40-yard line. Tannehill forced a pass over the middle. The ball was tipped into the air by Eli Apple and settled into the arms of Logan Wilson.

Burrow immediately went to work. On the first play out of the shotgun, he connected with Chase on the far sideline for a 19-yard gain. That's all they needed. After a couple practice swings, McPherson jogged onto the field. The snap and the hold were perfect. McPherson split the uprights from 52. The Bengals survived, 19–16. The euphoric sideline spilled onto the field. Cincinnati was advancing to the AFC Championship game for the first time in thirty-three years.

"Defense played unbelievable and we made plays when we needed to on offense," said an upbeat Burrow following the game. "It wasn't always pretty, but we got the job done. Like I've said all year, we can win a lot of different ways. Defense came up strong today."[693]

When asked about McPherson, Burrow relayed the following story. "So, he was talking to Brandon [Allen] when he was going out to kick. He gave a little warm-up swing and he said, 'Ah, looks like we're going to the AFC Championship.'"[694]

Joe closed the press conference by saying he was tired of the underdog narrative. The motto, "Why Not Us?" would now be "It Is Us!" "We're a really, really good team. We're here to make noise. Teams are going to have to pay attention to us. We're going for it all."[695]

Everyone was paying attention to the other AFC Divisional round game. The Bills and Chiefs played one for the ages, with the two teams combining for 25 points in the final two minutes of regulation. Kansas City won the overtime coin toss. And the game, 42–36.

It would be a Bengals-Chiefs rematch.

This time in Arrowhead.

Kansas City Here We Come

As the special teams videographer, Evan Cooley spends a lot of time with long snapper Clark Harris, punter/holder Kevin Huber and placekicker Evan McPherson. Maybe it's the similarity in age, but Cooley has forged an especially close bond with McPherson.

"Evan's my guy, my main buddy," says Cooley. "I've never seen him frown. He's happy-go-lucky. A great guy."[696]

The two Evans typically sit with each other on the plane or the bus. When the Bengals arrived at the Kansas City hotel, fans were there to greet the team. Naturally, the crowd started shouting out the names of their favorite players as they deboard.

Evan McPherson got a call out as he walked off the bus. Cooley was next. As he was unloading his video gear, he heard his name. Some Athenians were in the crowd. "Evan Cooley! Evan Cooley!" An impressed Mike Hilton turned to Cooley and said, "Damn, there are people who travel to watch you work?"[697]

While a few eyes were on Cooley, all eyes were on the other Athens High School Bengal, Joe Burrow. Especially on that particular Sunday. He planned his pregame outfit. And it went viral.

Earlier in the week, another photo of Burrow went viral—a picture of a smiling middle school Joe at the Athens County Fair. Demolition Derby night. He's wearing a sleeveless Kansas City Chiefs shirt with cut-off jeans. He looks proud.

And a bit goofy.

Robin remembered the day Joe called her and asked if he could cut up some clothes and go to the fair. "I have no idea what he was thinking when he did that," says Robin. "Growing up, Joe was just Joe. He never really cared about what other people thought about his clothes. He just did his own thing. I feel like that's what he's still doing. For some reason now people think it's cool."[698]

Kaitlin Baker and Joe Burrow at the Athens County Fair. *Photo credit: Kaitlin Baker*

When Joe stepped off the bus at Arrowhead, cameras locked on his pregame fashion statement—a black turtleneck, a JB9 Nike diamond studded pendant and Cartier glasses. The overcoat was a grey Sherpa jacket covered in hearts.

"Joe told me the night before he was going to wear it," recalls Zacciah Saltzman. "He wanted it to be a surprise for Micah."[699]

Micah is Zacciah's younger brother and the designer of the jacket. "Through me, Joe always saw Micah as another brother in a way," says Zacciah. "I think Joe wore the jacket because he's a great guy and wanted to help out Micah. But here's the thing: he never would have worn it if he didn't like it."[700]

Live2Love is the name of Micah's business. When Joe's pregame look went viral, Micah was inundated with orders. Especially the Sherpa jacket. He was even contacted by *The New York Times*, *LA Times*, and *GQ Germany*.[701]

From time-to-time Micah sends care packages to Joe. "When I design a line of clothing, I send something to Joe that I think he might like," says Micah. "Last year in the preseason, he wore one of my Live2Love hats and someone messaged me on Instagram. It was cool as the season went on to see Joe starting to think more carefully about his clothing rather than just wearing a SpongeBob sweatshirt."[702]

Joe's parents are happy to see their son expressing his personality. His fashion-merchandizing mom likes Joe's emerging aesthetic sensibilities. Jimmy is a bit more old-fashioned. "I'm partial to the pregame suits myself."[703] That said, Joe's dad does admit to having a t-shirt with a JB9 chain on it.

The Chiefs were seven-point favorites heading into the game, despite losing to the Bengals less than thirty days before. If the first quarter and a half was any indication, the odds-makers woefully underestimated the two-time defending AFC Champions.

Mahomes came out on fire, orchestrating 84-, 75- and 72-yard touchdown drives on the Chiefs' first three possessions. Cincinnati, on the other hand, could only muster a field goal in the opening twenty-nine minutes. The Bengals finally found the end zone when Samaje Perine took a screen pass 41 yards for a score.

But 1:05 remained on the clock—more than enough time for Mahomes to work his magic. The Chiefs moved efficiently down the field to the Bengal 1-yard line. With five seconds remaining, Andy Reid chose to go for it instead of taking the easy field goal. It would prove to be a costly mistake.

The first read was covered, so Mahomes tossed the ball in the flat to Tyreek Hill, who was quickly flipped to the ground by cornerback Eli Apple. The play was reminiscent of Jimmy Burrow's game-altering goal-line stand in the 1974 Sugar Bowl. Apple's stop would also prove to be a game-changer.

"That was a big play our defense made," said Joe after the game. "That stretch right there where we scored a touchdown and then they drive right down the field in a two-minute situation and our defense prevents any points from being put on the board. I think that was the turning point in the game."[704]

The Bengals came out of the locker room with new-found resolve. After both teams failed to score for the majority of the third quarter, a 31-yard Evan McPherson field goal with 2:58 remaining closed the gap to 8 points, 21–13.

On the next KC possession, B.J. Hill intercepted a short Mahomes' pass at the Chiefs 27-yard line. A mic'd up Ja'Marr Chase immediately grabbed his helmet and said, "Let's go, Joe. Let's go, Joe!" When they got to the huddle, Burrow instructed his offense: "When we score, we're goin' for 2." Chase responded, "Ah, yeah, I like that s***."[705]

After a 5-yard run by Mixon, Burrow found Chase for a 17-yard gain. After advancing the ball to the 2-yard line, Burrow threw a perfectly placed ball to Chase who snatched it out of the air for a touchdown. The two-point conversion—a short pass to sure-handed Trey Taylor—tied the game at 21 points.

Down the stretch, both defenses held their ground. After exchanging field goals, the game went into overtime. Representatives from opposing benches walked to midfield for perhaps the most important call of the game—the overtime coin toss. When the Chiefs won the flip the previous week against Josh Allen and the Buffalo Bills, Mahomes orchestrated the game-winning touchdown in a mere eight plays. Allen never saw the ball.

Chiefs' fans were desperately hoping and praying for a repeat.

The referee turned to the visiting team. Brandon Allen called heads. The coin twirled high into the air before landing softly on the Arrowhead Stadium turf.

Tails.

Arrowhead erupted.

Maybe the loudest moment of the day in the loudest stadium in the entire NFL.

Everyone knew what was coming next. Patrick Mahomes magic.

Right?

Wrong.

Mahomes opened the series with two incomplete passes. On third and 10, a deep ball down the near sideline to Tyreek Hill was high-pointed by safety Jessie Bates. The ball landed in the arms of fellow safety Vonn Bell.

The Bengal offensive players quickly grabbed their helmets. With the ball near mid-field, a few first downs would put the visitors within striking distance for the "baby-faced assassin," Evan McPherson. After a few passes to Tee Higgins and five punishing Joe Mixon runs, the Bengals were well within McPherson's range. It was a 31-yard attempt to win the game and send Cincinnati to the Super Bowl for the first time in thirty-three years.

The ball was snapped. A perfect hold. A perfect kick. When the ball split the uprights, McPherson's buddy Evan Cooley rejoiced on the sidelines. Burrow embraced Coach Taylor. Former LSU teammate Tyler Shelvin recreated a scene from the 2020 National championship game by lifting Joey Franchise onto his shoulders.

When he entered the press conference, a dapper Joe Burrow removed his Cartier glasses and carefully set them aside. Burrow expressed his gratitude for the Cincinnati supporters who traveled to Kansas City. "It was exciting to see all the fans who stayed around. It was tough to hear all the Bengals' fans in the stadium. But they showed up after everybody else filtered out so that was exciting."[706]

After a few game-related questions, reporters moved on to Joe's attire. One reporter asked about the chain. Burrow lit up. "Oh, you like this one? There's no story to it. I just think it's pretty cool.... This is probably my favorite outfit of the year." Another writer asked if the jewels were real. An exuberant Joe didn't hesitate. "They're definitely real. I think I make too much money to have fake ones."[707]

"Joe's core is still the same; There's nothing phony about him," says Don Cooley. "He has never made a big deal about trying to impress others. I think a lot of people thought Joe was being funny when he made the comment about the diamonds, but that's exactly the answer I would expect from him: 'Well, I'm rich. Of course, they're real.'"[708]

The world might think Burrow is a fashion trendsetter, but back in Athens he's just the same old Joe. Says Ryan Luehrman: "We'd give him such a hard time if he wore that outfit around here."[709]

As a long line of cars slowly wove its way out of the expansive parking lot, the tailgating continued for the Burrows. In a tribute to their sons, Jimmy Chase and Jimmy Burrow lit up a celebration cigar. They blew smoke rings in the shadow of Arrowhead, savoring one of the sweetest games their boys have ever won. Jimmy Chase and Jimmy Burrow smoking cigars and telling stories. It's a foretaste of a business idea Will Drabold has been pondering. Just a pipe dream. Literally.

"I say this kind of jokingly, but I really mean it," says Drabold. "Joe Burrow doesn't have to put in a penny. The Burrow family doesn't have to put in a penny. But I would love to create a stand-alone cigar shop/bar here in Athens. We'd call it 'Burreaux's' and Joe can have all the freakin' revenue for all I care. Humidor on the first floor. Second floor is a bar/smoking lounge. And the third floor is people just sitting around talking to Jimmy Burrow five days a week."[710]

Super Bowl LVI

Back in the The Plains, Fred Gibson, Les Champlin and Nathan White made their way through the snow over to the Grover "Jr." Stotts Bell Tower at Joe Burrow Stadium. They rang the bell with gusto. It was a glorious sound for the residents of The Plains. Their native son was going to Los Angeles and Super Bowl LVI.

Hometown spirit. *Photo credit: The Smathers Family*

In the two weeks leading up to the big game, Athens County was swept up in Bengal and Burrow mania. There was so much orange around town, it looked more like the end of October than the beginning of February.

A green and orange banner stretched across Court Street at the intersection of Washington. It read: "From Bulldog to Bengal: Who Dey – Let's Go Joe!" The Athens High School marching band spelled out "Who Dey" on the R. Basil Rutter Field at Joe Burrow Stadium. Homemade banners and signs filled the county. Even adjacent counties got in on the fun. About forty minutes away in neighboring Meigs County, there was a life-size cut-

The Athens High School Band spells out WHO DEY at Joe Burrow Stadium. *Photo credit: Ben Siegel*

out of the Bengals quarterback set up outside Eastern Elementary School, where Robin serves as principal.

It's a little surreal for the kids, seeing their principal on national TV on Sunday then in the school bus line the following morning. "That's 100 percent true," says Robin with a big laugh. "Kids will come up to me and say, 'You were on TV yesterday. What's going on?' I'm like, 'Yeah, that was me. I'm back!' In my mind, I'm just still going to Joe's games and working. It's what I've always done."[711]

Back in The Plains, Travis Brand and his team updated Gigi's marquee: "IT'S A BEAUTIFUL DEY IN THE NEIGHBORHOOD, WHO DEY!" On a frigid February morning, a reporter from sunny SoCal walked into the Country Kitchen. Jeff Miller was just one of the many reporters who descended upon The Plains that week.

Sam Smathers talking to the media about Joe Burrow. *Photo credit: Trisha Doudna*

"The *L.A. Times* showed up at 9 a.m. Sunday morning at Gigi's and asked, 'How do I get ahold of Sam,'" recalls Smathers. "They don't know how to find me because I'm not on any social media. So, they called my daughter, Trisha. She told me, 'This guy is sitting at Gigi's and wants to interview you.' I said, 'Send him over, I don't care. Nine o'clock Sunday morning, doesn't matter to me.'"[712]

So Smathers took Miller on a tour of the Dawg Pound. Photos and footage of young Joe, working his magic on the Peden Stadium turf. Sam showed the reporter the youth football Joe threw back in his formative years. Miller examined the ball with the same reverence the Burrows showed to the final Johnny Unitas touchdown ball.

Sam made some calls. They opened the weight room at the high school, so Miller could interview Jimmy Burrow and Nathan White in a heated area.

The national media couldn't get enough of the Joe Burrow story through the eyes of his hometown.

After a pep rally at Paul Brown Stadium, which drew around 30,000 die-hard fans, the team flew to Los Angeles. The Bengals practiced at UCLA's Drake Stadium in preparation for the game. At some point during the week, Ja'Marr Chase and Joe Burrow met with their personal jeweler, Leo Frost. Frost is responsible for the JB9 diamond-studded chain, as well as the number-9 pendant that Joe wore over his 740 shirt on draft night.

The meeting was to present Joe with a gift from Ja'Marr. "Chase reached out to me one week before the Super Bowl and said, 'Hey, I want to get Joe diamond grills for the Super Bowl," said Frost in a conversation with Kelsey Conway. "I got it done in four days and flew out to L.A. I met them at the hotel. When Joe put those grills on, that was probably one of the coolest moments of my jewelry career, because the sunlight just smacked his teeth. The diamonds in his mouth just glistened and blinded everybody who was there."[713]

Chase and Burrow both received some additional bling leading up to the game. On Thursday evening, the NFL Awards Show was held at the YouTube Theater in Inglewood. Chase was selected Offensive Rookie of the Year, while Burrow was named Comeback Player of the Year.

Troy Bolin was not only excited for Joe to receive the honor, but thrilled to cash in a bet he placed prior to the season. "I drove three hours to Pittsburgh and placed money on Joe to win Comeback Player of the Year," says Bolin. "I regretted not betting on Joe to win the Heisman Trophy, so I wasn't going to make that mistake again. I only won $800, though. Man, I wish I had bet the house. Why didn't I empty my bank account?"[714]

When Bolin arrived to place the bet, he was treated like royalty. "I took over $5,000 with me," recalls Bolin. "Most of it was other people's money, but the Barstool guys didn't know that. They thought I was some kind of big-roller. But only $200 was mine. When I went back over to collect my money, I lost about half of it on the Super Bowl. But I did bet on Tee Higgins to have the most receiving yards, so at least I won something that day."[715]

Kevin Goldsberry estimates around thirty to forty people from Athens County made the trip to Los Angeles. Kevin and Kristi were among the lucky Athenians who attended the game in person. "My cousin works for the Rams," says Goldsberry. "He's the vice president of marketing. We had standing-room-only tickets, but it worked out great. I had a portable beer vendor on one side and the men's room about 15 yards away on the other side. So, I was set."[716]

Nathan White and his wife, Sarah, received tickets from Joe. "It was unbelievable," recalls White. "We were planning on having ten or fifteen

Evan McPherson and Evan Cooley pose with Cooley's mother, Beth, leading up to the Super Bowl. *Photo credit: The Cooley Family*

people over to our house for the Super Bowl when Joe called. In his calm Joe voice, he just said, 'Hey Coach, if you're not busy next weekend, I came up with a couple tickets. Sorry for the late notice.' I just told him of course we wanted to go. I thanked him 100 times."[717]

The Bengals entered their first Super Bowl in thirty-three years as 4-point underdogs. But before they could kick off, Dwayne "The Rock" Johnson took the microphone at the 50-yard line. Like the announcer at a Big-Time Wrestling event, Johnson entertained the crowd to the bewilderment of many, including Joe Burrow.

"What's he doing out there?" A mic'd-up Burrow playfully asked Brandon Allen. "He's on kickoff return. They signed him."

Moments later, Joe enthusiastically added, "I like his shoes."[718]

As Burrow completed his final warm-up tosses, he pumped himself up: "Alright, Joe. This is what you've worked so hard for. It's why you do it."[719]

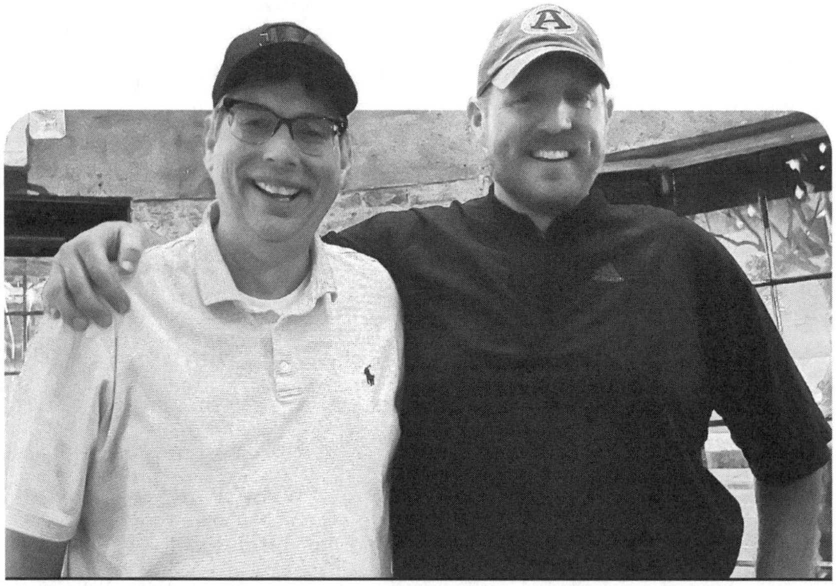

Don Cooley and Nathan White together at the hotel in Los Angeles. *Photo credit: The Cooley Family*

The Bengals' opening drive stalled at mid-field. On fourth and one, an aggressive Zac Taylor elected to go for it. The Rams stopped Samaje Perine short of the first-down marker, taking over at mid-field. On the sixth play of the drive, Matthew Stafford hit O'Dell Beckham Jr. in the end zone for the first score of the game. As the first quarter came to an end, the Bengals were on the board with a 29-yard Evan McPherson field goal.

In the early second quarter, The Rams extended their lead to 13–3 on an 11-yard Stafford to Cooper Kupp TD strike. The Bengals, however, put together a 7:04, 12-play drive down to the L.A. 6-yard line. On the next play, Burrow pitched the ball to Joe Mixon, who promptly lofted the ball into the end zone. Tee Higgins caught it. At the intermission, the Rams led 13-10.

On the first play of the second half, Burrow found Higgins on a go-route for a 75-yard touchdown. The Bengals had their first lead of the night, 17–13. On the next possession, a Chidobe Awuzie interception led to a 38-yard McPherson field goal. The Rams added a field goal of their own as the third quarter concluded.

As the fourth quarter wore on, the Rams defensive front was heating up and the Bengals offensive line was wearing down. Cincinnati failed to score on its final five drives of the game. The decisive drive for the Rams culminated with Stafford hitting Kupp for the go-ahead touchdown.

Burrow and the Bengals offense had 1:25 to work with which was plenty of time to get at least a game-tying field goal. The first two plays were promising: 17-yard completion to Chase, followed by a nine-yard connection to Tyler Boyd. But second and one turned into third and fourth and one. Burrow took the shotgun snap. Before he could take his next breath, Aaron Donald was upon him. A spinning Burrow tossed the ball forward in desperation. It hit the SoFi Stadium turf.

The game was over. The dream season came to an end.

In the postgame press conference, a somber Joe Burrow said, "We're a young team, so you'd like to think that we'll be back in this situation.... So, we take this and let it fuel you for the rest of our careers."[720]

Friends Don't Let Friends Down

After the AFC Championship game, James Rapien of "Locked on Bengals" asked Burrow if the win felt surreal. Burrow said the football part of it doesn't feel that way, but when NBA stars and Grammy-award winning musicians reach out to him, it does.

"You know the situation that I'm in, socially, doesn't really feel real to me," said Burrow. "Because in my head, I'm just the same old guy, but one of my idols growing up, Kid Cudi, yesterday reached out to me and you got LeBron tweeting at me...that part is surreal."[721]

When Cudi appeared on Late Night with Seth Meyers a month after the Super Bowl, he explained how he and Joe became friends. "Before the Chiefs game I reached out to him and told him good luck," said Cudi. "And I sent him a song to kind of get him pumped up for the game."

Meyers asked, "This is a pre-existing one of your songs?"

Cudi clarifies, "No, I wrote him a song. I wrote him a love song." He begins to sing it, "Joe, hello, you need to know you got the glow, Joe."

Cudi admitted to making an audacious request. "I got bold and I was just like, 'Man, I'm just gonna go ahead and ask him for the jersey.' He literally responded right away. He said, 'I'm sending it tomorrow.'" As promised, the game-worn AFC Championship Joe Burrow number 9 jersey, complete with blood, sweat and grass stains, arrived quickly at Kid Cudi's house.[722]

Burrow was instrumental in getting Cudi to play at the Bengals Super Bowl After Party. Joe now considers Cudi a "good friend."[723]

Why did Joe go the Super Bowl After Party? That's a question a lot of reporters were asking. One reason, as Joe stated in the postgame press conference, was because of what he learned from Kurt Warner. Even though the big game didn't turn out as you would have hoped, you can still celebrate the season.

A second reason Burrow chose to go to the After Party? Quite simply, Kid Cudi is now one of Burrow's friends. And friends don't let friends down.

Conclusion

SOUNDTRACK 2 MY LIFE

"That's something I want to do every year. Make sure that the guys we're looking to bring in feel at home in Cincinnati with the team because that's the culture we're building in the locker room. We're really, really close as a team."[724]

—Joe Burrow

Kid Cudi closed the private after party with "Soundtrack 2 My Life." It was the final song from Joe Burrow's curated list, bringing down the curtain on the Super Bowl LVI festivities.

It is also the perfect song to close this book. If we were to assemble a soundtrack to Joe Burrow's life, what tracks would make the cut? What memories would be attached? Who better to call than best friend Zacciah Saltzman. When asked to curate a few songs and moments that represent his friendship with Joe, Zacciah says, "Wow, very, very cool prompt."[725]

It doesn't take long for Saltzman to slip into his DeLorean. It turns out music is the elusive flux capacitor that can transport all of us back in time.

First stop for Zacciah and Joe, Athens High School. Joe is learning how to drive. Zacciah remembers Joe's running commentary while weaving around pedestrians, pets and pickups. "Dude would be like, 'Lookout mailman, watch out cat, get outta here truck!'" Music is blaring as the two cruise The Plains and Athens. Zacciah texts Joe to confirm his memory. Both agree. The artist who comes to mind is Future. The song is "Turn on the Lights."[726]

"We were the first guys to listen to Future in our area," says Zacciah, who thinks they discovered him on the AAU circuit. Zacciah also credits his dad for introducing them to new rap and hip hop artists. "When he was a basketball agent he'd always ask his players what they were listening to. Hanging out was always rap with me, Joe and Ibi."[727]

As Zacciah slips back into his time machine, he says, "You got me reminiscing all over the place." Next stop, summer before Joe's Heisman season with LSU. "A couple of us hung out on a summer night and listened to Tame Impala. We just watched the stars with the 'Currents' album playing in the background." Zacciah says the song that comes to mind is "Let It Happen" with the repetitive psychedelic chorus, "I'm ready for the moment and the sound, but maybe I was ready all along."[728]

Zacciah keeps traveling forward. Tame Impala remains the music of choice. "Ibi, Joe and I were in Vegas for UFC fights and we watched the

Ibi (20), Joe (10) and Zacciah (14) remain good friends. *Photo credit: Trisha Doudna*

sunset while listening to a shuffle of all Tame. It was a magical night."[729] Most recently, during the Summer of 2022, Joe, Ibi, Zacciah and brother Micah attend a Tame Impala concert in Columbus. Joe wasn't prepared for the non-stop rain. "He was in a t-shirt and getting absolutely drenched," says Zacciah. "He borrowed my rain jacket. After a while, I said, 'Dude, if you keep borrowing my jacket, people aren't going to think you're very tough.'" Joe didn't wear it the rest of the night.[730]

Finally, the DeLorean returns to Athens High School. Sophomore year for Joe. Zacciah and Ibi are freshmen. Walking into basketball practice, Zacciah pulls up some random Chinese flute music on his phone. All three break out into interpretative dance moves. "Man, that was the only time we danced like that. Ever," recalls Zacciah. "Hilarious moment."[731]

But through the years, Kid Cudi has always been a soundtrack mainstay. "Mr. Rager" might be their favorite Cudi song. "When we get together it always finds its way onto our playlist."[732] At the beginning of the song, Cudi says, "This here is dedicated to all of the kids like me." Zacciah reflects upon Cudi's influence. "He makes music because it's how he feels and he's being honest and pure with his fanbase," says Zacciah. "He sees himself as a big brother to middle schoolers or anyone who needs direction. Everyone goes through these emotions and transitions in life and he has the courage to put music to that."[733]

In a documentary entitled "A Kid Named Scott," Cudi explains that as his fame rose, more and more people wanted something from him. He finally realized, "I just want to be around good people. I want to look them in the eyes and see their souls and know they're real people and they're shooting me straight."[734]

Like Cudi, Burrow's fame has skyrocketed. Everyone wants something from him. And, like Cudi, he's careful to surround himself with people he can trust. His sudden fame makes it difficult to go out in public without persistent autograph and selfie requests. Zacciah assumes the role of planner so his friend doesn't become too reclusive. "I just make sure we go to a place where Joe feels comfortable," says Zacciah. "I think it's important that he keeps living his life."[735]

Cupcakes and Crackers

Everywhere Joe goes he cultivates a culture of character, relationships, brotherhood and family. He has genuine friendships with everybody in the locker room. Like in high school, he'll eat lunch with anybody in the Bengals' cafeteria. "Joe doesn't high hat anybody," says Don Cooley.[736]

The emphasis on community and trust has been and continues to be instrumental in the Bengals' historic turnaround. "How in the heck was he able to galvanize the Cincinnati Bengals' locker room?" asks Troy Bolin. "That's been one of the most dysfunctional locker rooms in football. And he goes in there with a snap of his fingers and almost changes it immediately."[737]

Building a relational culture has included wining and dining at The Precinct. When free agent right tackle Riley Reiff came to town during the Spring of 2021, Burrow and other team leaders took him to Jeff Ruby's iconic establishment for steaks and cigars. The deal was signed shortly thereafter.

In the Spring of 2022, offensive linemen Alex Cappa and Ted Karras were already in the fold, but Burrow still took them to The Precinct. He wanted to begin building rapport with his new right guard and center. As Robin always says, "It all starts with the center."

Later that night, Cappa and Karras found themselves sitting in Burrow's living room. Coveted free agent tackle La'el Collins strolls in. According to Collins, Burrow served cupcakes and crackers. After a wild social media ride the following day, which included Collins sightings all over town, the 6-foot-

4, 322-pound lineman signed on the dotted line. In the eleventh hour of negotiations, Burrow texted Collins, "Deal done????" Collins replied, "Yeah, your new bodyguard is in town. No one's going to touch you."[738]

In keeping with the theme of this chapter, here's a chance to cue "I Will Always Love You" by Whitney Houston. For the full effect, cruise on over to the Bengals Meme's Facebook page, where you'll find a slight modification to *The Bodyguard* movie poster (circa 1992). Instead of Kevin Costner holding Whitney Houston, La'el Collins is chivalrously cradling Joe Burrow.[739] Bengals fans are hoping Collins, like Costner, is willing to take a bullet for the star of the show.

Everyone was in a mirthful mood when Joe Burrow pulled his chair up to the microphone. It was mid-May, and Joe's first press conference since the Super Bowl. The media wasted no time asking about the night Joe served cupcakes and crackers to his future offensive linemen. Paul Dehner of *The Athletic* asked, "What exactly did that entail?" A light-hearted Burrow responded, "We just had some snacks." The room broke out in laughter. Dehner continued, "What kind of crackers were they?" Burrow said, "I don't remember. That was a while ago, but definitely made sure they had some snacks to eat."[740]

The conversation shifted to Joe's role in the recruiting of future free agents. "That's something I want to do every year," said Joe. "Make sure that the guys we're looking to bring in feel at home in Cincinnati with the team because that's the culture we're building in the locker room. We're really, really close as a team."[741]

Back in Athens

While Joe builds comradery among his teammates, the impact of his on-field performance and off-field generosity continues to be felt throughout Southeastern Ohio in a wide variety of ways. After more than $500,000 was initially generated through Will Drabold's Facebook fundraiser, the

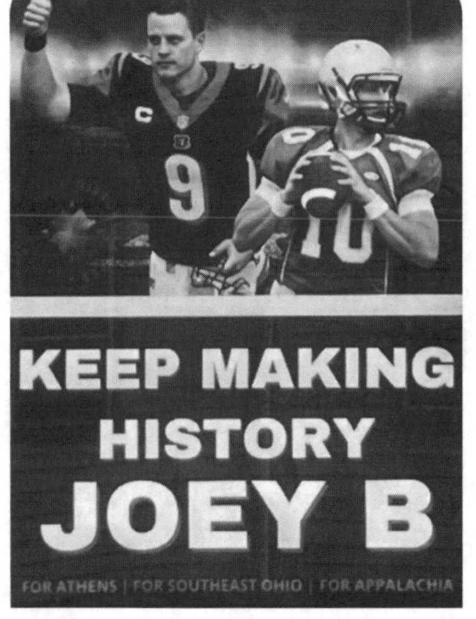

KEEP MAKING
HISTORY
JOEY B
FOR ATHENS | FOR SOUTHEAST OHIO | FOR APPALACHIA

A sign outside of the Southeast Ohio History Center. *Photo credit: Scott Burson*

Joe Burrow Hunger Relief Fund was established. At the time of this writing, nearly $2 million had been raised for food insecurity in the Athens area.

"Joe announced his Hunger Relief Fund on *Good Morning America*," said Karin Bright. "When he was injured, somebody started $9 donations in honor of Joe's number. I don't know how many $9 donations came in, but a lot. And then this past year, there were some really odd and quirky numbers people came up with. There was a $10 donation for the combination of Joe's [9] and Ja'Marr's [1] jerseys. Then the $31 donations for breaking the playoff curse and the $56 donations for the Super Bowl. We are amazed and grateful for all of the creative donations we continue to receive from people."[742]

Joe has been especially touched by how the stigma associated with the Food Pantry has fallen away. "Growing up we knew kids who had to go to the food bank because they didn't have a lot," remembers Joe. "I've heard stories from teachers that said little kids are [now] coming up to them and saying, 'Hey my family goes to the food bank.' They are excited about it. It isn't a thing where they are trying to hide it. That means a lot to me."[743]

Robin Burrow recently joined forces with Drabold and the Appalachian Children Coalition, an advocacy group for the needs of the region's children. As the principal of a small elementary school in Meigs County and mother of the "31-second" Heisman Trophy winner, Robin was the perfect fit. "We've been able to get state funding for expanding mental and behavioral health," says Robin, who serves on the board of directors and has been to the state house twice. "We are really just trying to bring awareness to the state legislature so we can receive some equity in funding down here. We're getting some strong traction."[744]

While Joe is not explicitly involved, Drabold believes the success of the Children Coalition can be traced back to Burrow's Heisman speech. "People want to see Joe succeed, which has created a real opportunity to say this is a great place, we need help and we deserve it," says Drabold. "You heard Joe talk about it, but that's the tip of the iceberg."[745]

When the NFL announced the "My Cause, My Cleats" initiative, providing players an opportunity to wear specially designed footwear in honor of their favorite charities, Joe reached out to the Athens High School art department. There would be a contest to design his customized cleats. The winner was Nikki Bean. Her design blended the two colors from the Athens County Food Pantry logo—green and orange, which also happen to be the primary colors of the Bulldogs and Bengals. Her eye-catching design also combined food cans and leaves from the Paul Brown Stadium Jungle. The autographed cleats were auctioned off with the proceeds going to the Joe Burrow Hunger Relief Fund.[746]

The Burrows continue to give back. On October 4, 2022, the Bengals' quarterback announced the launch of the Joe Burrow Foundation, which will focus on mental health and food insecurity in Southern Ohio and Louisiana. Burrow credits his parents, especially Robin for getting the foundation off the ground. "She spearheaded the whole thing. I wouldn't have done it at the time if I didn't have a mom and dad who are very passionate about what we're doing and are excited to help a lot of people in our community."[747]

While sports are not life and death, they can be life-giving for someone facing death. Athens Justice Robert Stewart had struggled with health

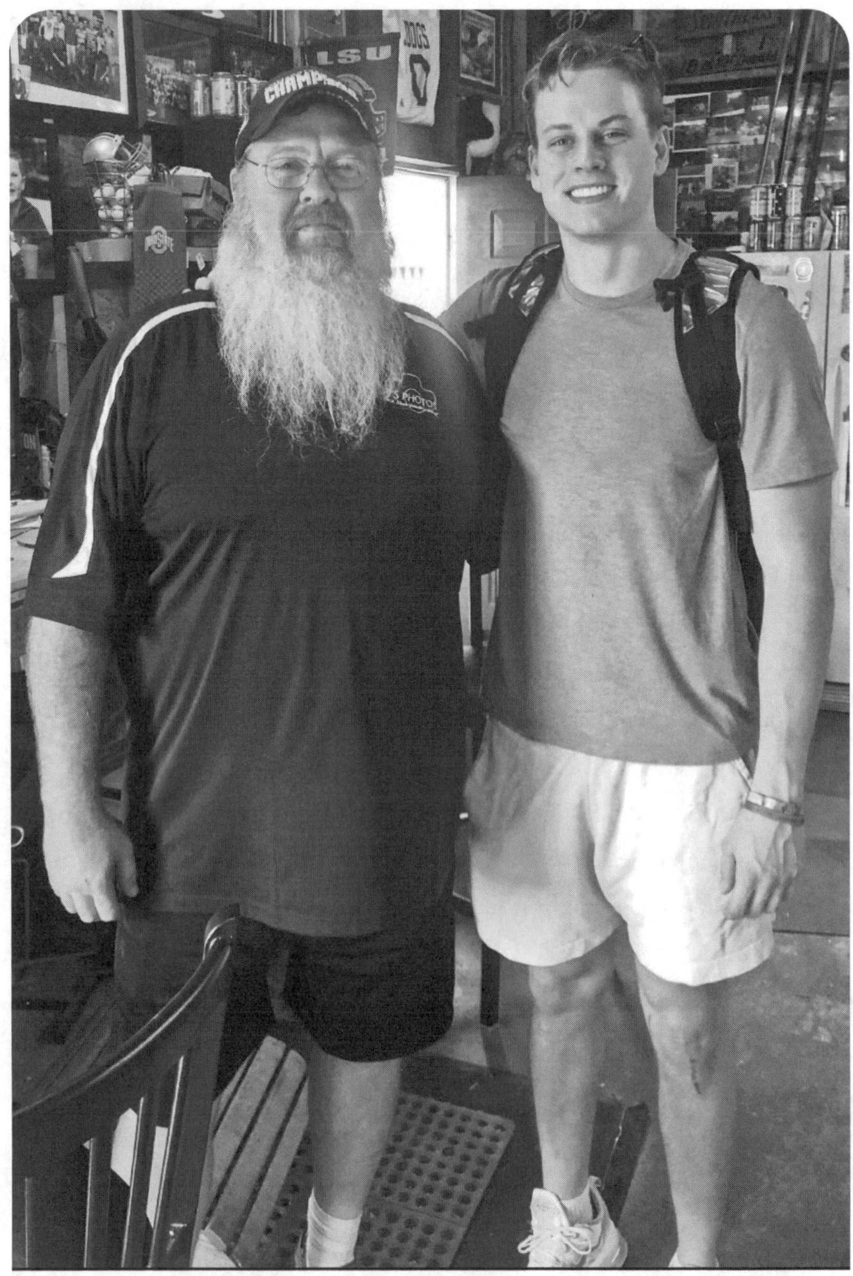

Joe often visits Coach Sam in the Dawg Pound when he returns to The Plains.
Photo credit: The Smathers Family

issues for many years. In the final year of his life, Joe Burrow posted the greatest individual season in college football history. Wife Machelle remembered how much each Saturday meant to Bob. It buoyed his spirit.

"While he was going through chemo and radiation, Bob was invigorated by looking forward to those games and hearing from Jimmy about what was happening at Joe's practices," says Machelle, "Bob's family was the most impactful factor in comforting him, but Joe provided a phenomenal diversion. He helped Bob think outside of himself and his pain and focus on someone else's success and joy. It was like a medicine the doctors hadn't invented."[748]

When Joe was drafted by Cincinnati, Bob was excited to see the Athens boy return to Ohio. Unfortunately, Bob didn't live long enough to see Joe play for the Bengals. He passed away the day before the opener against the Chargers in 2020. But Joe provided a priceless gift. The kid from Athens brought light, hope and joy into Bob's life in his final days.

From time to time, Joe quietly returns to The Plains. He occasionally reaches out to his former offensive coordinator Nathan White, now the head coach at Athens High School. "I usually get a text asking if he can get into the weight room and throw to some of the guys," says Coach White. "Of course, all of our receivers are lining up. Joe could easily go over to OU and do that, but it's cool he comes into our weight room and goes on the field with our current high school kids. It's awesome that this place still feels like home to him."[749]

Whether it's in the weight room or on the field, the Bengals' franchise quarterback gives maximum effort. "Our kids in the weight room get to look over and watch him lift and then on the field watch him go through his warm-up routine," continues White. "Three steps with a hitch, three steps escape right. Just to see a guy work at that level. It's invaluable. I tell them Joe didn't get to where he is by accident. Just look at him work."[750]

When he's finished at the high school, Joe swings by the Dawg Pound to visit with Sam Smathers. Joe pulls his Porsche into the driveway and asks Sam if he still details cars. Sam's happy to oblige. During the 90-minute visit, they don't discuss football. Just life.

One time, Sam's son Alan was in the garage when Joe stopped by. "We're hanging out and talking with him and my four-year-old boy, Jace, walks in," says Alan. "I said, 'Hey Jace, you want to get a picture with Joe?' Jace says, 'Nah, not really.' I turn and say, 'Not everybody knows you Joe.'"[751]

Bleed Green in 2014

Jace might not think Joe's a big deal, but nearly everyone else does. From Colorado to Croatia, people text Jimmy photos of people wearing Burrow attire. "Last time I checked, Joe's jersey is number-four among all NFL jersey sales," says Jimmy.[752]

In a "Football Morning in America" column, Peter King ranked Joe among the twenty-two most influential people in the NFL. While Burrow has been compared to Montana, King mentions a different Joe—Broadway Joe Namath.

"The reason why I think Burrow has shot to the top of NFL Q ratings is not only his ability and his Gen-Z-appealing fashion sense, but also his attitude," writes King. "He really has some Namath in him, the ability to play like the ultimate tough guy and at the same time having an I-could-not-care-less-what-you-think-of-me attitude. He doesn't get nervous or tight in big moments. And if his line could have blocked Aaron Donald down the stretch of Super Bowl LVI, he would have had the time to win it."[753]

Fred Gibson has first-hand knowledge of Joe's popularity. He has seen it stretch from Athens, Ohio, to Athens, Georgia. In early March 2022,

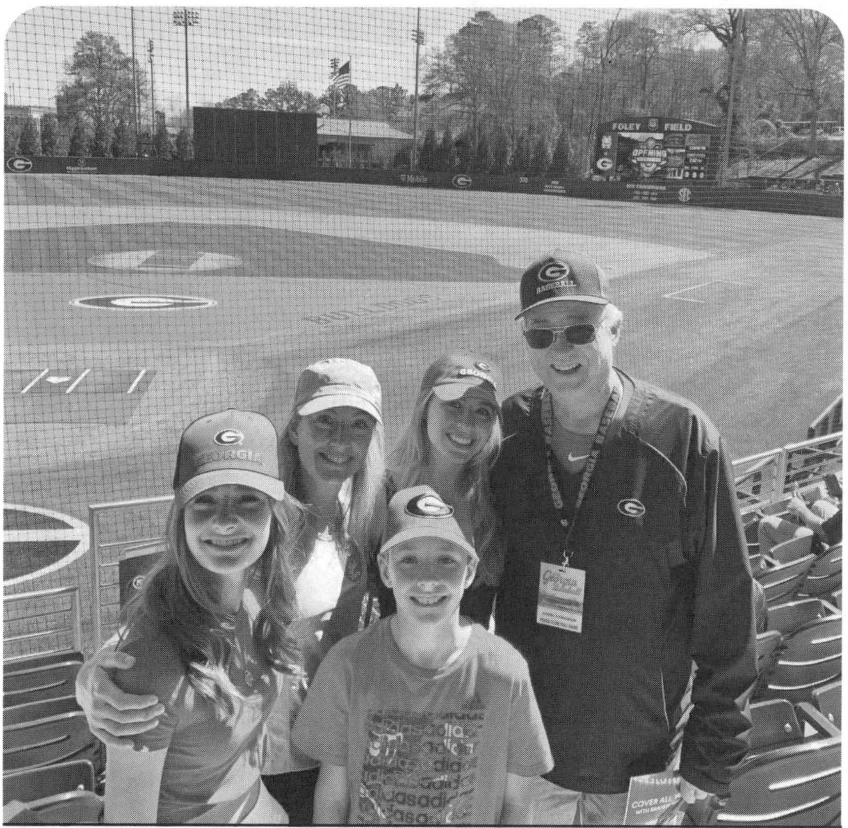

Gibby visits with friends at the University of Georgia baseball stadium. *Photo credit: The Gibson Family*

Gibby traveled to The Peach State to visit one of his former Athens High School players—Scott Stricklin, who has been the highly successful University of Georgia Bulldog baseball coach since 2014.

Stricklin's son is a high school baseball player, so they decide to go see him play. During one of the games, Gibby headed over to the concession stand. He noticed two kids with a football. One said to the other, "Go deep, I'm going to be Joe Burrow."

"Mind you, this is right after the University of Georgia won the national football title," says Gibby. "The kid wasn't pretending to be Georgia quarterback Stetson Bennett; He was imagining himself as Joe Burrow. That tells you something."[754]

Five months later the same two quarterbacks are paired on the front and back covers of the 2022 *Sports Illustrated* football preview issue. Bennett on the college side. Fresh-faced Joe Burrow on the NFL side. The headline reads: "Their Ultracool QB Has Transformed the Bengals' Vibe. Joe Burrow Knows the Job Isn't Done."[755]

Burrow won't be satisfied until he has a Super Bowl ring.

Joe is wearing a black Bengals jersey and holding a football with both hands. Staring thoughtfully into the distance. Contemplating another championship season perhaps. Or maybe reflecting upon the storybook journey that has landed him on the cover of the most prestigious sports magazine in the world.

There's a soundtrack to Joe's life, but on this day the Bengals' quarterback tells his story through wristbands. If you look closely at Joe's left wrist, you'll see a Scarlet red Buckeye band. On the right, a purple and gold Geaux Tigers. But the wristband closest to the ball and to his heart is green and weathered.

The lettering is mostly worn away, but his high school teammates know what it says: "Bleed Green in 2014" on one side. "Brotherhood" on the other.

"Joe remembers," says Troy Bolin. "He knows exactly who he is and where he's from."[756]

The rubber Bulldog band was on his wrist when he tossed six touchdowns in the Ohio high school state championship game. It was on his wrist when he accounted for another six touchdowns to win the college football national championship in New Orleans. It was on his wrist when he stunned Patrick Mahomes and the Kansas City Chiefs to claim Cincinnati's first Lamar Hunt AFC Championship Trophy in thirty-three years. There's no doubt that faded green band will be on his wrist if he ever lifts the biggest one of all—the Vince Lombardi Super Bowl Trophy.

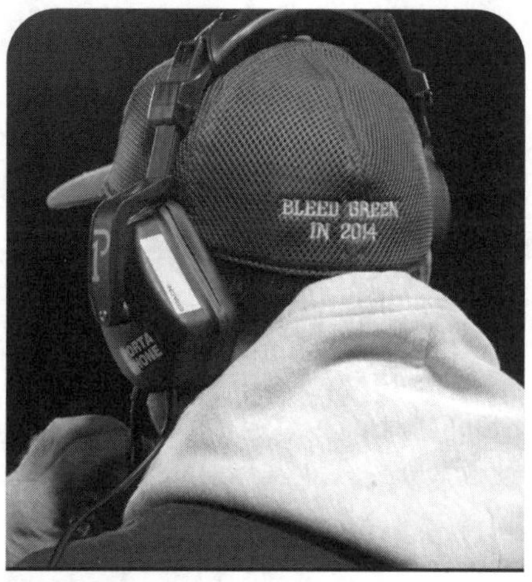

Ryan Adams wearing the "Bleed Green in 2014" hat. *Photo credit: Trisha Doudna*

For the people of Athens County, it's not a matter of *if*, but *when* Joe wins the Super Bowl. When it does happen, you can bet Fred Gibson, Les Champlin and Nathan White will be ringing the Bulldog victory bell and Sam Smathers will be blowing the A-train horn outside the Dawg Pound. And Joe Burrow Stadium will be lit up like Christmas, in Bulldog Green and Bengal Orange.

Epilogue

THE 2022–23 SEASON: THEY GOTTA PLAY US!

"I believe that we are in an era that is going to be the greatest era in Bengals history. And it's all because of one person. I challenge you to tell me why Joe Burrow is not going to take this team to the Promised Land at some point and very possibly multiple times."[757]

—Peter King
Football Morning in America

It's not much of a rivalry if one team wins every time.

The Bengals and Chiefs are now officially a rivalry.

After defeating Kansas City three times in a calendar year, Cincinnati fell short, 23–20, in the 2022–23 AFC title game. As expected, it was a back-and-forth slugfest, but in the end a 45-yard Harrison Butker field goal sent the Chiefs to their third Super Bowl in four years.

But the Bengals made it clear that their Super Bowl LVI appearance was no fluke. After setting several franchise records in 2022–23, they even converted doubting Thomas himself, Stephen A. Smith, who proclaimed, "The conversation has gone from Josh Allen and Patrick Mahomes to Joe Burrow and Patrick Mahomes. And Joe Burrow has put the world on notice. He's not going away."[758]

So, in honor of Joe, the 2022 NFL FedEx Air Player of the Year, here are nine highlights from one of the greatest seasons in Bengals franchise history.

9. Take a Deep Breath

"Let's all just take a deep breath and relax. We're going to be fine."[759]

Those were the confident words of Joe Burrow after the defending AFC Champion Cincinnati Bengals lost the first two games of the 2022 season to the Steelers and Cowboys. Both on last-second field goals.

While Burrow is never one to make excuses, there were two factors that contributed to the slow start. The first was a new offensive line. Without the benefit of any preseason snaps, it was inevitable that it would take time for the new line to gel. After giving up 13 sacks in the first two games, the Bengals would only give up 31 more during the rest of the regular season.

The second factor was an emergency trip to the hospital on the eve of training camp. Abdominal discomfort turned out to be a ruptured appendix for the Bengals' franchise quarterback. After nearly a week in the hospital, an emaciated Burrow appeared at practice—but was relegated to watching. He was noticeably thinner. And noticeably in pain. He had a pic line in his arm. The most he could do was participate in sprints—on his golf cart.

As the days moved closer and closer to September, Burrow returned to the field. It was a race against the clock to put weight back on his 6-foot-4 frame. "Gotta go back to high school days when you're trying to gain twenty pounds in a couple-week span," said Burrow. When asked what he had been eating, Joe responded, "Everything."[760]

The Enquirer's Kelsey Conway reminded Burrow that he had yet to have a normal training camp. Burrow just flashed a smile and shook his head: "I'd like to have a normal off season at some point. We'll try again next year."[761]

8. Joey Flowers

By the time Week Three rolled around, the offensive line was beginning to come together and Burrow was looking more like his pre-surgery self.

The result was a decisive 25–12 victory over the New York Jets. After tossing three touchdowns and registering his highest quarterback rating of the early season (114.9), Burrow returned to Paycor Stadium for a Thursday night showdown against old SEC nemesis Tua Tagovailoa and the visiting Miami Dolphins.

Joe Cool entered the stadium in a flowered suit and Cartier shades. His wardrobe choice was right on theme for a game in the Jungle against a team from South Florida.

In a conversation with Colin Cowherd, Burrow's most recent fashion selection was a topic of discussion. Cowherd said, "The fact that you like flowers warms my heart. Where does that come from?" Burrow replied, "I don't know where it started that you can only give girls flowers. If I got flowers I'd be pumped. Like if somebody came to me after a game and said, 'Hey, great game. Here's a rose.' I'd be excited about that."[762]

The very next day Burrow must have been ecstatic to find a bouquet of roses in his locker, courtesy of the Bengals' social media team.[763] A few months later, *The New York Times* tossed Burrow another bouquet by naming him one of their Ninety-three Most Stylish People of 2022.[764]

7. Back to the Bayou

After defeating Miami and losing at Baltimore on another walk-off field goal, the 2–3 Bengals traveled to New Orleans in what many labeled a must-win game.

Burrow's fashion statement was again on point. A few days before the game, he contacted Ja'Marr and asked if he could wear Chase's national championship game jersey. Numero Uno gladly complied, even though it meant pulling it off the wall and prying it out of its frame for the occasion.

The state of Louisiana had circled October 16th since the schedule dropped in May. Two of the best players from the best team in LSU history were coming home. But, unfortunately, they would be on the opposing sideline.

The last time the Bayou Bengals teammates played in the Super Dome, they connected for 221 yards, 9 catches and 2 touchdowns. Cincinnati would need a similar performance from their all-pro tandem. With 3:41 left on the clock and New Orleans clinging to a 26–24 lead, the Saints could put the game on ice with a few first downs. But the Bengals defense held, giving the ball back to Burrow with 1:57 remaining. On the first play from scrimmage, he found Ja'Marr on a 60-yard scoring pass to seal the victory.

Cincinnati improved to 3–3, but not without a cost. It was later revealed that Chase had fractured his hip earlier in the game. While he didn't go on Injured Reserve, the star receiver would eventually miss four games.

6. Havenly Wisdom

After winning two of the next three games, Cincinnati entered the Bye Week with the same record as last season: 5–4.

And, like last season, the Bengals came out of the Bye on a mission. Burrow was missing two of his top weapons (Chase and Joe Mixon). It didn't matter. He still threw for 355 yards and four touchdowns while spreading the ball around to nine receivers in a 37-30 victory over the Steelers.

As Cincinnati prepared to face the league's most difficult second-half schedule, Bengal superfan Haven Wolfe, a student at Northern Kentucky University, prepped for wisdom-tooth surgery. To calm her fears, she wore a Joe Burrow jersey.

After the procedure, Mom worked hard to keep her loopy daughter happy. A viral video would soon reveal a heavily medicated Haven talking like an informed Bengals beat writer.

Will Ja'Marr be ready soon?

Haven could offer no assurances: "I'm not a doctor. Never have been."

An emotional Haven then addressed the Bengals' impending gauntlet.

"We play the Titans on Sunday and Ja'Marr Chase isn't even a sure thing. And I miss him. But then, even if we get past that one, well then we've got the Kansas City Chiefs and Patrick Mahomes. He's so good and everyone knows it. And he makes those Subway commercials! Mom, I don't want to lose to the Browns. Joe Burrow's never beaten the Browns. And they are historically the worst franchise in NFL history. I mean my god-dang hero can't beat the Browns, Mom!"

Even the name of her favorite player couldn't stem the emotional tide.

"You love Joe Burrow don't you?" asked her mother. Through tears, Haven responded, "He's pretty, but dang it, he's talented. And let's be honest, I go for ambition, not looks!"[765]

A few days later, Burrow joined Peyton and Eli, on ESPN's Monday Night Football "Manning Cast." Haven's comments came up. After showing an edited portion of the clip, Eli said, "Let's repeat this, 'Let's be honest, I go for amibition, not looks.' Joe, I gotta know, is this flattering to you or is this an insult?" Burrow responded, "It sounds like I'm being called ugly there if you ask me."[766]

Haven took to Twitter to playfully defend herself: "Challenge flag thrown. After further review, Haven Wolfe NEVER called Joe Burrow UGLY. She said he is PRETTY and TALENTED. Illegal use of video. Roughing the wisdom tooth girl. Fifteen yard penalty. Automatic first down. Manning brothers ejected from game."[767]

Back in Nashville, the showdown with the Titans was hardly pretty, but Burrow's talent was on full display. The night before, Zac Taylor reminded the defending AFC champions that the remaining opponents on the schedule "Gotta Play Us!" The Bengals rewarded Haven and the rest of their fan base with victories over the Titans, Chiefs and Browns. The 27–24 conquest of the Chiefs was the third victory over Kansas City in a calendar year, making Burrow the first player to win his initial three meetings against Patrick Mahomes.

5. 89–1

In mid-December, the Bengals traveled to sunny Tampa to take on the Buccaneers. With victories over New Orleans, Atlanta and Carolina earlier in the season, Cincinnati was looking to make it a clean sweep of the NFC South. But the biggest attraction was watching Burrow go up against Tom Brady, the only other active quarterback with a winning record against Mahomes.

The Burrow-Brady Bowl did not go as planned. Brady and the 2022 Buccaneers had struggled to move the ball and score points all season. Not on this day. In the first half, the Bucs surged out to a 17–0 lead by scoring on three of their first four possessions. Tampa Bay ran twice as many plays as Cincinnati (40–20) in the opening half and entered the break with a commanding 17–3 lead.

But the Bengals regrouped and played their best second half of the season, scoring 31 unanswered points en route to a 34–23 victory. The Cincinnati defense forced four Brady turnovers (two fumbles, two interceptions) and Burrow threw touchdown strikes to Tee Higgins (5 yards), Tyler Boyd (3 yards), Ja'Marr Chase (8 yards) and Tampa-native Mitchell Wilcox (12 yards).

In his twenty-three-year career, Tom Brady had never lost a home game when leading by 17 or more points. Eighty-nine games. Zero losses. The GOAT was now 89–1.

4. The Game of Life

The Bengals traveled to frigid Foxboro for a Christmas Eve encounter with the playoff-contending Patriots. Cincinnati jumped out to a 22-0 first-half lead, but New England scored 18 unanswered points and was threatening again when Vonn Bell forced a redzone fumble. Cincinnati held on for its first victory in Foxboro in thirty-six years.

The Bengals won their seventh-straight game, but did not escape unscathed. After playing the first fifteen games with the same offensive line, Burrow's bodyguard, La'el Collins, suffered a season-ending knee injury. Over the next few games, the offensive line depth would be severely tested as right guard Alex Cappa and left tackle Jonah Williams would also go down with season-ending injuries.

After vanquishing Brady and Belichick in back-to-back weeks, Burrow and the Bengals returned home to take on Josh Allen and the Buffalo Bills. The Monday night encounter between two marquee quarterbacks was billed as the game of season.

Bengals radio announcer Dan Hoard likened the pre-game atmosphere, which included fireworks and an interactive light show, to the Super Bowl or Olympics. The electricity reached an early crescendo when Burrow threw a 14-yard touchdown dart to Tyler Boyd on the opening drive.

After holding Buffalo to a field goal, the Cincinnati offense was marching toward more points when Bills' safety Damar Hamlin tackled Tee Higgins. After initially getting to his feet, Hamlin collapsed. The medical team quickly started CPR.

Stunned Bills and Bengals players gathered together on the field. Some on a knee; others in a tearful embrace. As the severity of the situation sank in, prayers and pensive silence filled previously raucous Paycor Stadium.

After thirty minutes of on-field medical attention, an ambulance took Hamlin to the University of Cincinnati Medical Center. It was the second time this season that a player was rushed by ambulance to the nearby trauma center. Back in September, Tua Tagovailoa was also taken to UCMC after sustaining a head injury.

While the NFL discussed how to proceed, both teams left the field. When Burrow suffered his devastating knee injury during his rookie year, nearly every starting NFL quarterback reached out to him. It was the first time he had really experienced the NFL brotherhood. On this night, it was his turn to return the favor. With the status of the game still uncertain, Burrow led the Bengals' captains over to the Bills' locker room as a gesture of support and solidarity.

Meanwhile, the coaches had already spoken on the field. Bills' Head Coach Sean McDermott said he needed to be with Hamlin at the hospital. Taylor supported McDermott's decision and told him that he would treat Damar like one of his own players when the Bills returned to Buffalo.

The NFL officially postponed the game sixty-six minutes after Hamlin collapsed. It would be several days before the league decided whether or not to resume the game, but on this night the world saw the Bengals' organization and fanbase handle the crisis with compassion and class. In an interview with Dan Hoard, Peter King had nothing but praise for Zac Taylor and Joe Burrow: "As crazy as it sounds I almost get emotional when I think about both guys. And it was clear that they were the adults in the room."[768]

As Hamlin fought for his life, $8.6 million flooded into a toy drive fundraiser he had started two years prior. His initial goal was $2,500 to buy toys for needy kids.[769]

Remarkably, Damar improved each day. On Thursday, his doctors held a press conference. They announced that Damar was alert and communicating through writing. One of the first things he asked was "Did we win?" The doctor by his side responded, "Yes, Damar, you won. You've won the game of life."[770]

3. Fumble in the Jungle

Three days after the NFL postponed the Bengals-Bills game, the league officially ruled it a no contest. The announcement came with the following proviso: The Bengals would be awarded the AFC North title, but if Baltimore were to win the regular-season finale against Cincinnati, a coin-toss would decide the home field should the two teams square off in the first round of the playoffs.

Despite objecting to the league's decision, the Bengals turned their attention to preparing for a difficult Ravens team. While Damar's consistent improvement buoyed their spirits, several Bengals players openly discussed the challenge of playing while still emotionally processing Hamlin's near-death experience.

The league's coin-toss ruling forced the Bengals to play their starters in the season finale. The Ravens, on the other hand, chose to rest several key players who were nursing injuries. Despite building an early 17-point lead, the Bengals' offense stalled in the second half. The defense, however, forced four Baltimore turnovers on the day and held the Ravens to just three field goals down the stretch to secure a 27–16 victory.

No coin toss would be needed.

The sixth-seeded Ravens returned to Paycor Stadium to play the third-seeded Bengals the following Sunday night in the Super Wild Card round.

With just under twelve minutes remaining and the game tied at 17, Ravens' signal-caller Tyler Huntley attempted a quarterback sneak on third and goal from the 1-yard line. But instead of going low, as the play was designed, Huntley went high and extended the ball toward the goal line. Germaine Pratt held him up while Logan Wilson knocked the ball out of Huntley's hands.

The ball went straight into the fortuitous arms of Cincinnati Moeller grad Sam Hubbard, who rumbled 98 yards for a touchdown. Mike Tirico's call will be replayed by Bengals' fans for years to come: "Sam Hubbard, the Cincinnati kid, has a convoy chased by Andrews, at the 30, the 20, HE…

WILL...SCORE!"[771] It was the longest fumble return for a touchdown in NFL postseason history. And the loudest moment of the season in Paycor Stadium—registering 118 decibels.

Whether you call it "Hubbard to the House," "The Hubbard-Yard Run," or "The Fumble in the Jungle," Hubbard's heroics will go down as one of the most iconic moments in franchise history.

2. Better Send Those Refunds

The 24–17 victory over the Ravens sent the Bengals to Orchard Park for a divisional-round matchup against the Bills. Many thought the game should be played at a neutral site. After all, if the Bengals had won the cancelled game, the Bills would be headed to Cincinnati instead.

But the neutral-site arrangement would only apply to a Bills-Chiefs AFC title game. If needed, that game would be held in Atlanta. As Cincinnati prepared for Buffalo it was announced that 50,000 seats had already been sold to Bills and Chiefs season-ticket holders.

The Bengals' locker room was listening.

They were also listening to their head coach the night before the game. In a motivational speech, Taylor shared a statistic: the Bills' career home playoff record in Highmark Stadium was 13–1, dating all the way back to 1973. That'a a 93-percent winning percentage over the last fifty years. Nobody gave the Bengals a chance. The AFC North champions entered the game 5.5-point underdogs.

"We've never been an underdog," said D.J. Reader, who, like many in the Bengals' locker room, channeled the disrespect into fuel. "If people in Vegas want to keep losing their money, that's on them."[772]

As the clock ticked closer to kickoff, Western New York flakes began to coat the Highmark Stadium turf. How could the Bengals ever defeat the Bills in these conditions? Especially with a make-shift offensive line. By the end of the game, however, the Bengals had decisively answered all questions and doubters. And Joe Cool, Joe Shiesty, and Joe Brrr had acquired a new nickname: Snow Burrow.

While Bengals and Bills fans came together when Damar Hamlin was injured at Paycor Stadium *(above)*, that solidarity didn't hinder the intensity of the snowy rematch in Buffalo. *Photo credit: Scott Burson*

The 27–10 victory over the Bills was the most complete game of the year for the Bengals. They dominated in all three phases. First quarter touchdown passes to Ja'Marr Chase and Hayden Hurst sucked the energy out of the stadium. The Bills never found their footing on either side of the ball. The offensive line kept Burrow clean, allowing him time to find eight different receivers. The line also created gaping holes for Joe Mixon, who carried the ball 20 times for 105 yards.

The Bengals' defense held the vaunted Bills' offense to a meager 10 points—20 points under their home average. As the Bills' fans began to file out of the stadium midway through the fourth quarter, the celebration was on. "Who Deys" rang loudly throughout the stadium. Josh Allen's final pass of the season was intercepted by rookie Cam Taylor-Britt, leading to celebratory snow angels in the end zone.

After the game, sideline reporter Tracy Wolfson asked Burrow about all the neutral-site talk and how much it motivated the Bengals. Without missing a beat, Burrow said, "Better send those refunds."[773]

1. The Open Window

After the Bengals' decisive victory over the Bills, Peter King offered the following hopeful words: "I believe that we are in an era that is going to be the greatest era in Bengals history. And it's all because of one person. I challenge you to tell me why Joe Burrow is not going to take this team to the Promised Land at some point and very possibly multiple times."[774]

The Bengals fell a play or two short of going to their second consecutive Super Bowl. Nevertheless, the 2022–23 season was one of the greatest in team history. After an uneven start, the Bengals strung together a franchise-record ten consecutive victories, won back-to-back division titles and advanced to the AFC Championship game in consecutive seasons for the first time in team history.

Already an elite quarterback, Joe Burrow continued to ascend. For the first time in his short career, he was selected to the Pro Bowl and named the 2022 NFL FedEx Air Player of the Year.

Burrow solidified his spot among the top two or three quarterbacks in the league by leading the NFL in red-zone passer rating and finishing second in completion percentage and touchdown passes.

Former Bengals' quarterback Carson Palmer doesn't think Burrow is among the top two or three signal-callers in the league. Palmer thinks Burrow is number-one.

"I think Joe's the best quarterback in the league," said Palmer in a conversation with his brother, Jordan, who trains Burrow and Josh Allen in the off-season. "Patrick is phenomenal. But I just think Joe's more consistent. Talk about not having a weakness, mentally strong, physically tall, accurate, can throw it fast enough, gets the ball out quick. I think he's athletic outside the pocket. He can do a lot of the same things Patrick Mahomes has done. He hasn't done it and showed it yet. He's played well within his system and style but I think he's the best quarterback in the league."[775]

After the Bengals defeated the Ravens in the final regular-season game, Burrow fielded questions from the media. Joe was asked about the Bengals' current Super Bowl window. After all, he's still on a rookie contract. Once the extension is signed, it will be tough to keep the band together. A confident Burrow didn't hesitate: "The window's my whole career and everybody that we have in that locker room, all the coaches we have. Things are going to change year to year but our window's always open."[776]

2022–23 CINCINNATI BENGALS
AFC NORTH CHAMPIONS
14–5

WEEK 1: Steelers 23, Bengals 20 (OT)
WEEK 2: Cowboys 20, Bengals 17
WEEK 3: Bengals 27, Jets 12
WEEK 4: Bengals 27, Dolphins 15
WEEK 5: Ravens 19, Bengals 17
WEEK 6: Bengals 30, Saints 26
WEEK 7: Bengals 35, Falcons 17
WEEK 8: Browns 32, Bengals 13
WEEK 9: Bengals 42, Panthers 21
WEEK 10: BYE
WEEK 11: Bengals 37, Steelers 30
WEEK 12: Bengals 20, Titans 16
WEEK 13: Bengals 27, Chiefs 24
WEEK 14: Bengals 23, Browns 10
WEEK 15: Bengals 34, Buccaneers 23
WEEK 16: Bengals 22, Patriots 18
WEEK 17: Bengals-Bills—No Contest
WEEK 18: Bengals 27, Ravens 16
Wild Card Round: Bengals 24, Ravens 17
Divisional Round: Bengals 27, Bills 10
AFC Championship: Chiefs 23, Bengals 20

Endnotes

[1] Bally Sports Ohio & Great Lakes, "Future Ohio State Buckeye reflects on state title loss," https://www.youtube.com/watch?v=QsSUtblN0tI, December 8, 2014; accessed May 4, 2022.

[2] Ben Baby, ESPN, https://www.espn.com/nfl/story/_/id/33218282/tough-comes-why-bengals-joe-burrow-plays-qb-linebacker?device=featurephone; accessed May 7, 2022. Warren was the Ohio High School Player of the Year in 2016.

[3] Jimmy Burrow, interview with the author, Athens, Ohio, March 9, 2022.

[4] Bally Sports Ohio & Great Lakes, "Future Ohio State Buckeye reflects on state title loss."

[5] Ibid.

[6] Bill Landis, "Ohio State QB Commit Joe Burrow throws 6 TDs in Ohio Stadium debut, comes short of state title dream," https://www.cleveland.com/osu/2014/12/ohio_state_qb_joe_burrow_bucke.html, December 5, 2014; accessed May 6, 2022.

[7] Cincinnati Bengals, "Joe Burrow News Conference," https://www.youtube.com/watch?v=_xjJEUkaFbQ, December 1, 2022; accessed May 5, 2022.

[8] Jimmy Burrow, interview with the author, Athens, Ohio, March 9, 2022.

[9] Robin Burrow, interview with the author, The Plains, Ohio, May 27, 2022.

[10] Mark Pfaff, "He's Mr. City Recreation," *The Athens Messenger*, October 8, 1969.

[11] Sam Smathers, interview with the author, The Plains, Ohio, March 10, 2022.

[12] Ibid.

[13] Postgame Central, "Cincinnati Bengals Quarterback Joe Burrow Press Conference After Super Bowl LVI Loss to Rams," https://www.youtube.com/watch?v=ky4a4cdPvHE, February 14, 2022; accessed May 14, 2022.

[14] Mike Petraglia with Dan Hoard, Jungle Roar Podcast, "Jungle Roar with Dan Hoard: Why Jessie Bates Will Play and Why Joe Burrow Is Perfect for Cincinnati," May 18, 2022; accessed May 9, 2022.

[15] In fact, the feature film that tells the Kurt Warner story is entitled, "American Underdog."
[16] Jimmy Burrow, interview with the author, Athens, Ohio, March 9, 2022.
[17] Robin Burrow, interview with the author.
[18] Ibid.
[19] Mike Petraglia with Dan Hoard, "Jungle Roar with Dan Hoard."
[20] Fanatics View, "Odell Beckham Reacts to 'Cool' Joe Burrow & His First Impressions of Joe: 'You Can't Not Like Him,'" https://www.youtube.com/watch?v=l1I32qfqgwQ, February 8, 2022; accessed May 20, 2022.
[21] George Motz, host of Travel Channel's "Burger Land," lists Bill's as number two on his list of top burger joints from around the country. See Adam Baer, "18 Standout Burgers You Should Try Now," *Men's Journal*, https://www.mensjournal.com/food-drink/the-18-best-burgers-in-america-20131217/the-fried-burger-at-korzo-brooklyn-ny/, accessed June 3, 2022.
[22] Jimmy Burrow, interview with the author, The Plains, Ohio, May 27, 2022.
[23] Ben Portnoy, *The Commercial Dispatch*, "'I Still Have My Cowbell': LSU's Joe Burrow Returns Home to the State His Family Calls Home," https://cdispatch.com/sports/2019-10-18/i-still-have-my-cowbell-lsus-joe-burrow-returns-to-the-state-his-family-calls-home/, October 18, 2019; accessed May 15, 2022.
[24] ESPN College Football, "The Many Sides of LSU QB Joe Burrow, College GameDay," https://www.youtube.com/watch?v=PmxqT_QbXvc, October 12, 2019; accessed May 15, 2022.
[25] Jimmy Burrow, interview with the author, The Plains, Ohio, May 27, 2022.
[26] Bob Condotta, *The Seattle Times*, "Former WSU coach helped shape Joe Burrow's father's career," https://www.seattletimes.com/sports/wsu-cougar-football/former-wsu-coach-jim-walden-helped-shape-joe-burrows-fathers-career/, February 11, 2022; accessed May 15, 2022.
[27] Ibid.
[28] Michael Kelly, *Huskers Illustrated*, "The Burrow Who Geauxt Away," https://huskersillustrated.com/the-burrow-who-geauxt-away/, April 6, 2022; accessed June 3, 2022.
[29] Rick Cleveland, *Mississippi Today*, "Who knew? LSU quarterback sensation Joe Burrow has strong Mississippi ties," https://mississippitoday.org/2019/10/15/who-knew-lsu-quarterback-sensation-joe-burrow-has-strong-mississippi-ties/, October 15, 2019; accessed May 20, 2022.
[30] Condotta, "Former WSU coach helped shape Joe Burrow's father's career."
[31] Tim Rohan, *The New York Times*, "A Road Map for Penn State: How Two Coaches Dealt With Recruiting Limits," https://www.nytimes.com/2012/07/30/sports/ncaafootball/two-coaches-different-approaches-to-ncaa-sanctions.html?_r=0, July 29, 2012; accessed June 4, 2022.
[32] Kelly, "The Burrow Who Geauxt Away."
[33] Ibid.
[34] Ibid.
[35] "How Joe Burrow Got His Start Under Center," https://lsusports.net/news/2019/11/20/chapter-2-thats-joe/, November 20, 2019; accessed, June 5, 2022.
[36] Amanda Tomlinson, *The National News*, "Why the first five years of a child's development are the most important," https://www.thenationalnews.com/arts/why-the-first-five-years-of-a-child-s-development-are-the-most-important-1.127401, September 16, 2015; accessed June 5, 2022.
[37] Jimmy Burrow, interview with the author, The Plains, Ohio, May 27, 2022.
[38] Will Drabold, zoom interview with the author, June 1, 2022.
[39] Robin Burrow, interview with the author.

[40] Sam Smathers, interview with the author, The Plains, Ohio, May 24, 2022.

[41] Cincinnati Bengals, "Joe Burrow: 'We Made Plays When We Needed To,'" https://www.bengals.com/video/joe-burrow-we-made-plays-when-we-needed-to, January 15, 2022; accessed June 6, 2022.

[42] Ibid.

[43] Shubham Bhargava, First Sportz,"'Boy got style': Third-grader who chose Joe Burrow for his biography report is breaking the Internet for nailing the 'Joe Sheisty' look," https://firstsportz.com/nfl-third-grader-who-chose-joe-burrow-for-his-biography-report-is-breaking-the-internet-for-nailing-the-joe-sheisty-look/, April 4, 2022; accessed June 1, 2022.

[44] Robin Burrow, interview with the author.

[45] Sam Smathers, interview with the author, The Plains, Ohio, May 24, 2022.

[46] Jimmy Burrow and Sam Smathers, interview with the author, The Plains, Ohio, May 27, 2022.

[47] Jimmy Burrow, interview with the author, Athens, Ohio, March 9, 2022.

[48] Robin Burrow, interview with the author.

[49] Ibid.

[50] Keith McGrath, phone interview with the author.

[51] Ibid.

[52] Liz Luehrman, interview with the author, Athens, Ohio, May 26, 2022.

[53] The "hot corner" is another name for third base.

[54] Jimmy Burrow, interview with the author, The Plains, Ohio, May 27, 2022.

[55] Robin Burrow, interview with the author.

[56] Don Cooley, zoom interview with the author, June 4, 2022.

[57] Ibid.

[58] Evan Cooley, zoom interview with the author, June 6, 2022.

[59] Sam Vander Ven, zoom interview with the author, June 7, 2022.

[60] Tom Vander Ven, interview with the author, Athens, Ohio, May 27, 2022.

[61] Liz Luehrman, interview with the author.

[62] Ibid.

[63] Don Cooley, zoom interview with the author.

[64] Keith McGrath, phone interview with the author.

[65] Evan Cooley, zoom interview with the author.

[66] Sam Vander Ven, zoom interview with the author.

[67] Keith McGrath, phone interview with the author.

[68] Brody McGrath, zoom interview with the author, June 4, 2022.

[69] Don Cooley, zoom interview with the author.

[70] Off the Bench, "Joe Burrow Defeats Oklahoma In Basketball With Winning Shot," https://www.youtube.com/watch?v=t0WcqRGctWM, December 27, 2019; accessed June 9, 2022.

[71] Jimmy Burrow, interview with the author, Athens, Ohio, March 9, 2022.

[72] Brody McGrath, zoom interview with the author.

[73] Don Cooley, zoom interview with the author.

[74] Sam Vander Ven, zoom interview with the author.

[75] Mary Ann Welsh, interview with the author, The Plains, Ohio, May 26, 2022.

[76] Tom Vander Ven, interview with the author, Athens, Ohio, May 27, 2022.

[77] Cooley made it clear in the interview that this team was not from Wellston.

[78] Don Cooley, zoom interview with the author.

[79] Sam Vander Ven, zoom interview with the author. "Breaking someone's ankles" is a basketball colloquialism for making such a great move that the defender is completely thrown off balance.

[80] Cincinnati Bengals, "Joe Burrow News Conference: Off-Season Training Program," https://www.youtube.com/watch?v=iW_MJUflgHI, May 17, 2022; accessed June 11, 2022.

[81] Ben Linsey, "2022 NFL receiving corps rankings: Cincinnati Bengals take No. 1 spot, Philadelphia Eagles make top five," https://www.pff.com/news/nfl-receiving-corps-rankings-cincinnati-bengals-philadelphia-eagles-2022, June 9, 2022; accessed June 11, 2022.

[82] Sam Smathers, interview with the author, The Plains, Ohio, May 27, 2022.

[83] Sam Smathers, interview with the author, The Plains, Ohio, March 11, 2022.

[84] Ryan Luehrman, interview with the author, The Plains, Ohio, May 25, 2022.

[85] Sam Smathers, interview with the author, The Plains, Ohio, March 11, 2022.

[86] Ibid.

[87] Ibid.

[88] Sam Vander Ven, zoom interview with the author.

[89] The only exception was when a tornado damaged the field in 2010. We'll tell that story in the next chapter.

[90] Sam Vander Ven, zoom interview with the author.

[91] Sam Smathers, interview with the author, The Plains, Ohio, March 11, 2022.

[92] Ibid.

[93] Sam Smathers, interview with the author, The Plains, Ohio, May 27, 2022.

[94] Jimmy Burrow, interview with the author, The Plains, Ohio, May 27, 2022.

[95] John Pugh, interview with the author, The Plains, Ohio, May 24, 2022.

[96] Ibid.

[97] Sam Smathers, interview with the author, The Plains, Ohio, March 11, 2022.

[98] Ibid.

[99] Ibid.

[100] Les Champlin, interview with the author, The Plains, Ohio, May 24, 2022.

[101] Sam Smathers and John Pugh, interview with the author, The Plains, Ohio, May 24, 2022.

[102] Ibid.

[103] Sam Smathers, interview with the author, The Plains, Ohio, May 25, 2022.

[104] Ibid.

[105] Robin Burrow, interview with the author.

[106] Ibid.

[107] Liz Luehrman, interview with the author.

[108] Sam Smathers, interview with the author, The Plains, Ohio, May 25, 2022.

[109] Robin Burrow in conversation with John McCallister, "Meet Joe Burrow's 'Super Mom'–Robin Burrow," https://www.youtube.com/watch?v=VCWN32S3eBE, January 27, 2022; Accessed June 13, 2022.

[110] Sam Smathers, interview with the author, The Plains, Ohio, May 25, 2022.

[111] Pugh, interview with the author.

[112] Sam Smathers, interview with the author, The Plains, Ohio, May 25, 2022.

[113] Ibid.

[114] Sam Smathers, interview with the author, The Plains, Ohio, March 11, 2022.

[115] Don Cooley, zoom interview with the author.

[116] Marikay Vander Ven, zoom interview with the author, July 13, 2022.

[117] Tom Vander Ven, interview with the author, Athens, Ohio, May 27, 2022.

[118] Jeff Skinner, interview with the author, Athens, Ohio, May 26, 2022.

[119] lsufootball net, "2019 SEC Media Days – LSU's Joe Burrow," https://www.youtube.com/watch?v=SC4EGmNyilc, July 15, 2019; accessed June 15, 2022.

[120] Chase now plays for the Cincinnati Bengals, Jefferson for the Minnesota Vikings, and Marshall for the Carolina Panthers.

[121] lsufootball net, "2019 SEC Media Days – LSU's Joe Burrow."

[122] Chad Springer, interview with the author, The Plains, Ohio, March 10, 2022.

[123] Ibid.

[124] Zacciah Saltzman, zoom interview with the author, May 31, 2022.

[125] Ross Dellenger, *Sports Illustrated*, "Meet Joe Burrow: LSU's Toughest Renaissance Man and Maybe Savior," https://www.si.com/college/2019/07/16/joe-burrow-lsu-sec-media-days, July 15, 2019; accessed June 16, 2022.

[126] Fred Gibson, interview with the author, Athens, Ohio, March 8, 2022.

[127] Ibid.

[128] Ibid.

[129] Ibid.

[130] Ibid.

[131] Jimmy Burrow, interview with the author, The Plains, Ohio, May 27, 2022.

[132] If you are missing the references to Doc Brown, the DeLorean, and flux capacitor, you might want to add Steven Spielberg's classic *Back to the Future* to your movie queue.

[133] Bill Finnearty, Scott Burson's Facebook page, https://www.facebook.com/scott.burson.3, April 12, 2022; accessed September 6, 2022.

[134] Ryan Luehrman, interview with the author.

[135] Coach Gibson retired in 2012, but was still involved with the program in a different capacity when Joe was a senior. The road leading to the Athens High School baseball field was renamed "Gibby Way" in 2022.

[136] Jimmy Burrow, interview with the author, The Plains, Ohio, May 27, 2022.

[137] For some interesting comments from Burrow about Batman and Superman, check out this press conference: https://www.youtube.com/watch?v=_BClddnAEVw, June 14, 2022; accessed June 24, 2022.

[138] Dave Clark, *USA Today*, "Joey Votto in Instagram post: Joe Burrow asked 'aren't you a little old for TikTok?'" https://www.usatoday.com/story/sports/mlb/reds/2022/04/13/joe-burrow-joey-votto-meet-tiktok-cincinnati-reds-opening-day/7314711001/, April 13, 2022; accessed June 16, 2022.

[139] See Cincinnati Reds "@Amir_Garrett confirms: Joey Votto bangs on the basketball court," https://twitter.com/reds/status/1330915876468629504, November 23, 2020; accessed June 17, 2022.

[140] Jimmy Burrow, interview with the author, Athens, Ohio, March 9, 2022.

[141] Jeff Skinner, interview with the author, Athens, Ohio, May 26, 2022.

[142] Cleveland.com, "Ohio State QB Joe Burrow on Matthew Dellavedova," https://www.youtube.com/watch?v=j1zj4gUY9ok, August 11, 2016; accessed June 17, 2022.

[143] Doug Lesmerises@DougLesmerises, https://twitter.com/DougLesmerises/status/1205128753950724096, December 12, 2019; accessed June 16, 2022.

[144] Jeff Skinner, interview with the author, Athens, Ohio, May 26, 2022.

[145] Robin Burrow, interview with the author.

[146] Troy Bolin, zoom interview with the author, June 18, 2022.

[147] Jeff Skinner, interview with the author, Athens, Ohio, May 26, 2022.

[148] Ibid.

[149] Ibid.

[150] Jimmy Burrow, interview with the author, Athens, Ohio, March 9, 2022.

[151] Jeff Skinner, interview with the author, Athens, Ohio, May 26, 2022.

[152] Ibid.
[153] Ibid.
[154] Bolin, zoom interview with the author.
[155] Liz Luehrman, interview with the author.
[156] Jeff Skinner, interview with the author, Athens, Ohio, May 26, 2022.
[157] Bolin, zoom interview with the author.
[158] Jeff Skinner, interview with the author, Athens, Ohio, May 26, 2022.
[159] Bolin, zoom interview with the author.
[160] Jeff Skinner, interview with the author, Athens, Ohio, May 26, 2022.
[161] Ibid.
[162] Ibid.
[163] Ibid.
[164] Bolin, zoom interview with the author.
[165] Ibid.
[166] Jeff Skinner, interview with the author, Athens, Ohio, May 26, 2022.
[167] Ibid.
[168] Robin Burrow, interview with the author.
[169] Jeff Skinner, interview with the author, Athens, Ohio, May 26, 2022.
[170] Ibid.
[171] Ibid.
[172] Ibid.
[173] Nathan White, interview with the author, The Plains, Ohio, March 9, 2022.
[174] Jeff Skinner, story told to the author, Athens, Ohio, May 26, 2022.
[175] Bolin, zoom interview with the author.
[176] Ibid.
[177] Jeff Skinner, interview with the author, Athens, Ohio, May 26, 2022.
[178] Bolin, zoom interview with the author.
[179] TBD Tribute, "Let's Go" Podcast, "Tom Brady – Retirement Rumors & Joe Burrow," https://www.youtube.com/watch?v=JUttbP-iQLE, January 31, 2022; accessed June 27, 2022. At another time, Brady said the hit from Nate Clements was the hardest he's ever experienced. See Nick Wojton, Bills Wire, "Tom Brady says hit from Bills player long ago was hardest he's ever taken," https://billswire.usatoday.com/2022/06/02/tom-brady-hit-buffalo-bills-hardest-nate-clements/, June 2, 2022; accessed, June 28, 2022.
[180] Bill Finnearty, zoom interview with the author, June 27, 2022.
[181] White, interview with the author.
[182] Liz Luehrman, interview with the author.
[183] Ibid.
[184] Sam Smathers, interview with the author, The Plains, Ohio, May 27, 2022.
[185] Jimmy Burrow, interview with the author, The Plains, Ohio, May 27, 2022.
[186] Jack Glecker, *The Post*, "Ten years ago, Athens' stadium was destroyed by a tornado. It's community brought it back to life," http://projects.thepostathens.com/SpecialProjects/beyond-the-bubble-2020/athens-ohio-high-school-football-tornado-10-years-ago-basil-rutter-field.html, October 8, 2022; accessed August 28, 2022.
[187] Liz Luehrman, interview with the author.
[188] White, interview with the author.
[189] Ibid.
[190] Jeff Skinner, interview with the author, Athens, Ohio, May 26, 2022.
[191] White, interview with the author.

[192] Bolin, zoom interview with the author.
[193] White, interview with the author.
[194] Ibid.
[195] Ibid.
[196] Gibson, interview with the author.
[197] Ryan Luehrman, interview with the author.
[198] Finnearty, zoom interview with the author.
[199] Bolin, zoom interview with the author.
[200] Ibid.
[201] Finnearty, zoom interview with the author.
[202] Kevin Wiseman, *The Athens Messenger*, "Season ends for Bulldogs," https://www.athensmessenger.com/sports/local/season-ends-for-bulldogs/article_c2ad433e-fa5f-59d4-aa3a-ac6f57143388.html, November 17, 2012; accessed September 5, 2022.
[203] Robin Burrow, interview with the author.
[204] Bolin, zoom interview with the author.
[205] "Mitch Trubisky wins Ohio Mr. Football award for 2012 before heading to North Carolina," https://www.cleveland.com/highschoolsports/article/mentors-mitch-trubisky-wins-ohio-mr-football-award-for-2012-before-heading-to-north-carolina/, November 28, 2012; accessed June 30, 2022.
[206] Kevin Wiseman, *The Athens Messenger*, "Burrow back to lead Athens attack," https://www.athensmessenger.com/sports/local/burrow-back-to-lead-athens-attack/article_70d20a5c-48be-5bd2-9fac-d0fc3be64c74.html, April 29, 2013; accessed September 6, 2022.
[207] Zacciah Saltzman, zoom interview with the author, May 31, 2022.
[208] White, interview with the author.
[209] Sam Smathers, interview with the author, The Plains, Ohio, May 25, 2022.
[210] Bryce Graves, interview with the author, The Plains, Ohio, May 25, 2022.
[211] Sam Smathers, interview with the author, The Plains, Ohio, May 25, 2022.
[212] Matt Frazee, interview with the author, The Plains, Ohio, May 25, 2022.
[213] Gibson, interview with the author.
[214] Graves, interview with the author.
[215] Gibson, interview with the author.
[216] Ibid.
[217] Zacciah Saltzman, zoom interview with the author.
[218] Gibson, interview with the author.
[219] Jason Arkley, *The Athens Messenger*, "With Burrow, Athens knows anything is possible," https://www.athensmessenger.com/sports/local/with-burrow-athens-knows-anything-is-possible/article_09560e60-c5ff-549b-a27b-619b2b02fdbc.html, November 16, 2013; accessed September 6, 2022.
[220] Ibid.
[221] Jason Arkley, *The Athens Messenger*, "Bulldogs lose, but aren't defeated," https://www.athensmessenger.com/sports/local/bulldogs-lose-but-arent-defeated/article_7c74a93f-16a1-50f0-9cc1-25208b1f79b7.html, November 23, 2013; accessed September 6, 2022.
[222] White, interview with the author.
[223] Ibid.
[224] Sam Smathers, interview with the author, The Plains, Ohio, March 9, 2022.
[225] White, interview with the author.
[226] Ibid.
[227] Sam Smathers, interview with the author, The Plains, Ohio, March 9, 2022.

[228] Gibson, interview with the author.

[229] Ibid.

[230] Ibid.

[231] Ibid.

[232] Liz Luehrman, interview with the author.

[233] Kevin Wiseman, *The Athens Messenger*, "Bulldogs ready for Big Red," https://www.athensmessenger.com/sports/local/bulldogs-ready-for-big-red/article_c0d22f86-84ef-5273-ae43-9763b799e5ee.html, October 2, 2014; accessed September 6, 2022.

[234] Graves, interview with the author.

[235] Ryan Luehrman, interview with the author.

[236] Matt Frazee, interview with the author.

[237] Bill Kurelic, ScoutingOhio, "Athens/Joe Burrow vs. Steubenville Oct 3, 2014," https://www.youtube.com/watch?v=euqCA-RUMuk, January 10, 2018; accessed July 2, 2022.

[238] Bolin, interview with the author.

[239] Matt Frazee, interview with the author.

[240] Ryan Luehrman, interview with the author.

[241] Sam Vander Ven, zoom interview with the author.

[242] Ryan Mack, interview with the author, The Plains, Ohio, May 25, 2022.

[243] Graves, interview with the author.

[244] Adam Luehrman, interview with the author, The Plains, Ohio, May 25, 2022.

[245] Sam Smathers, interview with the author, The Plains, Ohio, May 25, 2022.

[246] Ryan Luehrman, interview with the author.

[247] Kevin Wiseman, *The Athens Messenger*, "Regional champions," https://www.athensmessenger.com/sports/local/regional-champions/article_62bb0bb9-6315-534f-8c61-f8e88715e917.html, November 22, 2014; accessed September 6, 2022.

[248] Ibid.

[249] Bolin, zoom interview with the author.

[250] Finnearty, zoom interview with the author.

[251] Kevin Wiseman, *The Athens Messenger*, "Burrow led fourth-quarter comeback in state semi-finals," December 19, 2019; accessed September 6, 2022.

[252] Bolin, zoom interview with the author.

[253] Sam Vander Ven, zoom interview with the author.

[254] Finnearty, interview with the author.

[255] Billy Witz, *The New York Times*, "Joe Burrow's Last Playoff Loss Was in High School. He Still Thinks About It." https://www.nytimes.com/2022/02/10/sports/football/bengals-joe-burrow-ohio.html, February 13, 2022; accessed July 3, 2022.

[256] Finnearty, zoom interview with the author.

[257] Witz, "Joe Burrow's Last Playoff Loss Was in High School."

[258] Gibson, interview with the author.

[259] Bally Sports Ohio & Great Lakes, "Future Ohio State Buckeye reflects on state title loss."

[260] Ryan Luehrman, interview with the author.

[261] Graves, interview with the author.

[262] White, interview with the author.

[263] Jason Arkley, *The Athens Messenger*, "Yo Joe, pick your head up," https://www.athensmessenger.com/sports/local/yo-joe-pick-your-head-up/article_aa16c4b5-6249-5f06-b8af-35eaa2acc6bb.html, December 5, 2014; accessed September 6, 2022.

[264] Don Cooley, zoom interview with the author.

[265] Robin Burrow, interview with the author.

[266] LSU Tiger TV, "'I eat a caramel apple sucker before every game.' – Joe Burrow on his pregame rituals," https://www.youtube.com/watch?v=52D0J_lwpy4, September 4, 2018; accessed July 5, 2022.

[267] Ibid.

[268] Mary Ann Welsh, interview with the author, The Plains, Ohio, May 26, 2022.

[269] Ibid.

[270] Jimmy Burrow, interview with the author, The Plains, Ohio, May 27, 2022.

[271] Robin Burrow, interview with the author.

[272] Jimmy Burrow, interview with the author, The Plains, Ohio, May 27, 2022.

[273] Kevin Wiseman, *The Athens Messenger*, "Burrow, Doseck reign supreme yet again," https://www.athensmessenger.com/sports/local/burrow-doseck-reign-supreme-yet-again/article_05de1ea3-0631-56e9-8857-989b329e1ab7.html, June 30, 2015; accessed September 6, 2022.

[274] Ibid.

[275] Robin Burrow, interview with the author.

[276] Wiseman, "Burrow, Doseck reign supreme yet again."

[277] Robin Burrow, interview with the author.

[278] Jimmy Burrow, interview with the author, The Plains, Ohio, May 27, 2022.

[279] Chad Springer, interview with the author, The Plains, Ohio, March 9, 2022.

[280] Kaitlin Baker, interview with the author, The Plains, Ohio, May 26, 2022.

[281] Welsh, interview with the author.

[282] Baker, interview with the author.

[283] Dominique Doseck, zoom interview with the author, June 23, 2022.

[284] lsufootball net, "2019 SEC Media Days – LSU's Joe Burrow," https://www.youtube.com/watch?v=SC4EGmNyilc, July 15, 2019; accessed July 6, 2022.

[285] Ben Shpigel, *The New York Times*, "Nice Fit: Joe Burrow Belongs to Everyone," https://www.nytimes.com/2022/02/12/sports/joe-burrow-style-super-bowl.html, February 13, 2022; accessed July 7, 2022.

[286] EI is shorthand for emotional intelligence. See Daniel Goleman, *Emotional Intelligence: Why it can matter more than IQ* (New York: Bantam Books, 1995).

[287] Kevin Wiseman, *The Athens Messenger*, "Former Athens teammates reveling in Burrow's success," https://www.athensmessenger.com/sports/local/former-athens-teammates-reveling-in-burrows-success/article_f01de54f-da29-5b9f-a5ad-1e4f7a64e7a8.htm, February 12, 2022; accessed September 6, 2022.

[288] Springer, interview with the author.

[289] For those interested in learning more about Kid Cudi's music and personal story, I suggest watching the documentary entitled "A Man Named Scott."

[290] Pardon My Take, "Joe Burrow #1 Pick & Bengals QB Sleeps in His Childhood Star Wars Bedroom," https://www.youtube.com/watch?v=BYUPTeYwJ_o, May 8, 2020; accessed July 7, 2022.

[291] Sam Vander Ven, zoom interview with the author.

[292] Zacciah Saltzman, zoom interview with the author, May 31, 2022.

[293] Full Send Podcast, "Joe Burrow on Partying After Super Bowl Loss, Brady's Future & Pre Game Outfits!" https://www.youtube.com/watch?v=8N4-0OaFB-c, May 18, 2022; accessed July 7, 2022.

[294] Zacciah Saltzman, zoom interview with the author, May 31, 2022.

[295] Bolin, zoom interview with the author.

[296] Gibson, interview with the author.

[297] Springer, interview with the author.

[298] Larry Di Giovanni, *The Athens Messenger*, "Locals react to seeing Athens grad as a Buckeye," https://www.athensmessenger.com/news/locals-react-to-seeing-athens-grad-as-a-buckeye/article_9f80bd89-f341-555b-acb1-27c0579a6c65.html, September 8, 2016; accessed September 6, 2022.

[299] Jeff Skinner, interview with the author, Athens, Ohio, May 26, 2022.

[300] Doseck, zoom interview with the author.

[301] Ibid.

[302] Brody Miller, NOLA.com, "His own kind of dude:' How quirky Joe Burrow won over Ohio State and will try to win over LSU," https://www.nola.com/archive/article_068f8ea8-32b4-5234-aae9-cba091b6d4ba.html, August 27, 2018; accessed July 8, 2022.

[303] Jason Arkley, *The Athens Messenger*, "Burrow says yes to Buckeyes," https://www.athensmessenger.com/sports/local/burrow-says-yes-to-buckeyes/article_39d5a29c-ab4a-555d-befb-65e37df2884a.html, May 27, 2014; accessed July 10, 2022.

[304] Ibid.

[305] "Tom Herman wins Broyles Award," https://www.espn.com/college-football/story/_/id/12004946/tom-herman-ohio-state-buckeyes-wins-broyles-award-nation-top-assistant-coach, December 9, 2014; accessed July 9, 2022.

[306] Wilson Alexander, *The Advocate*, "Just wait on it: How Joe Burrow's recruitment developed his bond with Texas coach Tom Herman," https://www.theadvocate.com/baton_rouge/sports/lsu/article_2026e6a0-ceaf-11e9-a097-7f71fab34b9d.html, September 3, 2019; accessed July 9, 2022.

[307] Jimmy Burrow, interview with the author, Athens, Ohio, March 9, 2022.

[308] Alexander, "Just wait on it."

[309] Kelly, *Huskers Illustrated*, "The Burrow Who Geauxt Away."

[310] Jimmy Burrow, interview with the author, Athens, Ohio, March 9, 2022.

[311] Ibid.

[312] Franklin Caltrider, "Urban Meyer Appears on the David Letterman Show," https://www.youtube.com/watch?v=BwnAYe9W1kI, January 16, 2015; accessed July 9, 2022.

[313] Jimmy Burrow, interview with the author, Athens, Ohio, March 9, 2022.

[314] Ibid.

[315] Kelly, *Huskers Illustrated*, "The Burrow Who Geauxt Away."

[316] theOzonedotnet, "Tim Beck Signing Day 2015," https://www.youtube.com/watch?v=OwQRATYXdSU, February 4, 2015; accessed July 9, 2022.

[317] Jimmy Burrow, interview with the author, Athens, Ohio, March 9, 2022.

[318] Arkley, "Burrow says yes to Buckeyes."

[319] ESPN College Football, "Joe Burrow's revenge tour has fueled his breakout season at LSU, College GameDay," https://www.youtube.com/watch?v=wkmTNTyhVxw, December 7, 2019; accessed July 10, 2022.

[320] Cleveland.com, "Joe Burrow on Ohio State's backup QB battle," https://www.youtube.com/watch?v=BBrOtH4yyeU, August 11, 2016; accessed July 10, 2022.

[321] Lantern TV, "Postgame press conference: Ohio State Spring Game," https://www.youtube.com/watch?v=BzpnTLv1dBM, April 16, 2016; accessed July 11, 2022.

[322] Billy George, "Joe Burrow Highlights 2016 Ohio State Spring Game," https://www.youtube.com/watch?v=qXIHhhZqGig; April 19, 2016; accessed July 11, 2022.

[323] Bolin, zoom interview with the author.

[324] Jimmy Burrow, interview with the author, Athens, Ohio, March 9, 2022.

[325] Mike Chiari, Bleacher Report, "Ohio State Spring Game 2016: Recap, Highlights and Twitter Reaction," https://bleacherreport.com/articles/2633394-ohio-state-spring-game-2016-recap-highlights-and-twitter-reaction, April 16, 2016; accessed September 6, 2022.

[326] Lantern TV, *The Bleacher Report*, "Postgame press conference: Ohio State Spring Game," https://bleacherreport.com/articles/2633394-ohio-state-spring-game-2016-recap-highlights-and-twitter-reaction, April 16, 2016; accessed July 11, 2022.

[327] Jason Arkley, *The Athens Messenger*, "Burrow takes advantage," https://www.athensmessenger.com/sports/local/burrow-takes-advantage/article_6b11e21b-8caa-53c3-bf5b-244222dbc0c5.html, April 16, 2016; accessed July 11, 2022.

[328] *Athens Messenger*, "Joe Burrow, 2016 Spring Game, " https://www.youtube.com/watch?v=IWeJIic-4A4, April 16, 2016; accessed July 11, 2022.

[329] NFL Highlights Channel, "Urban Meyer explains evolution of Dwayne Haskins and Joe Burrow," https://www.youtube.com/watch?v=Zd8sOxhy0EY, November 7, 2019; accessed July 11, 2022.

[330] Full Send Podcast, "Joe Burrow on Partying after the Super Bowl Loss, Brady's Future & Pre Game Outfits!"

[331] Liz Luehrman, interview with the author.

[332] Robin Burrow, interview with the author.

[333] Eleven Warriors, "Quarterback Joe Burrow after the annual Spring Game 4/15/17," https://www.youtube.com/watch?v=rVxrC2hHypE, April 15, 2017; accessed July 12, 2022.

[334] WBNS 10TV, "Urban Meyer Spring Game Press Conference," https://www.youtube.com/watch?v=Kg3RuCgme1I, April 15, 2017; accessed July 11, 2022.

[335] Jason Arkley, *The Athens Messenger*, "Burrow strong again in OSU spring game," https://www.athensmessenger.com/sports/local/burrow-strong-again-in-osu-spring-game/article_2c7b5a5c-dc92-56d4-ae33-0b43d0f98f6f.html, April 15, 2017; accessed September 6, 2022.

[336] Emphasis mine.

[337] Ibid.

[338] Dave Biddle, "Joe Burrow interview 8-14-17," https://www.youtube.com/watch?v=2kf9TUONmL0, accessed July 11, 2022.

[339] Jimmy Burrow, interview with the author, The Plains, Ohio, May 27, 2022.

[340] Robin Burrow in conversation with John McCallister, "Meet Joe Burrow's 'Super Mom'–Robin Burrow."

[341] NBC Sports, "Joe Burrow breaks down his QB process with Chris Simms, Chris Simms Unbuttoned," https://www.youtube.com/watch?v=s7aZQWo4QSw, June 21, 2022; accessed July 12, 2022.

[342] Jimmy Burrow, interview with the author, The Plains, Ohio, May 27, 2022.

[343] Jason Arkley, *The Athens Messenger*, "Burrow sends a message of his own," https://www.athensmessenger.com/search/?l=25&sort=relevance&f=html&t=article%2Cvideo%2Cyoutube%2Ccollection&app=editorial&nsa=eedition&q=Burrow+sends+a+message+of+his+own, April 14, 2018; accessed September 6, 2022.

[344] Lantern TV, "Ohio State HC Urban Meyer speaks after the 2018 game," https://www.youtube.com/watch?v=Xy8aD_m2WHs, April 14, 2018; accessed July 12, 2022.

[345] Ohio State football on Cleveland.com, "QB Joe Burrow after Ohio State's spring game," https://www.youtube.com/watch?v=YAIYDDFBhiw, April 14, 2018; accessed July 12, 2022.

[346] ESPN College Football, "Joe Burrow's revenge tour."

[347] Kelly, *Huskers Illustrated*, "The Burrow Who Geauxt Away."
[348] Jimmy Burrow, interview with the author, The Plains, Ohio, May 27, 2022.
[349] Kelly, *Huskers Illustrated*, "The Burrow Who Geauxt Away."
[350] Don Cooley, zoom interview with the author.
[351] Hank Williams, "Jambalaya." https://genius.com/Hank-williams-jambalaya-on-the-bayou-lyrics. Written in 1952, Public domain. We have taken the liberty to rearrange the lyrics in this epigraph to create a Burreaux arrangement.
[352] Joey Burrow@JoeyB, https://twitter.com/JoeyB/status/993884325383942144, May 8, 2018; accessed July 14, 2022.
[353] Glenn Guilbeau, "New LSU Offensive Coordinator Thought Burrow Was a Cincinnati Bearcat in 2018: 'That Was Over,'" https://www.outkick.com/new-lsu-offensive-coordinator-thought-burrow-was-a-cincinnati-bearcat-in-2018-that-was-over/, February 2022; Accessed July 14, 2022.
[354] Jimmy Burrow, interview with the author, The Plains, Ohio, May 27, 2022.
[355] Robin Burrow, interview with the author.
[356] Ed Orgeron with Bruce Feldman, *Flip the Script: Lessons Learned on the Road to a Championship* (Nashville: Nelson Books, 2020), 152.
[357] Guilbeau, "New LSU Offensive Coordinator Thought Burrow Was a Cincinnati Bearcat in 2018."
[358] Ibid.
[359] Jimmy Burrow, interview with the author, The Plains, Ohio, May 27, 2022.
[360] Orgeron with Feldman, *Flip the Script*, 151.
[361] Jimmy Burrow, interview with the author, The Plains, Ohio, May 27, 2022.
[362] Pardon My Take, "Pardon My Take Full Interview with LSU QB Joe Burrow," https://www.youtube.com/watch?v=dcrS-mF0Xhs, January 10, 2020; accessed July 15, 2022.
[363] Orgeron with Feldman, *Flip the Script*, 152–53.
[364] Ibid, 153–56.
[365] Ibid, 155.
[366] ESPN College Football, "The many sides of LSU QB Joe Burrow, College GameDay."
[367] Orgeron with Feldman, *Flip the Script*, 154.
[368] Jimmy Burrow, interview with the author, Athens, Ohio, March 9, 2022.
[369] Orgeron with Feldman, *Flip the Script*, 154–55.
[370] Pardon My Take, "Pardon My Take Full Interview with LSU QB Joe Burrow."
[371] Full Send Podcast, "Joe Burrow on Partying After Super Bowl Loss, Brady's Future & Pre Game Outfits!"
[372] Orgeron with Feldman, *Flip the Script*, 157.
[373] Off the Bench, "How Dan Burrow Helped Joe Burrow Become an LSU Tiger," https://www.youtube.com/watch?v=x-3Ij5KDUQs, April 1, 2020; accessed July 17, 2022.
[374] Orgeron with Feldman, *Flip the Script*, 159.
[375] Guilbeau, "New LSU Offensive Coordinator Thought Burrow Was a Cincinnati Bearcat in 2018."
[376] Liz Luehrman, interview with the author.
[377] Jimmy Burrow, interview with the author, The Plains, Ohio, May 27, 2022.
[378] This is a line from the Ohio University fight song, "Stand up and Cheer," https://www.ohio.edu/student-affairs/students/history-traditions/fight-song, accessed July 16, 2022.
[379] Sam Smathers, interview with the author, The Plains, May 25, 2022.
[380] ESPN, "Marty Smith walk and talk with LSU QB Joe Burrow," https://www.youtube.com/watch?v=PCVvpS7w-2w, September 13, 2018; accessed July 18, 2022.
[381] Robin Burrow, interview with the author.

[382] Jimmy Burrow, interview with the author, The Plains, Ohio, May 27, 2022.

[383] Mik'd Up w/ Mikie Mahtook, "LSU Football, Patrick Queen 'Joe Burrow Punched Me In The Face!" How A Fight Brought LSU To A Title," https://www.youtube.com/watch?v=MS8RdzrKLz0, April 7, 2022; accessed July 16, 2022.

[384] Cody Worsham, "The Truth: Joe Burrow Wins a Close QB Contest," https://lsusports.net/news/2018/08/27/211769604/, August 27, 2018; accessed July 16, 2022.

[385] Orgeron with Feldman, *Flip the Script*, 167.

[386] Ibid., 168.

[387] Zac Al-Khateeb, *The Sporting News*, "Joe Burrow is LSU's quarterback in 2018, even if Ed Orgeron won't say so (yet)," https://www.sportingnews.com/us/ncaa-football/news/lsu-quarterback-competition-joe-burrow-ed-orgeron-sec-media-days-lowell-narcisse/1nyp8on67z5w81q2hn20h9hzv4, July 16, 2018; accessed July 16, 2022.

[388] Orgeron with Feldman, *Flip the Script*, 170.

[389] Pardon My Take, "Pardon My Take Full Interview with LSU QB Joe Burrow."

[390] Ibid.

[391] White, interview with the author.

[392] Jimmy Burrow, interview with the author, Athens, Ohio, March 9, 2022. See OSU Overload, "Joe Burrow Vs Peter Warner [sic] In The Tire War," https://www.youtube.com/watch?v=mtIKhZo8i8s, January 27, 2022; accessed July 17, 2022.

[393] LSU Tigers on NOLA.com, "LSU head coach Ed Orgeron postgame following 33-17 win over Miami," https://www.youtube.com/watch?v=v_6hVwtTd2Y, September 3, 2018; accessed July 16, 2022.

[394] This reference comes from Oliver Goldsmith's poem, "The Deserted Village," in which the following line appears: "SWEET AUBURN! loveliest village of the plain." See Ian Berg, "Auburn Football: Breaking Down Tigers' Nickname, Battle Cry and Mascots," https://bleacherreport.com/articles/1277117-auburn-football-breaking-down-tigers-nicknames-battle-cry-and mascots#:~:text=The%20Auburn%20Tigers%20may%20have,loveliest%20village%20of%20the%20plain.%E2%80%9D, July 29, 2012; accessed July 18, 2022.

[395] LSU Tigers on TigerDetails, "LSU QB Joe Burrow discusses win over Auburn," https://www.youtube.com/watch?v=JSFvq8xovWE, September 15, 2018; accessed July 16, 2022.

[396] LSU Tigers on TigerDetails, "LSU Coach add [sic] Orgeron reacts to 22-21 upset of Auburn," https://www.youtube.com/watch?v=JSFvq8xovWE, September 15, 2018; accessed July 16, 2022.

[397] LSU Tigers on TigerDetails, "LSU QB Joe Burrow discusses win over Auburn."

[398] LSU Tiger TV, "Full Sound, QB Joe Burrow discusses LSU's dominant win over Ole Miss," https://www.youtube.com/watch?v=KJ2R00484P8, September 30, 2018; accessed July 17, 2022.

[399] LSU Tiger TV, "Full Presser, Coach Orgeron discusses highlights from the win against Georgia," https://www.youtube.com/watch?v=BLMqgCULklM, October 15, 2018; accessed July 17, 2022.

[400] LSU Tiger TV, "Full Sound, QB Joe Burrow talks LSU's upset win vs. #2 Georgia," https://www.youtube.com/watch?v=qybvjL6Rsvg, October 13, 2018; accessed July 17, 2022.

[401] Royce Wall, "LSU vs. UGA postgame comments from SEC Now," https://www.youtube.com/watch?v=JecGhlZZF4U, October 14, 2018; accessed July 17, 2022.

[402] LSU Tiger TV, "Full Presser, Coach Orgeron discusses highlights from the win against Georgia."

[403] Glenn Guilbeau, "LSU's Burrow returns to Mississippi, where his dad, uncle, grandparents were star athletes," *The Daily Advertiser*, https://www.theadvertiser.com/story/sports/college/lsu/2019/10/18/lsus-joe-burrow-could-have-become-miss-states-quarterback/3995696002/, October 18, 2019; accessed July 17, 2022.

[404] Jason Arkley, *The Athens Messenger*, "Burrow shows up to back Bulldogs," https://www.athensmessenger.com/search/?l=25&sort=relevance&f=html&t=article%2Cvideo%2Cyoutube%2Ccollection&app=editorial&nsa=eedition&q=Burrow+shows+up+to+back+Bulldogs, October 27, 2018; accessed July 17, 2022.

[405] Ryan Luehrman, interview with the author.

[406] CFB on Fox, "Haskins, Meyer Revisit Ohio State QB between Haskins & Burrow," https://www.youtube.com/watch?v=sp77ZiEoTu4, August 3, 2020; accessed July 17, 2022.

[407] Ibid.

[408] Full Send Podcast, "Joe Burrow on Partying After Super Bowl Loss, Brady's Future & Pre Game Outfits!"

[409] Sam Smathers, interview with the author, The Plains, Ohio, May 27, 2022.

[410] Bolin, zoom interview with the author.

[411] WWLTV, "Coach O talks LSU's 29-0 loss to Alabama," https://www.youtube.com/watch?v=gL_BUPZYDW4, November 3, 2018; accessed July 18, 2022.

[412] Ibid.

[413] Orgeron with Feldman, *Flip the Script*, 183.

[414] Ross Dellenger, *Sports Illustrated*, "Meet Joe Burrow: LSU's Toughest Renaissance Man and Maybe Savior."

[415] Stadium, "Fiesta Bowl Preview: UCF vs. LSU," https://www.youtube.com/watch?v=l2f4F9IOi78, December 11, 2018; accessed July 18, 2022.

[416] Dustin Schutte, "This awesome tweet from Joe Burrow went viral after leading LSU to Fiesta Bowl win," https://saturdaytradition.com/ohio-state-football/this-awesome-tweet-from-joe-burrow-went-viral-after-leading-lsu-to-fiesta-bowl-win/, January 1, 2019; accessed July 18, 2022.

[417] Fanatics View, "LSU Fiesta Bowl Press Conference Highlights feat. Ed Orgeron & Joe Burrow (Post-Game)," https://www.youtube.com/watch?v=GGxPkQ4ZuCk, January 2, 2019; accessed July 18, 2022.

[418] Orgeron and Feldman, *Flip the Script*, 184.

[419] All Pro Sports, "LSU Football: 2019 Season Movie: Something to Prove," https://www.youtube.com/watch?v=Xjp7tvhspFY, January 19, 2020; accessed July 22, 2022.

[420] Jim Kleinpeter, "How LSU got its purple and gold colors from Mardi Gras, and later the Tiger nickname," https://www.nola.com/sports/article_f3f07b4a-07c5-547d-9bab-10d5cc0d54a1.html, March 4, 2014; accessed July 22, 2022.

[421] Big Game Boomer, "50 Loudest College Football Stadiums Of All Time," https://twitter.com/BigGameBoomer/status/1521505006314213376?ref_src=twsrc%5Etfw%7Ctwcamp%5Etweetembed%7Ctwterm%5E1521505006314213376%7Ctwgr%5E%7Ctwcon%5Es1_&ref_url=https%3A%2F%2Fthespun.com%2Fmore%2Ftop-stories%2Flook-rankings-name-50-loudest-college-football-stadiums, May 2, 2022; accessed July 21, 2022.

[422] "Heritage and Songs of LSU," https://lsusports.net/news/2019/07/11/songs/, July 11, 2019; accessed July 23, 2022.

[423] "History of Mike the Tiger," https://www.mikethetiger.com/new-index, accessed July 23, 2022.

[424] Francis J. Fitzgerald, ed., *Greatest Moments in LSU Football History* (Champaign, IL: Sports Publishing LLC, 2002), 172.

[425] Crissy Froyd, LSU Wire, "Joe Burrow against LSU having live mascot, 'I'm anti animal in cage,'" https://lsutigerswire.usatoday.com/2020/05/08/joe-burrow-against-lsu-having-live-mascot-im-anti-animal-in-cage/, May 8, 2020; accessed July 23, 2022.

[426] "Mike the Tiger," https://www.mikethetiger.com/, accessed July 23, 2022.

[427] "History of Mike the Tiger."

[428] "Louisiana State University Traditions," https://en.wikipedia.org/wiki/Louisiana_State_University_traditions#cite_note-8, accessed July 23, 2022.

[429] Jimmy Burrow, interview with the author, Athens, Ohio, March 8, 2022.

[430] ESPN College Football, "Joe Burrow's father gave up coaching to watch him play at LSU, College GameDay," https://www.youtube.com/watch?v=-D508AWz9NM, December 28, 2019; accessed July 22, 2022.

[431] Ibid.

[432] Ibid.

[433] Zacciah Saltzman, zoom interview with the author, May 31, 2022.

[434] Kent Babb, *The Washington Post*, "Joe Burrow once made his Ohio town believe. Now he has Cincinnati dreaming," https://www.washingtonpost.com/sports/2022/01/29/joe-burrow-bengals-athens-ohio/, January 29, 2022; accessed July 19, 2022.

[435] Ibid.

[436] Jimmy Burrow, interview with the author, The Plains, Ohio, May 27, 2022.

[437] Graves, interview with the author.

[438] Mik'd Up w/ Mikie Mahtook, "LSU Football, Patrick Queen 'Joe Burrow Punched Me In The Face!" How A Fight Brought LSU To A Title."

[439] Ibid.

[440] Ibid.

[441] Ibid.

[442] Pardon My Take, "Coach O Just Led The Greatest College Football Team Ever To the Title," https://www.youtube.com/watch?v=t94iJj3ZX2E, January 16, 2020; accessed July 20, 2022.

[443] Orgeron with Feldman, *Flip the* Script, 194.

[444] Ibid., 195

[445] Ibid., 194

[446] All Pro Sports, "LSU Football: 2019 Season Movie: Something to Prove."

[447] SEC Network, "LSU Football: Summer of 10,000 Catches," https://www.facebook.com/watch/?v=394172051537583, October 12, 2019; accessed July 22, 2022.

[448] Ibid.

[449] Malcolm Gladwell, *Outliers: The Story of Success* (London: Penguin, 2008), 39–47.

[450] SEC Network, "LSU Football: Summer of 10,000 Catches."

[451] Jimmy Burrow, interview with the author, Athens, Ohio, March 8, 2022.

[452] Robin Burrow, interview with the author.

[453] 4th & Inches on Fanatic's View, "Joe Burrow talks Texas Longhorns Matchup, LSU's New Offense & Win vs. Georgia Southern," https://www.youtube.com/watch?v=qabay1rbdxs, September 4, 2019; accessed July 23, 2022.

[454] Bolin, zoom interview with the author.

[455] YurView - Gulf Sports South, "Joe Burrow looks at his record setting performance in week 1," https://www.youtube.com/watch?v=l6X_j3dFups, September 1, 2019; accessed July 23, 2022.

[456] LSU Tigers on TigerDetails, "FULL Ed Orgeron Press Conference after defeating Georgia Southern," https://www.youtube.com/watch?v=nzuetBMO5g4, August 31, 2019; accessed July 23, 2022.

[457] 4th & Inches on Fanatic's View, "Joe Burrow talks Texas Longhorns Matchup."

[458] ESPN College Football, "Lee Corso's headgear pick for LSU vs. 9 Texas with Matthew McConaughey, College Gameday," https://www.youtube.com/watch?v=REJnBcyC_2w, September 7, 2019; accessed July 23, 2022.

[459] LSU Tigers on TigerDetails, "Texas coach Tom Herman on LSU QB Joe Burrow," https://www.youtube.com/watch?v=2DajbzedYuY, September 2, 2019; accessed July 23, 2022.
[460] ESPN College Football, "LSU vs. Texas Highlights 2019, NCAAF Week 2, College Football Highlights," https://www.youtube.com/watch?v=aMZM6E6v3UQ, September 9, 2019; accessed July 24, 2022.
[461] Orgeron with Feldman, *Flip the Script*, 204.
[462] LSU Tigers on TigerDetails, "LSU coach Ed Orgeron postgame after Texas win," https://www.youtube.com/watch?v=phYeNyI3BPM, September 8, 2019; accessed July 24, 2022.
[463] Ibid.
[464] Wheels, "#4 LSU vs. Vanderbilt Highlights, NCAAF Week 4, College Football Highlights," https://www.youtube.com/watch?v=cwqmTeLdIjE, September 21, 2019; accessed July 24, 2022.
[465] Sam Smathers, email to the author, July 23, 2022.
[466] Jeff Skinner, zoom interview with the author, July 15, 2022.
[467] Paulsen, Sports Media Watch, "UF-LSU hits college football cable high," https://www.sportsmediawatch.com/2019/10/florida-lsu-ratings-espn-college-football-uga/, October 2019; accessed July 24, 2022.
[468] Orgeron with Feldman, *Flip the Script*, 204.
[469] ESPN College Football, "Joe Burrow opens up on his Heisman Trophy speech, facing Oklahoma in CFP, College Football on ESPN," https://www.youtube.com/watch?v=O-CJBHcAUOM, December 23, 2019; accessed July 24, 2022.
[470] LSU Tiger TV, "LSU HC Ed Orgeron on the Tiger's win against Florida," https://www.youtube.com/watch?v=ecz-iXWd3K0, October 13, 2019; accessed July 24, 2022.
[471] LSU Tigers on TigerDetails, "FULL LSU QB Joe Burrow press conference after beating Florida," https://www.youtube.com/watch?v=fGVsCRs_E54, October 13, 2019; accessed July 24, 2022.
[472] LSU Tigers on TigerDetails, "LSU QB Joe Burrow press conference ahead of Mississippi State game," https://www.youtube.com/watch?v=EOjf2EYo9Nw, October 14, 2019; accessed July 24, 2022.
[473] ESPN, "Tim Tebow Shocks Stephen A. by calling LSU QB Joe Burrow his Heisman Trophy favorite, First Take," https://www.youtube.com/watch?v=QYUzhFHcKh8, October 18, 2019; accessed July 24, 2022.
[474] Ben Portnoy, " 'I Still Have My Cowbell': LSU's Joe Burrow Returns Home to the State His Family Calls Home," *The Commercial Dispatch*, https://cdispatch.com/sports/2019-10-18/i-still-have-my-cowbell-lsus-joe-burrow-returns-to-the-state-his-family-calls-home/, October 18, 2019; accessed July 24, 2022.
[475] Glenn Guilbeau, "LSU's Burrow returns to Mississippi where his dad, uncle, grandparents were star athletes," https://www.theadvertiser.com/story/sports/college/lsu/2019/10/18/lsus-joe-burrow-could-have-become-miss-states-quarterback/3995696002/, *The Daily Advertiser*, October 18, 2019; accessed July 24, 2022.
[476] LSU Tigers on TigerDetails, "FULL LSU QB Joe Burrow press conference after win over Mississippi State," https://www.youtube.com/watch?v=XOFqQzc7LDU, October 19, 2019; accessed July 24, 2022.
[477] All Star Central, "Joe Burrow Takes Huge Hit Vs. Auburn 2019," https://www.youtube.com/watch?v=lRsD4ExwWZs, October 26, 2019; accessed July 24, 2022.
[478] WWLT, "LSU quarterback Joe Burrow post-game after Auburn win," https://www.youtube.com/watch?v=UVadqHWvIos, October 27, 2019; accessed July 24, 2022.
[479] Bolin, zoom interview with the author.

[480] Fenista Magic, "LSU Football 2020 National Championship Trophy Ceremony," https://www.youtube.com/watch?v=JmRgJcQ3clk, January 20, 2020; accessed July 19, 2022.
[481] ESPN, "Marty Smith walk and talk with LSU QB Joe Burrow."
[482] Jason Arkley, *The Athens Messenger*, "For Gigi's, Burrow fever has been 'wild,'" https://www.athensmessenger.com/spotlight/for-gigis-burrow-fever-has-been-wild/article_ce997508-70ff-5754-a8a0-d888368352c2.html, November 13, 2019; accessed July 27, 2022.
[483] Ibid.
[484] ESPN College Football, "Lee Corso's headgear pick for LSU vs. Alabama with Justin Thomas, College GameDay," https://www.youtube.com/watch?v=RxxEiJswrHg, November 9, 2019; accessed July 25, 2022.
[485] Orgeron with Feldman, *Flip the Script*, 213.
[486] Victors Valiant, "#2 LSU vs #3 Alabama Highlights, Week 11, College Football 2019," https://www.youtube.com/watch?v=VTSdow92S6c, November 9, 2019; accessed July 25, 2022.
[487] LSU Tigers on TigerDetails, "Joe Burrow recaps LSU's victory over Alabama," https://www.youtube.com/watch?v=cI8ATbNtyck, November 9, 2019; accessed July 25, 2022.
[488] Ibid.
[489] Victors Valiant, "#2 LSU vs #3 Alabama Highlights, Week 11, College Football 2019."
[490] LSU Tigers on TigerDetails, "Joe Burrow recaps LSU's victory over Alabama."
[491] Ibid.
[492] Keith Farner, Saturday Down South, "Party at the airport: Fan reaction to LSU beating Alabama even surprised Joe Burrow," https://www.saturdaydownsouth.com/lsu-football/party-at-the-airport-fan-reaction-to-lsu-beating-alabama-even-surprised-joe-burrow/, November 9, 2019; accessed July 27, 2022.
[493] Orgeron with Feldman, *Flip the Script*, 216.
[494] John Macon Gillespie, si.com, "Kirk Herbstreit Names Ole Miss Tailgating Scene as 'Mecca' of College Football," https://www.si.com/college/olemiss/football/ole-miss-the-grove-kirk-herbstreit-college-gameday, April 21, 2022; accessed July 26, 2022.
[495] Glenn Guilbeau, *The Daily Advertiser*, "LSU QB Joe Burrow's dad has strong ties to Ole Miss' favorite son Archie Manning," https://www.theadvertiser.com/story/sports/college/lsu/2019/11/16/lsu-ole-miss-burrows-and-mannings-have-much-common/4194989002/, November 16, 2019; accessed July 27, 2022.
[496] Jeff Skinner, interview with the author, Athens, Ohio, May 26, 2022.
[497] Brody Miller, *The Athletic*, "Tiger Tales: Untold stories of LSU's 2019 national championship run," May 20, 2020; accessed July 26, 2022.
[498] Travis Brand, phone call with the author, July 29, 2022.
[499] Ibid.
[500] Ibid.
[501] LSU Tigers on TigerDetails, "FULL Joe Burrow press conference after blowing out Texas A&M," https://www.youtube.com/watch?v=P9-Dto1Rl9Y, December 1, 2019; accessed July 30, 2022.
[502] Ibid.
[503] Brand, phone call with the author.
[504] Ibid.
[505] LSU Tigers on TigerDetails, "FULL Joe Burrow press conference after blowing out Texas A&M."
[505] Brand, phone call with the author.
[506] DawgNation, "LSU coach Ed Orgeron praises Georgia defense before 2019 SEC Championship Game," https://www.youtube.com/watch?v=8P1fiH2-aE8, December 6, 2019; accessed July 31, 2022.

[507] LSU Tigers on TigerDetails, "Watch Breiden Fehoko's dad perform special Haka for Joe Burrow's family before SEC Championship Game," https://www.youtube.com/watch?v=fOfWDuBw4aY, December 12, 2019; accessed July 30, 2022.

[508] Rusty Thomas, interview with the author, Athens, Ohio, March 9, 2022.

[509] Ibid.

[510] TD Staff Reporter, Tiger Droppings, "Video: Joe Burrow's Hometown In Ohio Had a Watch Party for the SEC Championship," https://www.tigerdroppings.com/lsu-football/video-joe-burrows-hometown-in-ohio-had-a-watch-party-for-the-sec-championship/87280555/, December 8, 2019; accessed July 30, 2022.

[511] Woubpbs, "Fans in Athens county hold Joe Burrow tailgate," https://www.youtube.com/watch?v=vGfsc34Vkxw, December 7, 2019; accessed July 30, 2022.

[512] NFL Season, "Joe Burrow HEISMAN MOMENT vs Georgia in SEC Championship Game!" https://www.youtube.com/watch?v=EY75swVleFU, December 7, 2019; accessed July 30, 2022.

[513] LSU Tigers on TigerDetails, "Ed Orgeron, Joe Burrow, Derek Stingley Jr. press conference after beating Georgia in SEC title game," https://www.youtube.com/watch?v=FLKwhtCP7aU, December 7, 2019; accessed July 31, 2022.

[514] Sam Smathers, phone interview with the author, July 31, 2022.

[515] Orgeron with Feldman, *Flip the Script*, 218.

[516] Thomas, interview with the author.

[517] Ben Pickman, SI.com, "Every Record LSU Set In Blowout Peach Bowl Win vs. Oklahoma," https://www.si.com/college/2019/12/28/joe-burrow-passing-records-lsu-first-half-vs-oklahoma, December 28, 2019; accessed July 31, 2022.

[518] LSU Tigers on TigerDetails, "FULL Joe Burrow press conference after dominating Oklahoma in Peach Bowl," https://www.youtube.com/watch?v=Hv4Eis6k12k, December 28, 2019; accessed July 31, 2022.

[519] Ibid.

[520] LSU Tigers on TigerDetails, "LSU's Ed Orgeron talks about beating Oklahoma in Peach Bowl, Steve Ensminger's family tragedy, more," https://www.youtube.com/watch?v=ijFQUqBFoDg, December 28, 2019; accessed July 31, 2022.

[521] LSU Tigers on TigerDetails, "FULL Joe Burrow press conference after blowing out Texas A&M," https://www.youtube.com/watch?v=P9-Dto1Rl9Y, December 1, 2019; accessed July 31, 2022.

[522] Hail Varsity, "Growing up Burrow," https://www.youtube.com/watch?v=LEYo1kRpE8w, February 2, 2022; accessed July 31, 2022.

[523] LSU Tiger TV, "LSU QB Joe Burrow has some 'weird' pregame rituals...including Lil Uzi and caramel apple suckers," https://www.youtube.com/watch?v=wPnko01VEZY, September 4, 2018; accessed July 31, 2022.

[524] Orgeron with Feldman, *Flip the Script*, 225–26.

[525] NBC4 Columbus, "Athens County excited to cheer for Joe Burrow in National Championship game," https://www.youtube.com/watch?v=wDMJOa-oHfU, January 13, 2020; accessed July 31, 2022.

[526] Ibid.

[527] Sam Smathers, phone interview with the author, July 31, 2022.

[528] Ibid.

[529] CBS Sports HQ, "LSU Post Game Press Conference: 2020 National Championship, CBS Sports," https://www.youtube.com/watch?v=daokE-eiJZs, January 14, 2022; accessed July 31, 2022.

[530] Fenista Magic, "LSU Football 2020 National Championship Trophy Ceremony," https://www.youtube.com/watch?v=JmRgJcQ3clk, January 20, 2020; accessed July 19, 2022.

[531] Eat my Noodlez, "LSU Get the Gat (full)," https://www.youtube.com/watch?v=_RdgtLak6YM, January 4, 2020; accessed August 1, 2022.

[532] Jimmy Burrow, interview with the author, Athens, Ohio, March 9, 2022.

[533] Jimmy Burrow, interview the author, The Plains, Ohio, May 27, 2022.

[534] Orgeron with Feldman, *Flip the Script*, 200.

[535] Jimmy Burrow, interview with the author, Athens, Ohio, March 9, 2022.

[536] Boys from the Boot, "LSU National Championship Celebration," https://www.youtube.com/watch?v=gdaL2FBbRf0, January 28, 2020; accessed August 1, 2022.

[537] Maria Luisa Paul, *The Washington Post*, "A Garth Brooks show was so loud it registered as an earthquake," https://www.washingtonpost.com/nation/2022/05/03/garth-brooks-concert-earthquake/, May 3, 2022; accessed August 1, 2022.

[538] ESPN College Football, "Joe Burrow's father gave up coaching to watch him play at LSU, College GameDay," https://www.youtube.com/watch?v=-D508AWz9NM, December 28, 2019; accessed August 1, 2022.

[539] ESPN, "Joe Burrow Wins 2019 Heisman Trophy, College Football on ESPN," https://www.youtube.com/watch?v=Zq68naJBdW0, December 14, 2019; accessed August 2, 2022.

[540] Jeremy Birmingham, Eleven Warriors, "Joe Burrow Wins Mr. Football in Ohio," https://www.elevenwarriors.com/ohio-state-football-recruiting/2014/12/45413/joe-burrow-wins-mr-football-in-ohio, December 3, 2014; accessed August 2, 2022.

[541] Pardon My Take, "Pardon My Take Full Interview with LSU QB Joe Burrow."

[542] Ibid.

[543] Robin Burrow, interview with the author.

[544] Sam Smathers, interview with the author, The Plains, Ohio, May 27, 2022.

[545] Johnny Unitas Golden Arm Award, "2019 Johnny Unitas Golden Arm Award: Joe Burrow," https://www.youtube.com/watch?v=V4rRmp4l9To, January 2, 2020; accessed August 4, 2022.

[546] Ibid.

[547] Ibid.

[548] 680TheFan, "LSU QB Joe Burrow at the ESPN College Football Awards," https://www.youtube.com/watch?v=01w0zsuWhHs, December 12, 2019; accessed August 4, 2022.

[549] Boys From the Boot, "December 12, 2019 – College Football Awards," https://www.youtube.com/watch?v=Z8eXnuc5CyI, December 16, 2019; accessed August 4, 2022.

[550] Ibid.

[551] John Taylor, NBC Sports, "Joe Burrow adds Manning Award to 2019 hardware haul," https://collegefootball.nbcsports.com/2020/01/29/joe-burrow-lsu-manning-award/, January 29, 2020; accessed August 4, 2022.

[552] Pardon My Take, "Pardon My Take Full Interview with LSU QB Joe Burrow."

[553] Ibid.

[554] Hallie Grossman, ESPN, "Heisman Trophy Winner Joe Burrow Electrifies LSU—and all of college football," https://www.espn.com/college-football/story/_/id/28285303/heisman-trophy-winner-joe-burrow-electrifies-lsu-all-college-football, December 16, 2019; accessed August 7, 2022.

[555] Marikay Vander Ven, zoom interview with the author, July 13, 2022.

[556] Heather Skinner, zoom interview with the author, July 15, 2022.

[557] Jeff Skinner, zoom interview with the author, July 15, 2022.

[558] Tom Vander Ven, zoom interview with the author, July 13, 2022.

[559] Marikay Vander Ven, zoom interview with the author.

[560] Brand, phone call with the author.
[561] Robin Burrow, interview with the author.
[562] Jimmy Burrow, interview with the author, The Plains, Ohio, May 27, 2022.
[563] Jimmy Burrow, interview with the author, Athens, Ohio, March 9, 2022.
[564] ESPN, "Joe Burrow Wins 2019 Heisman Trophy, College Football on ESPN."
[565] Jeff Skinner, zoom interview with the author, July 15, 2022.
[566] Heather Skinner, zoom interview with the author.
[567] Tom Vander Ven, zoom interview with the author, July 13, 2022.
[568] Marikay Vander Ven, zoom interview with the author.
[569] Tom Vander Ven, zoom interview with the author, July 13, 2022.
[570] Sam Vander Ven, zoom interview with the author.
[571] Ibid.
[572] Brooks Kubena, *The Advocate*, "Joe Burrow Q&A: LSU's Heisman hopeful on a broken hand, Billy Cannon letter, more," https://www.theadvocate.com/baton_rouge/sports/lsu/article_212170a4-1de5-11ea-9214-c7f2a9c10dfe.html, December 13, 2019; accessed August 7, 2022.
[573] Sam Smathers, phone interview with the author, August 7, 2022.
[574] Bolin, zoom interview with the author, June 18, 2022.
[575] Finnearty, zoom interview with the author.
[576] Ron Ricketts, phone interview with the author, August 8, 2022.
[577] Jason Arkley, *The Athens Messenger*, "Athens sends, and feels, the love on Heisman night," https://www.athensmessenger.com/spotlight/athens-sends-and-feels-the-love-on-heisman-night/article_6d8b2595-2b4b-50eb-bbef-5e0c765cc1f6.html, December 15, 2019; accessed August 9, 2022.
[578] Ricketts, phone interview with the author.
[579] Susan Wolfe, Facebook messenger exchange with the author, August 7, 2022.
[580] Drabold, zoom interview with the author.
[581] Karin Bright, zoom interview with the author, June 20, 2022.
[582] Jimmy Burrow, interview with the author, Athens, Ohio, March 9, 2022.
[583] Bright, zoom interview with the author.
[584] Ibid.
[585] Drabold, zoom interview with the author.
[586] Bright, zoom interview with the author.
[587] Ibid.
[588] Ibid.
[589] Ibid.
[590] Ibid.
[591] Drabold, zoom interview with the author.
[592] Ibid.
[593] Bright, zoom interview with the author.
[594] Ibid.
[595] Peter King, Peter King's Football Morning in America, "'Thank God for Joe Burrow,': A Heisman speech that raised nearly half a million for charity," https://sports.nbcsports.com/2019/12/23/thank-god-for-joe-burrow-a-heisman-speech-that-raised-nearly-half-a-million-for-charity/, December 23, 2019; accessed August 9, 2022.
[596] Matt Lawman, "Former Cardinals QB Kurt Warner likes comparisons to No. 1 pick Joe Burrow," Arizona Sports, https://arizonasports.com/story/2300985/former-cardinals-qb-kurt-warner-likes-comparisons-to-no-1-pick-joe-burrow/; accessed June 16, 2022.

597 Robin Miller, *The Advocate*, "Joe Burrow may have changed his stripes, but his namesake burrito remains the same," https://www.theadvocate.com/baton_rouge/entertainment_life/food_restaurants/article_f048cc0e-82df-11ec-8ec0-df15a2beb574.html, February 1, 2022; accessed August 10, 2022.

598 Izzy's Press Release, "Introducing 'The Bengal King' aka 'The Joe Burrow,'" https://izzys.com/bengal-king-joe-burrow/, April 27, 2020; accessed August 10, 2022.

599 Full Send Podcast, "Joe Burrow on Partying after Super Bowl Loss, Brady's Future & Pre Game Outfits."

600 Ian Rapoport, NFL Network, "Dolphins were willing to give up multiple first-round picks in 2020 NFL Draft for Joe Burrow," https://www.nfl.com/news/dolphins-were-willing-to-give-up-multiple-first-round-picks-in-2020-nfl-draft-fo, January 30, 2022; accessed August 13, 2022.

601 Hunter Bittinger, Stripe Hype, "Cincinnati Bengals: Every Joe Burrow Pro-Comparison so far," https://stripehype.com/2020/02/10/cincinnati-bengals-joe-burrow-pro-comparison/, no date provided; accessed August 13, 2022.

602 Ibid.

603 Dan Patrick Show, "CBS Sports' Gary Danielson: Burrow is Tom Brady, Tua is Kurt Warner, The Dan Patrick Show," https://www.youtube.com/watch?v=8n2y61wRQmw, December 2, 2019; accessed August 13, 2022.

604 Avery Yang, SI.com, "Joe Burrow: Please Don't Compare Me to Tom Brady," https://www.si.com/nfl/2020/03/04/joe-burrow-please-dont-compare-tom-brady, March 4, 2020; accessed August 13, 2022.

605 Nick Koscko, 247Sports, "Joe Burrow compared to NFL legend, according to Joel Klatt," https://247sports.com/Article/Joe-Burrow-compared-NFL-legend-Joe-Montana-LSU-Football-Notre-Dame-Football-142184827/, January 14, 2020; accessed August 14, 2022.

606 Lance Zierlein, NFL Network, "Joe Burrow Player Bio," https://www.nfl.com/prospects/joe-burrow/32004255-5267-9731-81c8-48673dcec5e2, no date provided; accessed August 13, 2022.

607 Jimmy Burrow, interview with the author, The Plains, Ohio, May 27, 2022.

608 Lawman, "Former Cardinals QB Kurt Warner likes comparisons to No. 1 pick Joe Burrow."

609 ESPN, "Joe Burrow goes No. 1 overall to the Cincinnati Bengals, 2020 NFL Draft," https://www.youtube.com/watch?v=CQm0n-9pixA, April 23, 2020; accessed August 15, 2022.

610 Ricketts, phone interview with the author.

611 Ibid.

612 Machelle Stewart, interview with the author, Athens, Ohio, March 10, 2022.

613 Heather Skinner, zoom interview with the author.

614 Robin Burrow, interview with the author.

615 Dave Clark, *Cincinnati Enquirer*, "Robin Burrow on Joe not wanting Bengals to draft him: 'No idea where that comes from,'" https://www.cincinnati.com/story/sports/nfl/bengals/2020/02/17/robin-burrow-shoots-down-report-joe-doesnt-want-bengals-draft-him/4788585002/, February 17, 2020; accessed August 15, 2022.

616 NFL, "Joe Burrow's Full NFL Combine Presser, 'I made a lot of relationships there,'" https://www.youtube.com/watch?v=lo9nRaA7PSs, February 25, 2020; accessed August 15, 2022.

617 Pro Football Focus, "Joe Burrow on his road to LSU, his rookie season with the Bengals, the knee injury and more," https://www.youtube.com/watch?v=dFyI03VAAXA, April 20, 2021; accessed August 15, 2022.

618 Jimmy Burrow, interview with the author, Athens, Ohio, March 9, 2022.

619 Sam Smathers, interview with the author, The Plains, Ohio, March 11, 2022.

[620] WCPO 9, "'Pride of Athens' Joe Burrow expected to be Bengals' pick," https://www.youtube.com/watch?v=Zm6O-HEhDHk, April 23, 2020; accessed August 15, 2022.

[621] Liz Luehrman, interview with the author.

[622] NFL, "Joe Burrow's Full NFL Combine Presser, 'I made a lot of relationships there.'"

[623] ESPN, "Joe Burrow calls number one a dream come true," https://www.youtube.com/watch?v=64kk_GnTO9Y, April 23, 2020; accessed August 15, 2022.

[624] Ibid.

[625] Sean Schmidt, River Beats New Orleans, "Joe Burrow Shows Off Diamond #9 Draft Necklace, A Gift From Lil Boosie," https://neworleans.riverbeats.life/joe-burrows-diamond-9-draft-necklace-a-gift-from-lil-boosie/, April 24, 2020; accessed August 15, 2022.

[626] Robin Burrow, interview with the author.

[627] Ibid.

[628] ESPN, "Joe Burrow describes first thought that went in his mind after Bengals picked him," https://www.youtube.com/watch?v=wOE1hj33Zns, April 24, 2020; accessed August 15, 2022.

[629] Dan Patrick Show, "Joe Burrow Talks Bengals, Dolphins, NFL Draft & More with Dan Patrick, Full Interview," https://www.youtube.com/watch?v=omJiMkaDLBU, January 31, 2020; accessed August 15, 2022.

[630] NFL on NBC, "NFL Draft 2020: Joe Burrow talks virtual draft, student-athletes, Pro Football Talk, NBC Sports," https://www.youtube.com/watch?v=4Z_4x1yUrWY, April 20, 2020; accessed August 15, 2022.

[631] Zacciah Saltzman, zoom interview with the author, May 31, 2022.

[632] Cincinnati Bengals, "Joe Burrow Introductory News Conference," https://www.youtube.com/watch?v=sWJuJB5Mb5w, July 31, 2020; accessed August 16, 2022.

[633] woubpbs, "Joe Burrow's continued impact in Southeast Ohio," https://www.youtube.com/watch?v=oNy-YYpyanM, April 27, 2020; accessed August 16, 2022.

[634] Ben Baby, ESPN Staff Writer, "Zoom calls, isolated meetings, no preseason: Joe Burrow's NFL education during a pandemic," https://www.espn.com/nfl/story/_/id/29753029/zoom-calls-isolated-meetings-no-preseason-joe-burrow-nfl-education-pandemic, August 29, 2020; accessed August 16, 2022.

[635] Cincinnati Bengals, "Joe Burrow News Conference, September 9, 2020," https://www.youtube.com/watch?v=HGdDQFZRpdI, September 9, 2020; accessed August 16, 2022.

[636] Joey Burrow@JoeyB, https://twitter.com/joeyb/status/1266404689203146754, May 29, 2020; accessed August 17, 2022.

[637] David Jablonski, *Dayton Daily News*, "Joe Burrow keeping in shape in hometown during pandemic," https://www.daytondailynews.com/sports/joe-burrow-keeping-shape-hometown-during-pandemic/zzVRKLFnjb937Kr1nh5yDK/, July 12, 2020; accessed August 16, 2022.

[638] Ohio University Fast Facts, https://www.ohio.edu/ohio-facts; accessed August 16, 2022.

[639] Zacciah Saltzman, zoom interview with the author, May 31, 2022.

[640] Cincinnati Bengals, "Joe Burrow: 'I'm Confident In Our Guys, Always Have Been," https://www.youtube.com/watch?v=0lK4_RPbfTU, September 13, 2020; August 18, 2022.

[641] Pro Football Focus, "Joe Burrow on his road to LSU, his rookie season with the Bengals, the knee injury and more." The actual words used in this exchange are disputed, but this is the gist.

[642] Tom Vander Ven, zoom interview with the author, July 13, 2022.

[643] Jeremy Rauch, "An extended chat with Joe Burrow's parents on his road back," https://www.youtube.com/watch?v=hVqXktNZgD8&t=8s, April 11, 2021; accessed August 20, 2022.

[644] Ibid.

[645] Dan Hoard, Bengals Booth Podcast, "Bengals Booth Podcast: Seen the Difference," April 7, 2022; accessed August 20, 2022.

[646] Ibid.

[647] Associated Press, Boston.com, "'See ya Next Year' Joe Burrow tweets after scary knee injury," https://www.boston.com/sports/nfl/2020/11/22/joe-burrow-cincinnati-bengals-quarterback-injury/, November 22, 2020; accessed August 20, 2022.

[648] Cincinnati Bengals, "Why Not Us?" https://www.youtube.com/watch?v=6ijyvDwz1CA, January 14, 2022; accessed September 4, 2022.

[649] Evan Cooley, zoom interview with the author.

[650] Ryan Luehrman, interview with the author.

[651] Evan Cooley, zoom interview with the author.

[652] Ibid.

[653] Ryan Luehrman, interview with the author.

[654] White, interview with the author.

[655] Zacciah Saltzman, zoom interview with the author, May 31, 2022.

[656] Don Cooley, zoom interview with the author.

[657] Jimmy Burrow, interview with the author, The Plains, Ohio, May 27, 2022.

[658] Robin Burrow, interview with the author.

[659] Evan Cooley, zoom interview with the author.

[660] Ibid.

[661] Sam Vander Ven, zoom interview with the author.

[662] Ibid.

[663] Ibid.

[664] Jalyn Bolyard, *Ohio News*, "Training Joe Burrow: OHIO alumnus Dak Notestine aids Bengals' star QB," https://www.ohio.edu/news/2022/02/training-joe-burrow-ohio-alumnus-dak-notestine-aids-bengals-star-qb, February 10, 2022; accessed August 25, 2022.

[665] Zacciah Saltzman, Facebook Messenger exchange with author, August 25, 2022.

[666] Bolyard, *Ohio News*, "Training Joe Burrow."

[667] Albert Breer, *Sports Illustrated*, "MMQB: Joe Burrow and the Long Road Back," https://www.si.com/nfl/2021/05/31/joe-burrow-inside-story-of-acl-rehab-monday-morning-quarterback-mmqb, May 31, 2022; accessed September 2, 2022.

[668] Cincinnati Bengals, "Joe Burrow Training Camp News Conference," https://www.youtube.com/watch?v=w0M77M3Y2fY, July 28, 2021; accessed September 4, 2022.

[669] Jeremy Rauch, "An extended chat with Joe Burrow's parents on his road back," https://www.youtube.com/watch?v=hVqXktNZgD8, April 11, 2021; accessed September 4, 2022.

[670] Cincinnati Bengals, "Why Not Us?" https://www.youtube.com/watch?v=6ijyvDwz1CA, January 14, 2022; accessed September 4, 2022.

[671] Ibid.

[672] Cincinnati Bengals, "Joe Burrow and Zac Taylor News Conference," https://www.youtube.com/watch?v=ZgubrcQKpTU, August 18, 2021; accessed September 4, 2022.

[673] Tyler Dragon, *Cincinnati Enquirer*, "NFL schedule reveal: Predicting Cincinnati Bengals' 2021 regular-season record," https://www.cincinnati.com/story/sports/nfl/bengals/2021/05/12/2021-nfl-schedule-cincinnati-bengals-regular-season-prediction/5059334001/, May 12, 2021; accessed September 4, 2022.

[674] Ben Baby, ESPN, "Cincinnati Bengals' 2021 Schedule: Tough slate stands in way of playoff push," https://www.espn.com/blog/cincinnati-bengals/post/_/id/33139/cincinnati-bengals-2021-schedule-tough-slate-stands-in-way-of-playoff-push, May 12, 2021; accessed September 4, 2022.

[675] BigR, "I'm going to VEGAS & betting on Bengals! Dan Orlovsky Predicted Joe Burrow winning the Superbowl!," https://www.youtube.com/shorts/1OxwpglHHqU, February 1, 2022; accessed September 4, 2022.

676 Cincinnati Bengals, "Joe Burrow Training Camp News Conference," July 28, 2022.
677 Jimmy Burrow, interview with the author, Athens, Ohio, March 9, 2022.
678 Cincinnati Bengals, "Joe Burrow Training Camp News Conference," July 28, 2022.
679 Cincinnati Bengals Talk, "CJ Uzomah on Cincinnati Bengals 24-21 win over Jacksonville Jaguars," https://www.youtube.com/watch?v=ZcG9QG06JMw, October 1, 2021; accessed September 4, 2022.
680 NFL on NBC, "Are the Cincinnati Bengals finally built to be contenders?" https://www.youtube.com/watch?v=1gK88945KF8, October 25, 2021; accessed September 5, 2022.
681 Cincinnati Bengals, "Bengals Postgame News Conference, Week 12 vs. Pittsburgh," https://www.youtube.com/watch?v=WOjY8Ptu3y8, November 28, 2021; accessed September 5, 2022.
682 Cincinnati Bengals, "Bengals Postgame News Conference, Week 14 vs. San Francisco," https://www.youtube.com/watch?v=seSILNOrNtU, December 12, 2021; accessed September 5, 2022.
683 Cincinnati Bengals, "Bengals Postgame News Conference, Week 16 vs. Baltimore," https://www.youtube.com/watch?v=vR6p8FigeZE, December 26, 2021; accessed September 5, 2022.
684 Cincinnati Bengals, "Bengals Postgame News Conference, Week 17 vs. Kansas City," https://www.youtube.com/watch?v=FmN9mBJIPCc, January 3, 2022; accessed September 5, 2022.
685 Ibid.
686 Tyler Dunne, "Joe Burrow is the most dangerous man in football: No quarterback is hotter right now. This combination of grit and brains—with a touch of swagger—could lift the Cincinnati Bengals to their first Super Bowl appearance since 1988. Here's why," https://www.golongtd.com/p/joe-burrow-is-the-most-dangerous?triedSigningIn=true, January 14, 2022; accessed August 27, 2022.
687 Dunne, "Joe Burrow is the most dangerous man in football."
688 Ibid.
689 Ibid.
690 Ibid.
691 Cincinnati Bengals, "Joe Burrow: 'We Made Plays When We Needed To," https://www.bengals.com/video/joe-burrow-we-made-plays-when-we-needed-to, January 15, 2022; accessed June 6, 2022.
692 WKRC, "Bengals Taylor discusses decision to pass out a game ball to fans at area bar," https://local12.com/sports/bengals/bengals-taylor-discusses-decision-to-pass-out-a-game-ball-to-fans-at-area-bar-cincinnati-nfl-pro-football-zac-press-conference-transcript-las-vegas-raiders-afc-playoffs, January 16, 2022; accessed September 8, 2022.
693 Postgame Central, "Cincinnati Bengals Quarterback Joe Burrow postgame press conference after playoff victory vs. Titans," https://www.youtube.com/watch?v=3NL60whRa0E, January 22, 2022; accessed September 5, 2022.
694 Ibid.
695 Ibid.
696 Evan Cooley, zoom interview with the author.
697 Don Cooley, zoom interview with the author.
698 Robin Burrow, interview with the author.
699 Zacciah Saltzman, zoom interview with the author, May 31, 2022.
700 Ibid.
701 Micah Saltzman, zoom interview with the author, June 6, 2022.
702 Ibid.
703 Robin and Jimmy Burrow, interview with the author, The Plains, Ohio, May 27, 2022.
704 PostGame Central, "Cincinnati Bengals Joe Burrow AFC Championship postgame after win onto Superbowl," https://www.youtube.com/watch?v=hx_7tK9xaucm, January 30, 2022; accessed September 7, 2022.

[705] Cincinnati Bengals, " 'It Is Us' – The Story of the 2021 Cincinnati Bengals, NFL Films," https://www.youtube.com/watch?v=548KO30-UBs, July 6, 2022; accessed September 8, 2022.
[706] PostGame Central, "Cincinnati Bengals Joe Burrow AFC Championship postgame after win onto Superbowl."
[707] Ibid.
[708] Don Cooley, zoom interview with the author.
[709] Ryan Luehrman, interview with the author.
[710] Drabold, zoom interview with the author.
[711] Robin Burrow, interview with the author.
[712] Sam Smathers, interview with the author, March 10, 2022.
[713] Kelsey Conway@KelseyLConway, "Ja'Marr Chase bought Joe Burrow grills ahead of Super Bowl 56 as a gift," https://twitter.com/kelseylconway/status/1514720020257030146?lang=en, April 14, 2022; accessed September 8, 2022.
[714] Bolin, zoom interview with the author.
[715] Ibid.
[716] Kevin Goldsberry, interview with the author, Athens, Ohio, March 9, 2022.
[717] White, interview with the author.
[718] NFL, "NFL Mic'up Super Bowl LVI 'Hey, I'm Joe,' Gameday ALL Access," https://www.youtube.com/watch?v=aKE4Pg71uJA; February 16, 2022; September 9, 2022.
[719] Ibid.
[720] PostGame Central, Cincinnati Bengals quarterback Joe Burrow postgame press conference after Super Bowl LVI loss to Rams," https://www.youtube.com/watch?v=ky4a4cdPvHE, February 13, 2022; accessed September 9, 2022.
[721] PostGame Central, "Cincinnati Bengals Joe Burrow AFC Championship postgame after win onto Superbowl."
[722] Late Night with Seth Meyers, "Kid Cudi Watches Horror Movies with His Daughter," https://www.youtube.com/watch?v=0rPspPIMrXM, March 16, 2022; accessed September 9, 2022.
[723] NFL on NBC, "Joe Burrow breaks down his QB process with Chris Simms," https://www.youtube.com/watch?v=s7aZQWo4QSw, June 21, 2022; accessed September 9, 2022.
[724] Cincinnati Bengals, "Joe Burrow News Conference, Offseason Training Program," https://www.youtube.com/watch?v=iW_MJUflgHI, May 17, 2022; accessed August 27, 2022.
[725] Zacciah Saltzman, Facebook messenger exchange with the author, August 24, 2022.
[726] Ibid.
[727] Ibid.
[728] Ibid.
[729] Ibid.
[730] Zacciah Saltzman, zoom interview with the author, May 31, 2022.
[731] Zacciah Saltzman, Facebook messenger exchange with the author, August 24, 2022.
[732] Ibid.
[733] Ibid.
[734] "A Man Named Scott."
[735] Zacciah Saltzman, zoom interview with the author, May 31, 2022.
[736] Don Cooley, zoom interview with the author.
[737] Troy Bolin, zoom interview with the author.
[738] Cincinnati Bengals, "Meet La'el Collins, Cincinnati Bengals," https://www.youtube.com/watch?v=ae9yVTHoPYg, March 29, 2022; accessed August 27, 2022.
[739] Bengals Meme's, https://www.facebook.com/BengalsMemes, March 21, 2022; accessed August 27, 2022.

[740] Cincinnati Bengals, "Joe Burrow News Conference, Offseason Training Program."
[741] Ibid.
[742] Karin Bright, zoom interview with the author.
[743] Cincinnati Bengals, "Joe Burrow News Conference, December 1, 2021," https://www.youtube.com/watch?v=_xjJEUkaFbQ, December 1, 2021; accessed August 28, 2022.
[744] Robin Burrow, interview with the author.
[745] Drabold, zoom interview with the author.
[746] Cole Behrens, *The Athens Messenger*, "Burrow auctioning cleats designed by Athens High student for food pantry, https://www.athensmessenger.com/news/burrow-auctioning-cleats-designed-by-athens-high-student-for-food-pantry/article_46e0167e-0a2f-5e0b-be86-1ef6bcc2ecbf.html, February 3, 2021; accessed August 28, 2022.
[747] Cincinnati Bengals Talk, "Joe Burrow on Cincinnati Bengals' Sunday Night Football Matchup With Baltimore Ravens, NFL Week 5," https://www.youtube.com/watch?v=Pq3UZlzjTxw, October 5, 2022; accessed October 6, 2022.
[748] Machelle Stewart, interview with the author, Athens, Ohio, March 10, 2022.
[749] White, interview with the author..
[750] Ibid.
[751] Alan Smathers, interview with the author, The Plains, Ohio, May 25, 2022.
[752] Jimmy Burrow, interview with the author, The Plains, May 27, 2022.
[753] Peter King's Football Morning in America, "FMIA: The 22 Most Influential NFL People This Season Includes Sean McVey, Trey Lance and an Amazon VP," https://profootballtalk.nbcsports.com/2022/06/06/22-nfl-most-influential-fmia-peter-king/, June 6, 2022; accessed August 28, 2022.
[754] Gibson, interview with the author.
[755] Conor Orr, *Sports Illustrated*, "Their Ultracool QB Has Transformed the Bengals' Vibe. Joe Burrow Knows the Job Isn't Done." Vol. 133, No. 8 (September 2022): Front Cover.
[756] Bolin, zoom interview with the author.
[757] Peter King on Dave Lapham In The Trenches, "NFL Insider Peter King: We Are In An Era That Is Going To Be The Greatest Era in Bengals History," https://www.youtube.com/watch?v=YDYOmtfqkUo, January 26, 2023; accessed January 26, 2023.
[758] ESPN, "Joe Burrow has put the world on NOTICE! He's not going away! – Stephen. A., First Take," January 23, 2023; accessed January 28, 2023.
[759] Cincinnati Bengals, "Joe Burrow: We're Going To Be Fine," https://www.youtube.com/watch?v=M8KIUfbKMWc, September 21, 2022; accessed February 3, 2023.
[760] Ibid.
[761] WCPO 9, "Cincinnati Bengals QB Joe Burrow speaks for the first time since appendix surgery," August 18, 2022; accessed January 28, 2023.
[762] The Volume, "Joe Burrow on Tua injury, Bengals-Ravens rivalry, Kid Cudi friendship: The Colin Cowherd Podcast," https://www.youtube.com/watch?v=5ce_pZfYcag, October 4, 2022; accessed February 4, 2023.
[763] Cincinnati Bengals@Bengals, https://twitter.com/Bengals/status/1577763596691554304/photo/1, October 5, 2022; accessed February 4, 2023.
[764] *The New York Times*, "Styles's 93 Most Stylish People of 2022," https://www.nytimes.com/2022/12/11/style/most-stylish-people.html, December 12, 2022; accessed February 4, 2023.
[765] WCPO 9, "Bengals fan posts hilarious post-wisdom teeth surgery video," https://www.youtube.com/watch?v=qqRIuzG3d0A, December 2, 2022; accessed February 4, 2023.
[766] NFL, "Joe Burrow joins the Manning Cast on 'MNF' to talk about his favorite nicknames,

Week 14," https://www.youtube.com/watch?v=JeLNqAD5rOo, December 12, 2022; accessed February 4, 2023.

[767] Dave Clark, *Cincinnati Enquirer*, "'Wisdom tooth girl' Haven Wolfe: 'Never called Joe Burrow ugly ... Mannings ejected," https://www.cincinnati.com/story/sports/nfl/bengals/2022/12/14/haven-wolfe-on-manningcast-review-of-wisdom-teeth-viral-video-never-called-joe-burrow-ugly/69726712007/, December 14, 2022; accessed February 4, 2023.

[768] Dan Hoard, Bengals Booth Podcast, "Prayers for Damar," https://podcasts.apple.com/us/podcast/bengals-booth-podcast/id1278501610, January 5, 2023; accessed February 5, 2023.

[769] Thalia Beaty, Associated Press, "Damar Hamlin's toy drive: What's the plan for $8.6M?" https://apnews.com/article/buffalo-bills-nfl-sports-damar-hamlin-fae1a8983657be78c931731a30648ac1, January 10, 2023; accessed February 5, 2023.

[770] T*he Buffalo News*, "Excerpts from news conference with doctors on Bills' Damar Hamlin," https://buffalonews.com/sports/bills/excerpts-from-news-conference-with-doctors-on-bills-damar-hamlin/article_87927220-8d40-11ed-91d2-0b81c6e11910.html, January 6, 2023; accessed February 5, 2023.

[771] NFL on NBC, "Sam Hubbard sprints fumble 98 yards for crucial Bengals touchdown," https://www.youtube.com/watch?v=zDnn0xylHKA, January 15, 2023; accessed February 5, 2023.

[772] Kelsey Conway, *Cincinnati Enquirer*, "Analysis: Bengals show why it's time they should stop being treated as an underdog," https://www.cincinnati.com/story/sports/nfl/bengals/2023/01/23/afc-championship-game-after-beating-buffalo-bills-bengals-shouldnt-be-underdogs-vs-kansas-city/69830725007/, January 22, 2023; accessed February 5, 2023.

[773] Highlight Heaven, "Joe Burrow: 'better send those refunds,'" https://www.youtube.com/watch?v=C4axNCoags8, January 22, 2023; accessed February 5, 2023.

[774] Peter King on Dave Lapham In The Trenches..

[775] The Room Podcast, Jordan Palmer and Kyle Allen, "I Finally Had My Brother On, Full Show With Carson Palmer," https://podcasts.apple.com/us/podcast/the-room/id1639912196, February 1, 2023; accessed February 5, 2023.

[776] Cincinnati Bengals Talk, "Joe Burrow on Beating Ravens, Celebrating As Back-to-Back AFC North Champions," https://www.youtube.com/watch?v=NX4uKVCTy_w, January 8, 2023; accessed February 5, 2023.

Index